NEW YORK

Stratford
Milford
King's

Horse
Neck
Fairfield
Norwalk
Hudson
CONN.

Rye
Stamford

Setauket
Hubbard's

New
Rochelle
Brewster's
Fanning's

Kings Bridge
Huntington
LONG ISLAND

New York
Jamaica

Elizabeth
Baker's
Hempstead

Woodbridge

Perth Amboy

New
Brunswick

ATLANTIC

OCEAN

N

HAMILTON'S
ITINERARIUM
1744

Southwestern Section, Starting at Annapolis

Based upon the map in A.B. Hart's edition of HAMILTON'S
ITINERARIUM in which the names of places are modernized

5   0   5   10   15   20   25   30 MILES

SCALE

GENTLEMAN'S PROGRESS

Alexander Hamilton armiger
Societatis vulgo Tuesday Club, nuncupatæ, Secretarius
et orator, nec non ejusdem, Socius veteranus et Longo-staticus.

Nostri ab archivis consortii cuspice Scribam,
Qui tua verba, Cole, Stylo perenni arah,
Nec non facta tua, placido Sermone perorah,
Nestora quem lingua, vincere posse putes.

Gentleman's Progress

THE ITINERARIUM
OF DR. ALEXANDER HAMILTON

1744

EDITED WITH AN INTRODUCTION BY

Carl Bridenbaugh

Published for the Institute of
Early American History and Culture

AT WILLIAMSBURG, VIRGINIA

By the University of North Carolina Press

CHAPEL HILL, 1948

Contents

ILLUSTRATIONS

NOTE: All of these sketches are the property of the Maryland Historical Society and are reproduced here through the courtesy of the Director, Mr. James W. Foster. The frontispiece is taken from page 257 of the Minutes of the Tuesday Club, of which Hamilton was secretary. The parallel lines in the illustration are caused by the handwriting on page 258.

Introduction

BY CARL BRIDENBAUGH

INTRODUCTION

Dr. ALEXANDER HAMILTON'S *Itinerarium* is one of the happiest combinations of liveliness, wit, and instructive information written in colonial America. The description of his journey from Maryland to Maine and back in 1744 is unequalled by any other writer. As a rule travelers, like fishermen, think to enliven their accounts by fanciful invention, by embellishing the truth, by gross exaggeration of adventures encountered and hardships experienced—all for the amazement of contemporaries and the deluding of posterity. They traffic in the incredulous. The better the tale the greater the sale is their maxim. Not so with Dr. Alexander Hamilton. He is that seldom encountered person, the truthful traveler. Moreover his accurate and comprehensive reporting, to my knowledge unequalled in any other colonial travel account, enhances rather than detracts from the fascination of his narrative. In the cogent phrase of his day this veracious tourist was an *original.*

What manner of man was this unique doctor who refused "to play the traveler," and who so charmingly and intimately wrote an Inside the Colonies in 1744?

Alexander Hamilton was foreign enough to be interested in all aspects of the American colonies and yet sufficiently familiar with their civilization to look beyond the spectacular

and the temporary and seize upon its fundamental and endur-
ing traits.[1] His birth, at or near Edinburgh in 1712, into the
highly respected family of Dr. William Hamilton, Professor of
Divinity and Principal of the University of Edinburgh, assured
him a secure place in the Scottish gentry, who alone among
aristocracies valued intellectual eminence equally with land and
family connections.[2]

In this Presbyterian stronghold young Hamilton, one of
nine children, was given the best education available in the
early eighteenth century. Attracted no doubt by the great fame
of the University as a center for medical training, he learned
pharmacy in the shop of Dr. David Knox, surgeon, perhaps as
an apprentice, before entering the Medical School.[3] Upon the
presentation of his thesis, *De Morbis Ossium* (Treatise on the
Diseases of Bones), in 1737 he was granted the degree of
Doctor of Medicine, and there are indications in his journal
that he may have spent some time in Holland where he possibly met Dr. Hermann Boerhaave, the great physician and
teacher of Leyden.[4]

Why, one may ask, would a cultured Scottish gentleman
choose to exchange the urbane society of Edinburgh for a
semi-rural existence in a tiny American colonial capital at the
outset of a promising professional career? Benjamin Franklin
provided the classic answer to this question when he replied
to David Hume's letter deploring the departure of so eminent
a philosopher from London for comparative exile at Philadelphia: "You have here at present . . . such a plenty of wisdom.
Your people are, therefore, not to be censured for desireing
no more among them than they have; and if I have *any*, I
should certainly carry it where, from its scarcity, it may probably come to a better market."[5] Certain it is that able, well-edu-
cated young Scots, particularly physicians, were going out to

America at this time in search of a better market. We shall meet many of them in the pages that follow.

Attracted to Maryland by the presence there of an older brother, the Reverend John Hamilton, the young doctor settled in Annapolis, capital of the province, early in 1739.[6] This little community had need of a good physician, and Hamilton's ability in his profession soon brought him a large and lucrative practice. As a well-connected gentleman, and a university graduate to boot, he was immediately and eagerly received into the society of the Chesapeake tobacco aristocrats, and in a very short time he had become a well-known figure in Maryland.[7]

Although Hamilton quickly recovered from the "seasoning" to which the Maryland climate subjected all Europeans, he found the summer heats trying to his none too robust constitution, and in the late spring of 1743 he suffered a prolonged illness, accompanied by "fevers and a bloody spitting," that caused his friends, including Dr. Adam Thomson, to despair of his life.[8] Rallying sufficiently to plan a return to the British Isles, in September he issued a broadside advertisement for "all Persons indebted to him to discharge their respective Debts; and likewise such as have Demands upon him, to come and receive what is due." [9]

As his health continued to improve Dr. Hamilton decided not to close out his practice. Perhaps it was his favorite prescription for patients that brought about a measure of recovery. "What is the best drink for health?" the young painter Charles Willson Peale once inquired. "Toddy, mun," replied the medico."The spirit must hae something to act on, and therefore acts on the sugar and does nae injury to the stomach." [10]

Could anything less than this invigorating potation have so restored the ailing physician that by October he felt spry enough to accede to the request of many fellow-citizens and stand as a candidate for the City Council of Annapolis in opposition to "a certain creature of the Court," whom the Proprietor was attempting to force on the city? The contest waxed hot, and on the afternoon of election day the polling place in the Mayor's Court was in an uproar. When partisans "went to Cudgelling and breaking of heads" the frightened officials had to close the polls to quiet the mob. The election was still incomplete on October 20, when the doctor wryly remarked in a letter to his brother Gilbert that dearly as he loved liberty and abhorred "force of any kind," he doubted whether he would continue to stand for election. "I like better to be a peace maker, than an Instrument of disturbance in any Shape." Unfortunately, the records do not tell us the outcome.[11]

Alexander Hamilton wrote to a friend in Scotland on November 3 that "I am not well in health and for that reason chiefly I continue Still a Batchellor." After a detailed description of his sickness to his brother he concluded in a tone of discouragement: "I am now considerably better, but am followed up by an Incessant cough, which no medicine whatsoever can abate or diminish; this makes me apprehensive that the consequences will be a confirmed Consumption," which has not yet formed, "but I run a great Risque." [12] That he was suffering from tuberculosis there can be no doubt.

A journey northward as far as York, in what is now Maine, "intended only for health and recreation," seemed to offer a pleasant and effective antidote to personal indisposition and the torrid strife of Maryland politics as well as relief from ennui and an opportunity to see the colonies. In 1744 such a trip as the doctor proposed required careful planning months in advance of departure; it was an adventure little comprehended today. Each colony had its own paper money, which passed at different rates, and arrangements for credit had to be made in order to avoid the danger of traveling with large sums of cash on one's person. Letters of introduction to prominent gentlemen in the places to be visited were essential both as financial and as social passports. Maps were poor and hard to come by, and the only available guide book was the *Vade-Mecum for America: Or a Companion for Traders and Travellers,* which listed existing roads and taverns from Maine to Virginia and contained a directory of Boston streets for the year 1732.

At eleven o'clock on Wednesday morning, May 30, 1744, Dr. Hamilton set out on horseback accompanied by his Negro slave Dromo, and, because bad weather prevented crossing the Chesapeake, they took "a very circumflex course" by land around the head of the bay. Traveling by leisurely stages to Philadelphia, they tarried there a week before continuing on to New York. After spending six days at Manhattan, Dr. Hamilton determined upon a side trip by boat up the Hudson to Albany. On his return to New York two weeks later he picked up Dromo and the horses and set out for New England by way of Long Island, crossing from its eastern end to New London and proceeding to Boston by way of Newport, Rhode Island. Following a protracted stay at the Bay Town he rode down east through Marblehead, Salem, Newbury, and Portsmouth as far as York in the Massachusetts province of Maine.

Hamilton's return journey was made along the Connecticut shore rather than on Long Island, but was otherwise unchanged. He reached the end of his trip on Thursday, September 27. "In this itineration," he concluded philosophically, "I compleated, by land and water together, a course of 1624 miles. The northeren parts I found in generall much better settled than the southeren. As to politeness and humanity, they are much alike except in the great towns where the inhabitants are more civilized, especially at Boston."[13]

Greatly restored in health and spirits and exhilarated by his adventure, Alexander Hamilton resumed his medical practice, and when his boon companion, Printer Jonas Green, established the *Maryland Gazette* the next year he ran an advertisement for four issues which indicates that much of his income came from compounding medicines:[14]

TO BE SOLD,
At the Subscriber's Shop in *ANNAPOLIS*,
JESUIT'S BARK, at Twelve Shillings,
Currency, the Pound; Where sundry other Medicines
may be had, at reasonable Prices.
ALEXANDER HAMILTON

A puckish sense of humor, not infrequently tinged with irony or sarcasm, was one of Hamilton's outstanding traits. Another was his love of sociability. Memories of the "whinbush Club" in Scotland and of many convivial evenings spent with the "set clubs" to which he had been introduced during his travels must have revealed to this gay bachelor an opportunity to exercise the highly developed comic spirit that had impelled his sister to write when he left home: "Alas! how much scotch drollery is now transplanted into American soil." [15] On May 14, 1745, eight gentlemen, of whom four were Scots, met at Hamilton's house in Annapolis to form "The Ancient and Honourable Tuesday Club." Limited to fifteen members, dedicated to raillery, and "designed for humor, and . . . a sort of farcical Drama of Mock Majesty," this group assembled weekly at the home of a "long-standing member." The club's most arresting rule was one providing that if anyone ever brought up the subject of Maryland politics, "no answer shall be given thereto, but . . . the society shall laugh at the Member offending in order to divert the discourse." [16]

Within a short time the organization was flourishing with

Charles Cole as president, Jonas Green as poet laureate and
P.P.P.P.P. (poet, printer, punster, purveyor, and punchmaker),
and Alexander Hamilton, jocularly known as Loquacious
Scribble, Esq., for secretary and historiographer. Only one dish,
customarily a gammon of bacon, was served at a meeting and
no fresh liquor was prepared after eleven P.M. One detects a
certain Hamiltonian canniness in the by-law requiring each
member to provide his own sand-box as a spittoon in order
to spare the floors at members' houses. According to the ritual
the first toast was always "the Ladies," followed by "the King's
Majesty," and then came "the Deluge." It was a coarse age,
and the language and pranks of the Tuesday Club were in
keeping with it. Copious draughts of Dr. Hamilton's punch
must have been required to make some of Jonas Green's puns
seem funny.[17] Here is his toast to President Cole, addressed
by the members as Jole:

> Wishing this ancient club may always be
> Promoters of facetious mirth and glee,
> And that our members all may be expert
> At the great punning and connundrum art,
> And that our Laureate's muse may ever warble,
> Our fame to last as grav'd on brass or marble,
> And while gay laughter furbishes each soul,
> Let each a bumper drink to noble Jole.

These effusions of wit, and more also, formed the raw
materials out of which their "cheerful, facetious companion,"
Loquacious Scribble, fashioned the History of the Tuesday
Club, a chronicle that ran to three volumes totalling 1900
closely-written pages, including the club's songs set to music.[18]
On June 2, 1747, Jonas Green's *Maryland Gazette* announced that "Friday last [May 29] Dr. Alexander Hamilton
of this City, was married to Miss Margaret Dulany (Daughter

of the Hon. Daniel Dulany, Esq.) a well accomplish'd and agreeable young Lady, with a handsome Fortune." Thus did the thirty-five-year-old physician ally himself with one of the foremost families in all the thirteen colonies. His wife's father, Daniel Dulany the Elder, as rich as any man in Maryland, was a force to reckon with in politics, being at this time the Proprietor's agent and receiver-general as well as a member of the Council. For a brother-in-law Hamilton acquired haughty Daniel Dulany the Younger, who had just been admitted to the bar on his return from a genteel education at Eton, Clare College, Cambridge, and the Middle Temple, and who within two years would further cement family alliances by marrying Rebecca, daughter of Benjamin Tasker of the Council.[19]

The physician's defection from bachelor ranks proved a great disappointment to certain members of the Tuesday Club. Since you left for England, Stephen Bordley wrote to Witham Marshe, a charter member, things have come to a pretty pass, "for poor Hamilton is gone—not dead, but married. He was the day before yesterday obliged to throw himself up to the Mony of Peggy Dulany, and is already what you wd from your knowledge of this Lady now suppose him to be, a very Grave sober fellow." [20]

Inasmuch as Hamilton had chosen the path to respectability and preferment we are not surprised to discover that he exchanged membership in the rigorous Presbyterian Church for communion with the more fashionable Church of England which was also far more congenial to his latitudinarian tastes. This shift must have occurred before his marriage, and on March 27, 1749, he was rewarded with election to the vestry of St. Ann's Church in Annapolis.[21] He was led to it no doubt as much by the influence of his fellow-member of the Tuesday Club and rector of St. Ann's, the Reverend John Gordon, as from any aspiration for social recognition. So intimate were he and the Scottish parson that the doctor went bond for Mr. Gordon when he borrowed £50 in currency from the provincial Loan Office in 1748.[22]

But Alexander Hamilton's favorite crony was Jonas Green whose wit and sociability always evoked a response in him. These two were the moving spirits of the Tuesday Club and it is not surprising to find them presiding at the founding of the Annapolis Lodge of the Freemasons in 1749. As secretary, Green looked after all the details, including the printing and publishing in 1751 of the sermon preached by the Reverend William Brogden before the Masons in St. Ann's Church, December 27, 1749, and appropriately "Dedicated to the right Honorable Alexander Hamilton, M.D. Master." [23]

As one would expect of a man of his education and position, Dr. Hamilton generously encouraged and supported the Reverend Thomas Bacon's scheme for a charity school in Talbot County, where poor children of both sexes were to be lodged, fed, clothed, and instructed "in the Knowledge and Fear of God, and inured to useful Labour" before being put out as apprentices. This aristocratic Scot agreed whole-heartedly with the contention of Mr. Bacon that "Ignorance and Indolence among the Lower Class of People in these Colonies are no less prejudicial to the common Interest, or dangerous to the Constitution, than Popery and Idleness were in Ireland," as he subscribed £2 annually to the school.[24]

Medical pursuits engrossed much of the doctor's attention in the early 'fifties.[25] At Philadelphia Hamilton's acquaintance, Dr. Adam Thomson, published in 1750 a *Discourse on the Preparation of the Body for the Small Pox: and The Manner of receiving the Infection* in which he advocated the use of mercury, antimony, and quinine as preparatives for inoculation.

This pamphlet elicited from the dean of Pennsylvania medicos, Dr. John Kearsley, the sneering charges that Thomson's liberal use of "Catholic Bark" was but "the common Refuge of Ignorance," and that he was substituting for scientific procedure the "vain Chimeras of a doubtful Hypothesis." Support from a practitioner of intercolonial repute came to Dr. Thomson the next year when William Bradford of Philadelphia published Alexander Hamilton's able *Defence of Dr. Thomson's Method*.[26] His views were also upheld by most of the Philadelphia faculty and before long even Dr. Kearsley was forced to abandon his fierce dogmatism and partially apologized in the columns of the *Pennsylvania Journal*.[27]

Political cauldrons brewed incessantly, and often with violence, in colonial Maryland. "We hear from Baltimore County," a Philadelphia newspaper reported laconically in May, 1752, "that two Men who got hurt at the last Election there, are since died of their wounds." [28] Notwithstanding poor health and an aversion to strife, Hamilton blithely disregarded this obvious warning and in 1753 embarked on a campaign for one of the two Annapolis seats in the Assembly. The Dulanys evidently spurred him to this action in order to bring about the defeat of the Calverts' candidate. A merry contest it was, with both aspirants physicians and both Scots!

When the balloting was over and the votes were counted Mayor Michael Macnemara (from Erin!) certified Hamilton to the Assembly as having been duly elected, but the Aldermen thought otherwise and issued their certificate of election to Dr. George Steuart. The Upper House listened on October 9 to the petition of Hamilton "complaining of an undue Return, made by the Aldermen," and ordered that Dr. Steuart be given notice by his opponent to appear on the morrow when "Lists of controverted Votes shall be mutually exchanged." Steuart countered by securing a postponement of appearance in order to prepare his defense.[29]

Meanwhile on October 10 the Lower House examined the claims of the two men and discovered that while Mayor Macnemara had signed Hamilton's return, the Recorder whose endorsement made the Corporation's papers legal had signed neither return. While this discussion was going on Dr. Hamilton, accompanied by Messrs. Carroll and Gassaway of the Lower House, went before the Upper House where he swore his oath, abjured the pope, took the religious test oaths, qualified for office, and retired

A week later the Lower House began consideration of the dispute and on October 19, "after the most mature Deliberation on the Merits of the said Election," decided that Dr. George Steuart was "not duly elected" and that Dr. Alexander Hamilton was. In his capacity of Clerk of the House, not as Mayor, Michael Macnemara was ordered to "regulate" the return of the recalcitrant Aldermen by erasing Steuart's name and inserting "that of Dr. Alexander Hamilton, who is the Person that ought at first to have been mentioned therein." This being done, "the Gentleman took his seat in the House," which on November 1 directed both of the contestants to pay £7.10.0 in fees to cover the summoning of thirty witnesses in their case.[30] Since his brother-in-law, Walter, occupied the other Annapolis seat, the Dulany family's control of the capital's vote was assured.

Dr. Hamilton's career in the Lower House, 1753-54, was that of a conscientious and competent conservative member representing the Dulany interest. It is to his credit that his vote was cast with the minority that desired to vote £4000 to support Virginia's war effort against the French instead of £3000. We might expect a former Presbyterian to take a bigoted stand on the bill to prevent the spreading of popery in Maryland, but Hamilton voted against it, although he did side with those who sought to imprison "interloping peddlers" rather than to fine them. He deserves the greatest praise for stoutly backing the plan for the "Erection of One Public Seminary of Learning" in the province—a proposal which, however, never bore fruit.[31]

Evidently realizing that his time was short, Hamilton made his will on October 7, 1754, and had it witnessed by his old Scottish friends the Reverend John Gordon and Henry Cummings. It is a refreshingly brief document, merely leaving all of his property to Margaret Dulany Hamilton, unless there should be a posthumous child, who was to have two-thirds of the estate.[32] The end came within two years' time, on May 11, 1756. In the *Maryland Gazette* his devoted fellow-clubman, Jonas Green, paid him a sincere tribute in more restrained language than one ordinarily finds in the florid obituaries of the day.[33]

"On Tuesday last in the morning, died at his house, in this city, Alexander Hamilton, M.D., aged 44 years. The death of this valuable and worthy gentleman is universally and justly lamented. His medical abilities, various knowledge, strictness of integrity, simplicity of manners, and extensive benevolence, having deservedly gained him the respect and esteem of all ranks of men. No Man in his sphere, has left fewer enemies or more friends."

Colonial America, as well as Maryland, had lost a rare spirit; realizing this the members of the Tuesday Club never met again.

II

The spectacle of the human race with all its vagaries fascinated Alexander Hamilton. Instinctively he divided people into sheep and goats. Nearly everyone he met on his travels was characterized in an incisive sentence or two. At Head of Elk "one of the ferry men, a young fellow, plyed his tongue faster than his oar;" Mr. Shakesburrough, surgeon to the garrison at Albany, "by his conversation, seemed to have as little of the quack in him as any half hewn doctor ever I met with;" and in a tavern debate at Boston "one Mr. Clackenbridge (very properly so named upon account of the volubility of his tongue) was the chief disputant as to verbosity and noise but not as to sense or argument." "For rural scenes and frank pritty girls," the doctor found Newport "the most agreeable place I had been in," while at Albany "their women in generall, both young and old, are the hardest favoured ever I beheld." When the gallant bachelor paid Miss Arbuthnot of Boston a fulsome compliment in the presence of her father, he recorded that "I breathed a little after this speech, there being something romantick in it and, considdering human nature in the propper light, could not be true. The young lady blushed; the old man was pleased and picked his teeth, and I was conscious that I had talked nonsense."

If we would understand our forefathers of the mid-eighteenth century the *Itinerarium* provides a unique introduction to them.

Dr. Hamilton viewed colonial life with the detachment of the scientist. He analyzed the social traits of the people he met much as he would have diagnosed their maladies. It is highly significant that this detachment was based upon an acute class consciousness in an age when gradations in society were openly recognized and accepted by all ranks.

A European-bred gentleman of culture and refinement sure of his position at the top of the social scale, he accepted it quietly and unostentatiously, but at the same time demanded that others recognize it and duly accord him deference and respect. As he rode through the colonies dressed in fine clothes, laced hat, and sword, and accompanied by his body servant Dromo, people instantly knew him to be a person of quality. When one Morison, ("clad in a greasy jacket and breeches and a dirty worsted cap, and withal a heavy forward clownish air and behaviour"), who was "desirous to pass as a gentleman," took offense at the landlady of Curtis's in Newcastle for serving him a countryman's breakfast, Hamilton noted that he angrily swore: " 'Damm him, if it w'ant out of respect to the gentleman in company,' (meaning me) he would throw her cold scraps out att the window and break her table all to pieces should it cost him 100 pounds for damages." Clothes may not have made, but they signified the gentleman.

There are overtones of this awareness of place in all of the physician's observations of men and manners. In the great towns he encountered many colonial parvenus, pretenders to gentility, who reminded him of those Manhattan "dons . . . who imagined few or none were their equals." Such vulgar behavior impelled him to set down his social creed: "But this I found always proceeded from their narrow notions, ignorance of the world, and low extraction, which indeed is the case with most of our aggrandized upstarts in these infant countrys of America who never had an opportunity to see, or if they had, the capacity to observe the different ranks of men in polite nations or to know what it is that really constitutes that difference of degrees."

Eighteenth-century custom assigned people to one of three established ranks: the gentry constituted "the better sort;" yeomen farmers and artisans composed "the middling sort;" and sailors, laborers, indentured servants, and negro slaves made up "the inferior sort." Transition from one class to another was not infrequent, but nonetheless distinctions between the groups were clearly made and defined. Concentration of land in the hands of a few of "the better sort" and the presence of a large body of white bonded servants, transported convicts, and negro slaves in the Chesapeake tidewater society where Dr. Hamilton lived combined to buttress the barriers between classes to a greater degree than in the large commercial cities or the small-farm regions to the northward.

As he traveled along, Hamilton became increasingly aware of the declining subordination of inferiors to superiors. At a tavern near Saybrook in Connecticut he observed "I find they are not quite so scrupulous about bestowing titles here as in Maryland. My landlady goes here by the name of Madam Lay. I cannot tell for what, for she is the homeliest piece both as to mein, make, and dress that I ever saw, being a little round shouldered woman, pale faced and wrinkly, clothed in the coarsest home spun cloth; but it is needless to dispute her right to the title since we know many upon whom it is bestowed who have as little right as she." New England, he discovered, was not like the Lower Counties (Delaware) or the Hudson Valley, "where the country people stared at me like sheep when I inquired of them the way."

Without realizing it Alexander Hamilton was witnessing in the American colonies the beginnings of one of the greatest revolutions of modern times—the breakdown of the medieval class structure and the liberation of the common man. In 1744 the decline of the "Great Law of Subordination" was just setting in. A striking indication of the change was the non-European boldness of the middling and inferior sorts in asking him innumerable personal questions. As a gentleman, reared with the innate Scottish resentment of curiosity in others, he regarded such interrogations as rude and boorish, and often gave impatient and sarcastic replies. Yet he is not to be blamed for a failure to perceive that a levelling process was going on among what he sardonically called "the *mobile,* that many headed heart," and that it would in three decades hence reject monarchy and eventually rule in the democratic society of our own day. Read in this light the *Itinerarium* becomes one of the most illuminating documents of the colonial period.

Dr. Hamilton's account of his travels presents impressive evidence of the growing unity of the colonies. Its emphasis is upon the common elements rather than the divisive forces in a burgeoning society. Wherever he journeyed he found the people of each class much the same as those with whom he was familiar in Maryland. In particular this was true of the aristocracy. Before setting out on his trip he procured letters of introduction to prominent gentlemen in each community he proposed to visit. That he could do this is proof that the northern gentry were well known in polite circles at Annapolis and that there existed as early as 1744 an intercolonial solidarity among the better sort in striking contrast to the comparative absence of contacts among those of the middling or inferior sort. In part this interchange at the top came from economic relations by land and sea, and in Hamilton's case also from his professional connections with clannish Scottish doctors who had almost monopolized the practice of medicine in the larger towns. But most of all it stemmed from the ready welcome and hospitality one gentleman always accorded to another. Among men of wealth, political influence, and culture a sort of freemasonry prevailed. Historically class consciousness in America took its rise in the gentry who were the first to recognize their community of interest.

Yet a surprising number from all ranks were on the move in 1744. Journeys by sea continued as in earlier years, but since Madam Sarah Kemble Knight's remarkable and hazardous

trip from Boston to New York and back in 1704, overland travel
had improved amazingly. At no time did Dr. Hamilton com-
plain of bad roads, or of either danger or poor service in the
fifty ferry crossings he carefully recorded. Moreover, his personal safety was never once threatened as it would have been
along the highways of the British Isles by robbers like Dick
Turpin and his fellows. For the most part country inns offered satisfactory accommodations, although they were usually
noisy and privacy was an unknown luxury. In the cities good
food and service were available at taverns and coffee-houses,
and a gentleman could always find comfortable private lodgings
through the good offices of those to whom he bore letters of
introduction. Throughout the country there obtained along
the highroad a traveler's camaraderie that crossed over class
boundaries and made even a valetudinarian's tour agreeable.

Alexander Hamilton ran the gamut of colonial life;
little that was interesting or significant escaped him. Although
he describes provincial rural society, he bestows most of his
attention on the urban centers—Philadelphia, New York, Newport, Boston. There an American culture was germinating.

This was an age of clubs. In the seaboard cities it had
become possible to assemble "Knots of men rightly sorted," and
mere conviviality was being challenged by gatherings devoted
to more exalted purposes—the improvement of useful knowledge in medicine and natural philosophy, the discussion of
literature (at one club Cervantes and the English poets provided the topic), and the performance of chamber music. Book
auctions flourished in Boston and at Newport Hamilton discovered in Robert Feke colonial America's first talented painter.
In these communities, too, he found the first evidences of a
developing public architecture as town halls, market houses, and
provincial capitols rose beside the churches. Almost alone the

theater was missing. Wealth wrung from land and commerce had made it possible for gentlemen to patronize the arts, despite the strain of a war which threatened the very existence of these seaports.

Dr. Hamilton's report on the America of 1744 reveals more unity than diversity. Each province had its own individuality, its local foibles, and its peculiar characteristics, to be sure, but the differences were those of detail, not fundamentals. Uniformity was hardly a virtue of the eighteenth century. Yet, there was a lesser chasm in outlook and customs between a Massachusetts Yankee and a Tidewater Marylander than between a Prussian and a Wurttemberger, a Breton and a Gascon, or even a Londoner and a North Briton. Although political differences often tended to force them apart, social and economic bonds were even more firmly welding them together into one people.

A final feature of the *Itinerarium* is the unconscious portrait its author draws of himself as a typical cultured gentleman of the age. He was what was known as a *virtuoso*. Success in his profession had brought this bachelor the wealth needed for leisure to indulge in sociability, travel, wide reading and settling the elements of taste. Upon one occasion we discover him in a Philadelphia tavern reading Shakespeare's *Timon of Athens,* "which, tho' not written according to Aristotle's rules, [is] yet abounding with inimitable beauties peculiar to this excellent author." In a Boston studio he dispenses what passes for art criticism among the *cognoscenti* upon viewing John Smibert's copy of Poussin's *Continence of Scipio:* "The passions are all well touched in the severall faces. . . . But what I admired most of the painter's fancy . . . is an image or phantome of chastity behind the solium where Scipio sits." Again, at New York he attends a concert where "the violin was by far the best I had heard played since I came to America." When Dr.

Moffatt of Newport lent him a copy of Mercius, "a most lusci-
ous piece," he "did not read this book upon account of its
liquorice contents, but only because I knew it to be a piece
of excellent good Latin, and I wanted to inform my self of
the propper idiom of the language upon that subject."

Gay, facetious, and affable, Alexander Hamilton enjoyed
nothing on his travels so much as to foregather with a gentleman's club about a convivial bowl where the conversation might
begin with a discussion of war, trade or politics, progress to
women, and then, as he readily admitted, end "in a smutty
strain." Hamilton, himself, had the well-bred gentleman's
knack of being gross without being disgusting, and, consequently, of entertaining a company sunk below the level of
Attic refinement. The "toapers" of Manhattan, however, proved
to much for him, and he often left their company "pritty well
flushed . . . and ruminating on my folly."

Because he was alert, fairminded and tolerant the doctor
reviewed the colonial scene with an amused eye. Inclined to a
fashionable deism like so many of his class, he resented religious enthusiasm, and poured out his irony on the followers of
George Whitefield, "our New Light biggots," whom he could
infallibly detect by "a particular down hanging look." Creeds
held no interest for him and as a result he indifferently confused Presbyterians and Congregationalists in his comments on
the Great Awakening, then at its height in New England.
Among "men of sense, ingenuity, and learning" he gave free
rein to the delightful humor that sparkles in the pages of
the *Itinerarium*. He was impatient of all pretense, human
ignorance and stupidity (of which he encountered much in his
travels), from whatever rank it came, and either "laughed a
little handkerchief fashion," or, if sufficiently aroused, exposed the object of his contempt with deliberate raillery or
scorn.

Alexander Hamilton everywhere found life arresting and entertaining, and just as he generously shared his experience with contemporaries he also recorded it with sprightliness and humor for the enjoyment of posterity.

III

The manuscript of the *Itinerarium* has had an unusually interesting history. Commerical contacts between the English colonies and the Italian states were few and far between in the eighteenth century. Occasionally a colonial vessel ventured to Leghorn, and even less frequently did a native of Italy reach American shores. When Dr. Hamilton returned from his tour in September, 1744, he met an Italian gentleman, Onorio Razolini, for whom he came to have a great affection which he expressed felicitously in the Latin dedication of his journal. When the signor left Maryland he carried with him the manuscript of the *Itinerarium,* containing the inscription: "Presented by Alexander Hamilton, Doctor of Medicine, to Onorio Razolini, Annapolis, Nov. 29, 1744."

Early in the present century the journal was acquired by Frank T. Sabin, bookseller of London, who thus described its history:

"The manuscript remained in the possession of the family of the Italian gentleman to whom it was dedicated, and to whom it was originally given, until within a few years. It then passed into the hands of an Italian bookseller, who sent it to a correspondent in London, from whom I purchased it.

"Doubtless, owing to the rather obscure lettering on the back, it remained almost unnoticed for the last hundred years, or, on the other hand, it may have been preserved with reverent care by a generation or two of descendants, who finally, tempted by a good offer, parted with it. It will not do for me to indulge in too much fanciful conjecture. So far as facts are concerned, they are as stated above."[34]

Messrs. B. F. Stevens and Brown of London bought the *Itinerarium* from Mr. Sabin and sold it to the well-known American collector, Mr. William K. Bixby of St. Louis. Impressed by the intrinsic interest of Hamilton's journal as well as by its historical value, Mr. Bixby engaged Albert Bushnell Hart to transcribe and edit the volume, which was published at St. Louis in 1907 with the title: *Hamilton's Itinerarium: Being a Narrative of a Journey From Annapolis, Maryland, Through Delaware, Pennsylvania, New York, New Jersey, Connecticut, Rhode Island, Massachusetts, and New Hampshire from May to September, 1744*. By Dr. Alexander Hamilton. This de luxe edition, printed on paper specially manufactured in Holland and limited to 487 signed copies, was "issued only for Private Distribution by W. K. Bixby" to his friends. Today the *Itinerarium* is a collector's item that appears only rarely in dealers' catalogues. Since most of the gift copies have remained in private hands even some of the largest libraries do not possess one. Thus it seems appropriate for the Institute of Early American History and Culture to offer this scarce and valuable travel diary to a wider reading public.

In preparing the present edition for publication the original text of the manuscript has been scrupulously followed with three exceptions: modern rules of paragraphing, punctuation, and capitalization have been adopted in the interest of clarity and readability. Dr. Hamilton wrote for his own amusement in an age less delicate than our own. Although he never intended his journal for publication, I have not thought it part of my duty to act as his censor. The *Itinerarium* is here reproduced in its entirety.

To insure the reader's full enjoyment of Hamilton's racy

account of his travels without annoying interruptions, the notes have been placed at the end of the volume where they may be readily consulted by means of the numbering at the head of each page. Such an arrangement, moreover, permits a somewhat fuller annotation than would otherwise have been decently permissable in a volume intended for the general public. As far as possible every person or place mentioned is identified and complete references have been given to establish the author's accuracy, so unexpected in a travel book, in order to provide a standard reference work for this period of colonial history.

The manuscript of the Itinerarium (HM 922) is now owned by the Henry E. Huntington Library of San Marino, California, whose officials supplied the Institute of Early American History and Culture with a microfilm copy and generously granted permission to publish it. Through the courtesy of Mr. James W. Foster of the Maryland Historical Society Alexander Hamilton's sketches of the meetings of the Tuesday Club were made available to me. Mr. Lester J. Cappon gave me the benefit of his editorial advice, Mr. Arthur P. Middleton made several helpful suggestions, and Miss Mary Wright of the Institute checked the text and notes. Publication of this volume was made possible in part by a grant from the Richmond Area University Center. My wife, Roberta Herriott Bridenbaugh, patiently undertook the laborious task of transcribing the text from the microfilm copy and also gathered much of the material for the notes. To all of them I am deeply grateful for their readiness to come to my assistance.

CARL BRIDENBAUGH

Williamsburg, Virginia
February 23, 1948.

The Itinerarium

OF DR. ALEXANDER HAMILTON

1744

AMICO SUO HONORANDO, DIVINITISSIMO DOMINO
ONORIO RAZOLINI, MANUSCRIPTUM HOCCE ITINERARIUM,
OBSERVANTIAE ET AMORIS SUI QUALCUMQUE SYMBOLIUM,
DAT CONSECRATIQUE.

ALEXANDER HAMILTON

*[To his honorable friend, the most excellent Signor
Onorio Razolini, Alexander Hamilton gives and
dedicates this manuscript the Itinerarium as a
token of his esteem and affection.]*

ITINERARIUM

DIE MERCURII TRIGESIMO MENSIS MAII INCHOATUM ANNO MDCCXLIV

ANNAPOLIS, Wednesday, May 30th. I set out from Annapolis in Maryland upon Wednesday, the 30th of May, att eleven a'clock in the morning, contrary winds and bad weather preventing my intended passage over Chesapeak Bay, so taking the Patapscoe road, I proposed going by way of Bohemia to Newtown upon Chester,[1] a very circumflex course, but as the journey was intended only for health and recreation, I was indifferent whether I took the nearest or the farthest route, having likewise a desire to see that part of the country. I was in seeming bad order att my first seting out, being suspicious that one of my horses was lame, but he performed well and beyond my expectation. I travelled but 26 miles this day. There was a cloudy sky and an appearance of rain. Some miles from town I met Mr. H[ar]t[2] going to Annapolis. He returned with me to his own house where I was well entertained and had one night's lodging and a country dinner.

Mr. H[asel]l,[3] a gentleman of Barbadoes, with whom I expected to have the pleasure of travelling a good part of my intended journey, had left Annapolis a week or ten days before me and had appointed to meet me att Philadelphia. He went to Bohemia by water and then took chaise over land to Newcastle and Willimington, being forbid for certain physicall reasons to travell on horseback. This was a polite and facetious gentleman, and I was sorry that his tedious stay in some places put it out of my power to tarry for him; so I was deprived of his conversation the far greatest part of the journey.

Mr. H[ar]t and I, after dinner, drank some punch and conversed like a couple of virtuosos. His wife had no share in the conversation; he is blessed indeed with a silent woman, but her muteness is owing to a defect in her hearing, that, without bawling out to her, she cannot understand what is spoke, and therefor not knowing how to make pertinent replys, she chuses to hold her tongue. It is well I have thus accounted for it; else such a character in the sex would appear quite out of nature. Att night I writ to Annapolis and retired to bed att 10 a'clock.

Thursday, May 31. I got up by times this morning pour prendre le frais, as the French term it, and found it heavy and cloudy, portending rain. Att 9 o'clock I took my leave of Mr. H[ar]t, his wife and sister, and took horse. A little before I reached Patapscoe Ferry, I was overtaken by a certain captain of a tobacco ship, whose name I know not, nor did I inquire concerning it lest he should think me impertinent.

Patapscoe Ferry

We crossed the ferry together att 10 o'clock.[4] He talked inveteratly against the clergy and particularly the Maryland clerks of the holy cloth, but I soon found that he was a prejudiced person, for it seems he had been lately cheated by one of our parsons.[5]

Baltimore Town—Gunpowder Ferry—Joppa

This man accompanied me to Baltimore Town,[6] and after I parted with him, I had a solitary journey till I came within three miles of Gunpowder Ferry[7] where I met one Mathew Baker, a horse jockey.

Crossing the ferry I came to Joppa, a village pleasantly situated and lying close upon the river.[8] There I called att one Brown's, who keeps a good taveren in a large brick house.[9] The landlord was ill with intermitting fevers, and understanding from some there who knew me that I professed physick, he asked my advice, which I gave him.

Here I encountered Mr. D[ea]n,[10] the minister of the parish, who (after we had dispatched a bowl of sangaree)[11] carried me to his house. There passed between him, his wife, and I some odd rambling conversation which turned chiefly upon politicks. I heard him read, with great patience, some letters from his correspondents in England, written in a gazett stile, which seemed to be an abridgement of the politicall history of the times and a dissection of the machinations of the French in their late designs upon Great Brittain. This reverend gentleman and his wife seemed to express their indignation with some zeal against certain of our st[ate]sm[e]n and c[ouncillo]rs att Annapolis who, it seems, had opposed the interest of the clergy by attempting to reduce the number of the taxables. This brought the proverb in my mind, The shirt is nearest the skin. Touch a man in his private interest, and you immediately procure his ill will.

Leaving Joppa I fell in company with one Captain Waters and with Mr. D———gs, a virtuoso in botany. He affected some knowledge in naturall philosophy, but his learning that way was but superficiall.

Description of the Gensing

He showed me a print or figure of the gensing which, he told me, was to be found in the rich bottoms near Susquehanna.[12] The plant is of one stemm, or stalk, and jointed. From each joint issues four small branches. At the extremity of each of these is a cinquefoil, or 5 leaves, somewhat oblong, notched and veined. Upon the top of the stemm, it bears a bunch of red berries, but I could not learn if it had any apparent flower, the colour of that flower, or att what season of the year it blossomed or bore fruit. I intended, however, to look for it upon the branches of Susquehanna; not that I imagined it of any singular virtue, for I think it has really no more than what may be in the common liquorice root mixed with an aromatick or spicy drug, but I had a curiosity to see a thing which has been so famous.

After parting with this company, I put up att one Tradaway's about 10 miles from Joppa. The road here is pritty hilly, stonny, and full of a small gravell. I observed some stone which I thought looked like limestone.

Just as I dismounted att Tradaway's, I found a drunken club dismissing.[13] Most of them had got upon their horses and were seated in an oblique situation, deviating much from a perpendicular to the horizontal plan[e], a posture quite necessary for keeping the center of gravity within its propper base for the support of the superstructure; hence we deduce the true physicall reason why our heads overloaded with liquor become too ponderous for our heels. Their discourse was as oblique as their position; the only thing intelligible in it was oaths and God dammes; the rest was an inarticulate sound like Rabelais' frozen words a thawing, interlaced with hickupings and belchings. I was uneasy till they were gone, and my landlord, seeing me stare, made that trite apology—that indeed he did not care to have such disorderly fellows come about his house; he was always noted far and near for keeping a quiet house and entertaining only gentlemen or such like, but these were country people, his neighbours, and it was not prudent to dissoblige them upon slight occasions. "Alas, sir!" added he, "we that entertain travellers must strive to oblige every body, for it is our dayly bread." While he spoke thus, our Bacchanalians, finding no more rum in play, rid off helter skelter as if the devil had possessed them, every man sitting his horse in a see-saw manner like a bunch of rags tyed upon the saddle.

I found nothing particular or worth notice in my landlord's character or conversation, only as to his bodily make. He was a fat pursy man and had large bubbies like a woman. I supped upon fry'd chickens and bacon, and after supper the conversation turned upon politicks, news, and the dreaded French war;[14] but it was so very lumpish and heavy that it disposed me mightily to sleep. This learned company consisted of the landlord, his overseer and miller, and another greasy thumb'd fellow who, as I understood, professed physick and particularly surgery. In the drawing of teeth, he practiced upon the house maid, a dirty piece of lumber, who made such screaming and squalling as made me imagine there was murder going forwards in the house. However, the artist got the tooth out att last with a great clumsy pair of black-smith's forceps; and indeed it seemed to require such an instrument, for when he showed it to us, it resembled a horsenail more than a tooth.

The miller, I found, professed musick and would have tuned his crowd[15] to us, but unfortunatly the two middle strings betwixt the bass and treble were broke. This man told us that he could play by the book. After having had my fill of this elegant company, I went to bed att 10 o'clock.

Friday, June 1st. The sun rose in a clear horizon, and the air in these highlands was, for two hours in the morning, very cool and refreshing. I breakfasted upon some dirty chocolate, but the best that the house could afford, and took horse about half an hour after six in the morning. For the first thirteen miles the road seemed gravelly and hilly, and the land but indifferent.

Susquehanna Ferry

When I came near Susquehanna, I looked narrowly in the bottoms for the gensing but could not discover it. The lower ferry of Susquehanna,[16] which I crossed, is above a mile broad. It is kept by a little old man whom I found att vittles with his wife and family upon a homely dish of fish without any kind of sauce. They desired me to eat, but I told them I had no stomach. They had no cloth upon the table, and their mess was in a dirty, deep, wooden dish which they evacuated with their hands, cramming down skins, scales, and all. They used neither knife, fork, spoon, plate, or napkin because, I suppose, they had none to use. I looked upon this as a picture of that primitive simplicity practiced by our forefathers long before the mechanic arts had supplyed them with instruments for the luxury and elegance of life. I drank some of their syder, which was very good, and crossed the ferry in company with a certain Scots-Irishman by name Thomas Quiet. The land about Susquehanna is pritty high and woody, and the channell of the river rockey.

Mr. Quiet rid a little scrub bay mare which he said was sick and ailing and could not carry him, and therefor he 'lighted every half mile and ran a couple of miles att a footman's pace to spell the poor beast (as he termed it). He informed me he lived att Monocosy[17] and had been out three weeks in quest of his creatures (horses), four of which had strayed from his plantation. I condoled his loss and asked him what his mare's distemper was, resolving to prescribe for her, but all that I could gett out of him was that the poor silly beast had choaked herself in eating her oats; so I told him that if she was choaked, she was past my art to recover.

This fellow, I observed, had a particular down hanging look which made me suspect he was one of our New Light biggots.[18] I guessed right, for he introduced a discourse concerning Whitfield and inlarged pritty much and with some warmth upon the doctrines of that apostle, speaking much in his praise. I took upon me, in a ludicrous manner, to impungn some of his doctrines, which, by degrees, put Mr. Quiet in a passion. He told me flatly that I was damnd without redemption. I replyed that I thought his name and behaviour were very incongruous and desired him to change it with all speed, for it was very impropper that such an angry, turbulent mortall as he should be called by the name of Thomas Quiet.

Principio Iron Works—North East

In the height of this fool's passion, I overtook one Mr. B[axte]r,[19] a proprietor in the iron works there, and, after mutual salutation, the topic of discourse turned from religious controversy to politicks; so putting on a little faster, we left this inflammed bigot and his sick mare behind. This gentleman accompanied me to North East and gave me directions as to the road.

Elk Ferry

I crossed Elk Ferry att 3 in the afternoon.[20] One of the ferry men, a young fellow, plyed his tongue much faster than his oar. He characterized some of the chief dwellers in the neighbourhood, particularly some young merchants, my countrymen, for whom he had had the honour to stand pimp in their amours. He let me know that he understood some scraps of Latin and repeated a few hexameter lines out of Lilly's Grammar.[21] He told me of a clever fellow of his name who had composed a book for which he would give all the money he was master of to have the pleasure of reading it. I asked him who this name sake of his was. He replied it was one Terence, and, to be sure, he must have been an arch dog, for he never knew one of the name but he was remarkable for his parts.

9

Bohemia

Thus entertained, I got over the ferry and rid to Bohemia, and calling att the mannor house there, I found no body att home.[22] I met here a reverend parson who was somewhat inquisitive as to where I came from and the news, but I was not very communicative. I understood afterwards it was Parson W[y]e.[23]

Bohemia Ferry

I crossed Bohemia Ferry and lodged att the ferry house.[24] The landlord's name I cannot remember, but he seemed to be a man of tollerable parts for one in his station. Our conversation run chiefly upon religion. He gave me a short account of the spirit of enthusiasm that had lately possessed the inhabitants of the forrests there and informed me that it had been a common practise for companys of 20 or 30 hair brained fanaticks to ride thro' the woods singing of psalms. I went to bed att 9 att night; my landlord, his wife, daughters, and I lay all in one room.

Saturday, June 2d. In the morning there was a clear sky over head but a foggy horizon and the wind att south, which presaging heat, I set out very early.

Sassafrax Ferry

I took the road to Newtown upon Chester River, crossed Sassafrax Ferry att 7 o'clock in the morning, where I found a great concourse of people att a fair. The roads here are exceeding good and even, but dusty in the summer and deep in the winter season. The day proved very hot. I encountered no company, and I went three or four miles out of my way.

Newtown

I reached Newtown[25] att 12 o'clock and put up att Dougherty's, a publick house there. I was scarce arrived when I met severall of my acquaintance. I dined with Dr. Anderson and spent the rest of the day in a sauntering manner. The northeren post arrived att night.[26] I read the papers but found nothing of consequence in them; so after some comicall chat with my landlord, I went to bed att eleven o'clock att night.

Sunday, June 3d. I stayed all this day att Newtown and breakfasted with Th. Clay, where I met with one W——b, a man of the law, to appearance a civil, good natured man but set up for a kind of connoiseur in many things. I went to visit some friends and dined att the taveren where I was entertaind by the tricks of a female baboon in the yard. This lady had more attendants and hangers on att her levee than the best person (of quality as I may say) in town. She was very fond of the compliments and company of the men and boys but expressed in her gestures an utter aversion att women and girls, especially negroes of that sex—the lady herself being of a black complexion; yet she did not att all affect her country women.

Att night I was treated by Captain Binning[27] of Boston with a bowl of lemmon punch. He gave me letters for his relations att Boston. Whiele we put about the bowl, a deal of comicall discourse pass'd in which the landlord, a man of a particular talent att telling comic storys, bore the chief part.

Monday, June 4th. The morning being clear and somewhat cool, I got up before 5 a'clock and soon mounted horse. I had a solitary route to Bohemia and went very much out of my way by being too particular and nice in observing directions.

Sassafrax and Bohemia Ferries

I reached Mr. Alexander's[28] house on the mannor att 12 o'clock. There I stayed and dined and drank tea with Miss C[ours]ey.[29] After some talk and laugh, I took my leave att 5 a'clock designing 12 miles farther to one Vanbibber's[30] that keeps a house upon the Newcastle road, but instead of going there, I went out of my way and lay att one Hollingsworth's[31] att the head of Elk.

Head of Elk

There is a great marsh upon the left hand of his house, which I passed in the night, thro the middle of which runs Elk. The multitude of fire flys glittering in the dark upon the surface of this marshe makes it appear like a great plain scattered over with spangles.

In this part of the country I found they chiefly cultivated British grain, as wheat, barley, and oats.[32] They raise, too, a great deal of flax, and in every house here the women have two or three spinning wheels a going. The roads up this way are tollerably levell but, in some places, stonny. After a light supper I went to bed att 10 a'clock.

Pensylvania—Newcastle[33]

Tuesday, June 5th. I took horse a little after 5 in the morning, and after a solitary ride thro stonny, unequall road, where the country people stared att me like sheep when I enquired of them the way, I arrived att Newcastle[34] upon Delaware att 9 a'clock in the morning and baited my horses att one Curtis's att the Sign of the Indian King,[35] a good house of entertainment.

This town stands upon stonny ground just upon the water, there being from thence a large prospect eastward towards the Bay of Delaware and the province of the Jerseys. The houses are chiefly brick, built after the Dutch modell, the town having been originally founded and inhabited by the Dutch when it belonged to New York goverment.[36] It consists chiefly of one great street which makes an elbow att right angles. A great many of the houses are old and crazy. There is in the town two publick buildings, viz., a court house[37] and church.[38]

Att Curtis's I met company going to Philadelphia and was pleased att it, being my self an utter stranger to the roads. This company consisted of three men: Thomas Howard, Timothy Smith, and William Morison. I treated them with some lemmon punch and desired the favour of their company. They readily granted my request and stayed some time for me till I had eat breakfast. Smith, in his hat and coat, had the appearance of a Quaker, but his discourse was purged of thee's and thou's tho his delivery seemed to be solemn and slow paced. Howard was a talkative man, abounding with words and profuse in compliments which were generally blunt and came out in an awkward manner. He bestowed much panegyrick upon his own behaviour and conduct.

Morison (who, I understood, had been att the Land Office in Annapolis enquiring about a title he had to some land in Maryland) was a very rough spun, forward, clownish blade, much addicted to swearing, att the same time desirous to pass for a gentleman; notwithstanding which ambition, the conscientiousness of his naturall boorishness obliged him frequently to frame ill tim'd apologys for his misbehaviour, which he termed frankness and freeness. It was often, "Damn me, gentlemen, excuse me; I am a plain, honest fellow; all is right down plain dealing, by God." He was much affronted with the landlady att Curtis's who, seeing him in a greasy jacket and breeches and a dirty worsted cap, and withall a heavy, forward, clownish air and behaviour, I suppose took him for some ploughman or carman and so presented him with some scraps of cold veal for breakfast, he having declared that he could not drink "your damnd washy tea." As soon as he saw his mess he swore, "Damn him, if it wa'n't out of respect to the gentleman in company," (meaning me) he would throw her cold scraps out at the window and break her table all to pieces should it cost him 100 pounds for dammages. Then taking off his worsted night cap, he pulled a linnen one out of his pocket and clapping it upon his head, "Now," says he, "I'm upon the borders of Pensylvania and must look like a gentleman; 'tother was good enough for Maryland, and damn my blood if ever I come into that rascally province again if I don't procure a leather jacket that I may be in a trim to box the saucy jacks there and not run the hazard of tearing my coat." This showed, by the bye, that he payed more regard to his coat than his person, a remarkable instance of modesty and self denyall.

He then made a transition to politicks and damnd the late Sr. R[obert] W[alpole] for a rascall.[39] We asked him his reasons for cursing Sr. R[obert], but he would give us no other but this, that he was certainly informed by some very good gentlemen, who understood the thing right well, that the said Sr. R[obert] was a damnd rogue. And att the conclusion of each rodomontade, he told us that tho he seemed to be but a plain, homely fellow, yet he would have us know that he was able to afford better than many that went finer: he had good linnen in his bags, a pair of silver buckles, silver clasps, and gold sleeve buttons, two Holland shirts,[40] and some neat night caps; and that his little woman att home drank tea twice a day; and he himself lived very well and expected to live better so soon as that old rogue B——t dyed and he could secure a title to his land.

The chief topic of conversation among these three Pensylvanian dons upon the road was the insignificancy of the neighbouring province of Maryland when compared to that of Pensylvania. They laid out all the advantages of the latter which their bungling judgement could suggest and displayed all the imperfections and dissadvantages of the first. They inlarged upon the immorality, drunkeness, rudeness and im-

moderate swearing so much practised in Maryland and added
that no such vices were to be found in Pensylvania. I heard
this and contradicted it not, because I knew that the first part
of the proposition was pritty true. They next fell upon the goodness of the soil as far more productive of pasturage and grain.
I was silent here likewise, because the first proposition was
true, but as to the other relating to grain, I doubted the truth
of it. But what appeared most comical in their criticisms was
their making a merit of the stonnyness of the roads. "One may
ride," says Howard, "50 miles in Maryland and not see as
many stones upon the roads as in 50 paces of road in Pensylvania." This I knew to be false, but as I thought there was
no advantage in stonny roads, I even let them take the honour
of it to themselves and did not contradict them.

Att Newcastle I heard news of Mr. H[asel]l, my intended
fellow traveller. They told me he was att Willmington upon
Cristin River.

Cristin Ferry—Willmington—Brandywine

We crossed that ferry[41] att twelve a'clock and saw Willmington[42]
about a mile to the left hand. It is about the largeness of
Annapolis but seemingly more compactly built, the houses all
brick. We rid seven miles farther to one Foord's, passing over
a toll bridge in bad repair att a place called Brandywine. Att
Foord's we dined and baited our horses. There one Usher, a
clergiman, joined our company, a man seemingly of good naturall parts and civil behaviour but not overlearned for the
cloth. While dinner was getting ready, a certain Philadelphian
merchant called on Mr. Howard, and with him we had a dish
of swearing and loud talking.

After dinner we fell upon politicks, and the expected
French war naturally came in, whence arose a learned dispute

in company which was about settling the meaning of the two words, declaration and proclamation. Mr. Smith asserted that a proclamation of war was an impropper phraze, and that it ought to be a declaration of war, and on the other hand, a proclamation of peace. Mr. Morison affirmed with a bloody oath that there might be such a thing as a proclamation of a declaration and swore heartily that he knew it to be true both by experience and hearsay. They grew very loud upon it as they put about the bowl, and I retired into a corner of the room to laugh a little, handkerchef fashion, pretending to be busied in blowing my nose; so I slurd a laugh with nose blowing as people sometimes do a fart with coughing.

Att last the parson determined all by a learned definition to this purpose: that a proclamation was a publication of any thing by authority, and a declaration only a simple declaring of any thing without any authority att all but the bare assertion of a certain fact, as if I should declare that such a one was drunk att such a time, or that such a person swore so and so.

This dispute ended, we took our horses and rid moderately, it being excessive hot. I observed the common stile of salutation upon the road here was How d'ye? and How is't?

The people all along the road were making of hay which, being green and piled up in rucks, cast a very sweet and agreeable smell. There are here as fine meadows an[d] pasture grounds as any ever I saw in England. The country here is not hilly, nor are the woods very tall or thick. The people in generall follow farming and have very neat, brick dwelling houses upon their farms.

Chester

We passed thro' Chester[43] att 7 a'clock att night, where we left Morison, Smith, and Howard, and the parson and I jogged on intending to reach Darby, a town about 9 or 10 miles from Chester. Chester is a pritty, neat, and large village, built chiefly of brick, pleasantly situated upon a small river of the same name that discharges it self into Delaware about half a mile below where the village stands. Over this river is a wooden bridge built with large rafters and plank in form of an arch.[44] The State House is a pritty enough building. This put me in mind of Chelsea near London, which it resembles for neatness but is not near so large.

Darby

The parson and I arrived att Darby,[45] our resting place, att half an hour after eight att night. This village stands in a bottom and partly upon the ascent of a hill which makes it have a dull, melancholly appearance. We put up att a publick house kept by one Thomas where the landlady looked after every thing herself, the landlord being drunk as a lord. The liquor had a very strange effect upon him, having deprived him of the use of his tongue. He sat motionless in a corner smoking his pipe and would have made a pritty good figure upon arras.

We were entertained with an elegant dispute between a young Quaker and the boatswain of a privateer concerning the lawfullness of using arms against an enimy. The Quaker thee'd and thou'd it thro' the nose to perfection, and the privateer's boatswain swore just like the boatswain of a privateer, but they were so far from settling the point that the Quaker had almost acted contrary to his principles, clenching his fist att his antagonist to strike him for bidding God damn him. Att nine Mr. Usher and I went to bed.

Skuylkill Ferry

Wednesday, June 6th. We mounted horse att 5 in the morning, crossed Skuylkill Ferry[46] att 6, and in half an hour more put up our horses att one Cockburn's att the Sign of the Three Tons in Chestnut Street.[47]

Philadelphia

The country round the city of Philadelphia is level and pleasant, having a prospect of the large river of Delaware and the province of East Jersey upon the other side. You have an agreeable view of this river for most of the way betwixt Philadelphia and Newcastle. The plan or platform of the city lyes betwixt the two rivers of Delaware and Skuylkill, the streets being laid out in rectangular squares which makes a regular, uniform plan, but upon that account, altogether destitute of variety.

Att my entering the city, I observed the regularity of the streets, but att the same time the majority of the houses mean and low and much decayed, the streets in generall not paved, very dirty, and obstructed with rubbish and lumber, but their frequent building excuses that.[48] The State House, Assembly House,[49] the great church in Second Street,[50] and Whitefield's church[51] are good buildings.

I observed severall comicall, grotesque phizzes in the inn wher[e] I put up which would have afforded variety of hints for a painter of Hogarth's turn.[52] They talked there upon all subjects—politicks, religion, and trade—some tollerably well, but most of them ignorantly. I discovered two or three chaps very inquisitive, asking my boy who I was, whence come, and whether bound.

I was shaved by a little, finicall, hump backd old barber who kept dancing round me and talking all the time of the operation and yet did his job lightly and to a hair. He abounded in compliments and was a very civil fellow in his way. He told me he had been a journyman to the business for 40 odd years, notwithstanding which, he understood how to trim gentlemen as well (thank God) as the best masters and dispaired not of preferment before he dyed.

I delivered my letters, went to dine with Collector Alexander,[53] and visited severall people in town. In the afternoon I went to the coffee house[54] where I was introduced by Dr. Thomas Bond[55] to severall gentlemen of the place, where the ceremony of shaking of hands, an old custom peculiar to the English, was performed with great gravity and the usuall compliments. I took private lodgings att Mrs. Cume's in Chestnut Street.[56]

Thursday, June 7th. I remarked one instance of industry as soon as I got up and looked out att my chamber window, and that was the shops open att 5 in the morning. I breakfasted with Mrs. Cume and dined by invitation with Dr. Thomas Bond where, after some talk upon physicall matters, he showed me some pritty good anatomical preparations of the muscles and blood vessels injected with wax.

After dinner Mr. V[ena]bles,[57] a Barbadian gentleman, came in who, when we casually had mentioned the free masons, began to rail bitterly against that society as an impudent, assuming, and vain caball pretending to be wiser than all mankind besides, an *imperium in imperio,* and therefor justly to be discouraged and suppressed as they had lately been in some foreign countrys. Tho I am no free mason myself, I could not agree with this gentleman, for I abhorr all tyrannicall and arbitrary notions. I believe the free masons to be an innocent and harmless society that have in their constitution nothing mysterious or beyond the verge of common human understanding, and their secret, which has made such a noise, I imagine is just no secret att all.[58]

In the evening att the coffee house, I met Mr. H[asel]l,[59] and enquiring how he did and how he had fared on his way, he replied as to health he was pritty well, but he had almost been devoured with buggs and other vermin and had met with mean, low company which had made him very uneasy. He added that he had heard good news from Barbadoes concerning his friends there—from one, who he imagined called himself Captain Scrotum, a strange name indeed, but this gentleman had always some comicall turn in his discourse. I parted with him and went to the taveren with Mr. Currie[60] and some Scots gen[t]lemen where we spent the night agreeably and went home sober att eleven a'clock.

Friday, June 8. I read Montaign's Essays in the forenoon which is a strange medley of subjects and particularly entertaining.

I dined att a taveren with a very mixed company of different nations and religions. There were Scots, English, Dutch, Germans, and Irish; there were Roman Catholicks, Church men, Presbyterians, Quakers, Newlightmen, Methodists, Seventh day men, Moravians, Anabaptists, and one Jew. The whole company consisted of 25 planted round an oblong table in a great hall well stoked with flys. The company divided into comittees in conversation; the prevailing topick was politicks and conjectures of a French war. A knott of Quakers there talked only about selling of flower and the low price it bore. The[y] touched a little upon religion, and high words arose among some of the sectaries, but their blood was not hot enough to quarrell, or, to speak in the canting phraze, their zeal wanted fervency. A gentleman that sat next me proposed a number of questions concerning Maryland, understanding I had come from thence. In my replys I was reserved, pretending to know little of the matter as being a person whose business did not lye in the way of history and politicks.

In the afternoon I went to see some ships that lay in the river. Among the rest were three vessels a fitting out for privateers—a ship, a sloop, and a schooner. The ship was a large vessel, very high and full rigged; one Capt. Mackey intended to command her upon the cruise.[61] Att 6 a'clock I went to the coffee house and drank a dish of coffee with Mr. H[asel]l.

After staying there an hour or two, I was introduced by Dr. Phineas Bond[62] into the Governour's Club, a society of gentlemen that met at a taveren[63] every night and converse on various subjects. The Governour gives them his presence once a week, which is generally upon Wednesday, so that I did not see him there. Our conversation was entertaining; the subject was the English poets and some of the foreign writers, particularly Cervantes, author of Don Quixot, whom we loaded with elogiums due to his character. Att eleven a'clock I left this club and went to my lodging.

Saturday, June 9th. This morning there fell a light rain which proved very refreshing, the weather having been very hot and dry for severall days. The heat in this city is excessive, the sun's rays being reflected with such power from the brick houses and from the street pavement which is brick. The people commonly use awnings of painted cloth or duck over their shop doors and windows and, att sun set, throw buckets full of water upon the pavement which gives a sensible cool. They are stocked with plenty of excellent water in this city, there being a pump att almost every 50 paces distance.[64] There are a great number of balconies[65] to their houses where sometimes the men sit in a cool habit and smoke.

The market in this city is perhaps the largest in North-America. It is kept twice a week upon Wednesdays and Saturdays.[66] The street where it stands, called Market Street, is large and spacious, composed of the best houses in the city.

They have but one publick clock here which strikes the hour but has neither index nor dial plate. It is strange they should want such an ornament and conveniency in so large a place, but the chief part of the community consisting of Quakers, they would seem to shun ornament in their publick edifices as well as in their aparrell or dress.

The Quakers here have two large meetings,[67] the Church of England one great church in Second Street, and another built for Whitfield in which one Tennent,[68] a fanatick, now preaches, the Romans one chapell,[69] the Anabaptists[70] one or two meetings, and the Presbyterians two.[71]

The Quakers are the richest and the people of greatest interest in this goverment; of them their House of Assembly is chiefly composed. They have the character of an obstinate, stiff necked generation and a perpetuall plague to their governors. The present governour, Mr. Thomas,[72] has fallen upon a way to manage them better than any of his predecessors did and, att the same time, keep pritty much in their good graces and share some of their favours. However, the standing or falling of the Quakers in the House of Assembly depends upon their making sure the interest of the Palatines in this province, who of late have turned so numerous that they can sway the votes which way they please.

Here is no publick magazine of arms nor any method of defence, either for city or province, in case of the invasion of an enimy. This is owing to the obstinacy of the Quakers in maintaining their principle of non-resistance. It were a pity but they were put to a sharp triall to see whether they would act as they profess.[73]

I never was in a place so populous where the gout for publick gay diversions prevailed so little.[74] There is no such thing as assemblys of the gentry among them, either for dancing or musick; these they have had an utter aversion to ever since Whitefield preached among them. Their chief employ, indeed, is traffick and mercantile business which turns their thoughts from these levitys. Some Virginia gentlemen[75] that came here with the Commissioners of the Indian Treaty were desirous of having a ball but could find none of the feemale sex in a humour for it. Strange influence of religious enthusiasm upon human nature to excite an aversion at these innocent amusements, for the most part so agreeable and entertaining to the young and gay, and indeed, in the opinion of moderate people, so conducive to the improvement of politeness, good manners, and humanity.

I was visited this morning by an acquaintance from Annapolis of whom, inquiring the news, I could not learn any thing material.

I dined att the taveren, and returning home after dinner I read part of a book lately writ by Fielding entituled The Adventures of Joseph Andrews,[76] a masterly performance of its kind and entertaining; the characters of low life here are naturally delineated, and the whole performance is so good that I have not seen any thing of that kind equal or excell it.

This proved a rainy afternoon which, because it abated the sultry heat, was agreeable. I drank tea with Collector Alexander, where I saw Mr. H[asel]l. Their conversation turned upon the people in Barbadoes, and as I knew nothing of the private history of that island, I only sat and heard, for they went upon nothing but private characters and persons. This is a trespass on good manners which many well bred people fall into thro' inadvertency, two engrossing all the conversation upon a subject which is strange and unknown to a third person there.

At six in the evening I went to my lodging, and looking out att the window, having been led there by a noise in the street, I was entertained by a boxing match between a master and his servant. The master was an unweildy, pott-gutted fellow, the servant muscular, rawbon'd, and tall; therefor tho he was his servant in station of life, yet he would have been his master in single combat had not the bystanders asisted the master and holp him up as often as the fellow threw him down. The servant, by his dialect, was a Scotsman; the names he gave his master were no better than little bastard, and shitten elf, terms ill apply'd to such a pursy load of flesh. This night proved very rainy.

Sunday, June 10th. This proved a very wet morning, and there was a strange and surprizing alteration of the temperature of the air from hot and dry (to speak in the stile of that elegant and learned physitian, Dr. Salmon[77] and some other antient philosophers) to cold and moist.

I intended to have gone to church, or meeting, to edify by the Word but was diverted from my good purpose by some polite company I fell into who were all utter strangers to churches and meetings. But I understood that my negro Dromo very piously stept into the Lutheran Church[78] to be edified with a sermon preached in High Dutch, which, I believe, when dressed up in the fashion of a discourse, he understood every bit as well as English and so might edify as much with the one as he could have done with the other.

I dined att a private house with some of my countrymen, but our table chat was so trivial and trifling that I mention it not. After dinner I read the second volume of The Adventures of Joseph Andrews and thought my time well spent.

I drank tea with Mrs. Cume at 5 a'clock. There was a lady with her who gave us an elegant dish of scandal to relish our tea. At 6 a'clock I went to the coffee-house where I saw the same faces I had seen before. This day we had expresses from N.

York which brought instructions to proclaim war against France, and there was an express immediatly dispatched to Annapolis in Maryland for the same purpose.

Monday, June 11th. The morning proved clear, and the air cool and refreshing, which was a great relaxation and relief after the hot weather that had preceeded. I read Montaigne's Essays in the morning and was visited by Dr. Lloyd Zachary, a physitian in this place.[79]

I dined with Collector Alexander and went in the afternoon in the company of some gentlemen to attend the Governour to the Court House stairs where war was publickly to be proclaimed against France.[80] There were about 200 gentlemen attended Governour Thomas. Coll. Lee of Virginia walked att his right hand, and Secretary Peters[81] upon his left; the procession was led by about 30 flags and ensigns taken from privateer vessels and others in the harbour, which were carried by a parcell of roaring sailors. They were followed by 8 or 10 drums that made a confounded martiall noise, but all the instrumental musick they had was a pitifull scraping negroe fiddle which followed the drums and could not be heard for the noise and clamour of the people and the rattle of the drums. There was a rabble of about 4,000 people in the street and great numbers of ladies and gentlemen in the windows and balconies. Three proclamations were read: 1st, the King of England's proclamation of war against the French king; 2d, a proclamation for the encouragement of such as should fit out privateers against the enimy; 3d, the Governour of Pensylvania's proclamation for that province in particular, denouncing war and hostility against France.

When Secretary Peters had read these, the Governour, with a very audible voice, desired all such persons as were fit to carry arms to provide themselves—every man with a good musket, cartouch box, powder and shot, and such implements as were requisite either to repell or annoy the enimy if there should be any necessity or occasion—adding that he should surely call upon each of them to see that they were provided. "For depend upon it," says he, "this Province shall not be lost by any neglect or oversight of mine."[82]

The Governour having thus spoke, a certain bold fellow in the croud with a stentorian voice made this reply. "Please your Honour," says he, "what you say is right, but I and many others here, poor men, have neither money nor credit to procure a musket or the third part of a musket, so that unless the publick takes care to provide us, the bulk of the people must go unfurnished, and the country be destitute of defence." The Governour made no reply but smiled; so went into his chariot with Coll. Lee and the Secretary and drove homewards.

In the evening I drank tea with Mrs. Cume and went to the coffee house. Att 7 a'clock I went to the Governour's Club where were a good many strangers, among the rest Captain Macky, commander of the privateer ship. The conversation run chiefly upon trade and the late expedition att Cartagene.[83] Severall toasts were drank, among which were some celebrated ones of the female sex.

Tuesday, June 12. This seemed to me an idle kind of a day, and the heat began to return. I prepared my baggage, intending to morrow to proceed on my journey towards New York, which city I proposed to be my next resting place. I breakfasted abroad and dined att the taveren where I met another strange medley of company and, among the rest, a trader from Jamaica, a man of an inquisitive disposition who seized me for half an hour, but I was upon the reserve.

I drank tea with Mrs. Cume att 5 a'clock. There was with her a masculin faced lady, very much pitted with the small pox.

I soon found she was a Presbyterian, and a strait laced one too. She discovered my religion before I spoke. "You, sir," said she, "was educated a Presbyterian, and I hope you are not like most of your country men of that perswasion who, when they come abroad in the world, shamefully leave the meeting and go to church." I told her that I had dealt impartially betwixt both since I came to the place, for I had gone to neither. "That is still worse," said she.

I found this lady pritty well versed in the church history of Maryland. "I am surprized," said she, "how your goverment can suffer such a rascally clergy. Maryland has become a receptacle and, as it were, a common shore for all the filth and scum of that order. I am informed that taylors, coblers, blacksmiths, and such fellows, when they cannot live like gentlemen by their trade in that place, go home to take orders of some latitudinarian bishop and return learned preachers, setting up for teachers of the people, that have more need of schooling themselves; but that might bear some excuse if their lives were exemplary and their morals good, but many of them are more compleatly wicked than the most profligate and meanest of the laity. It is a shame that such fellows should be inducted into good livings without any further ceremony or enquiry about them than a recommendation from L[or]d B[altimo]re.[84]

"The English think fit sometimes to be very merry upon the ignorance and stupidity of our Presbyterian clerks. I am sorry indeed that it is too true that many of them have exposed themselves in ridiculous colours, but, notwithstanding this, can the generality of their clergy, as wise and learned as they are, show such good behaviour and moral life? Besides, generally speaking, in Scotland where the Presbyterian constitution is the national church, they admitt none now to holy orders who have not had a college education, studied divinity regularly, and undergone a thorrow examination before a presbytery of clerks. Do the English do so? No, their inferior clergy are rascally fellows who have neither had a fit education nor had their knowledge put to the tryall by examination, but undergoing some foolish ceremony or farce from a bishop, commence teachers presently and prove afterwards inferior to none for ignorance and vice. Such are your Maryland clerks."

I heard this long harangue with patience and attempted to speak in defence of our clergy, but this lady's instructions bore such credit with her that she would not be contradicted. I quoted the maxim of Constantin the Great who used to say that when a clergiman offended, he would cover him with his cloak; but her charity for the order, I found, did not extend so far; so I allowed her to run on in this kind of criticall declamation till her stock was exhausted.

I must make a few remarks before I leave this place. The people in generall are inquisitive concerning strangers. If they find one comes there upon the account of trade or traffic, they are fond of dealing with him and cheating him if they can. If he comes for pleasure or curiosity, they take little or no notice of him unless he be a person of more than ordinary rank; then they know as well as others how to fawn and cringe. Some persons there were inquisitive about the state of religion in Maryland. My common reply to such questions was that I studied their constitutions more than their consciences so knew something of the first but nothing of the latter.

They have in generall a bad notion of their neighbouring province, Maryland, esteeming the people a sett of cunning sharpers; but my notion of the affair is that the Pensylvanians are not a whit inferior to them in the science of chicane, only their method of tricking is different. A Pensylvanian will tell a lye with a sanctified, solemn face; a Marylander, perhaps, will convey his fib in a volley of oaths; but the effect and point in view is the same tho' the manner of operating be different.

In this city one may live tollerably cheap as to the articles of eating and drinking, but European goods here are extravagantly dear. Even goods of their own manufacture such as linnen, woolen, and leather bear a high price. Their goverment is a kind of anarchy (or no goverment), there being perpetual jarrs betwixt the two parts of the legislature. But that is no strange thing, the ambition and avarice of a few men in both partys being the active springs in these dissentions and altercations, tho a specious story about the good and interest of the country is trumpt up by both; yet I would not be so severe as to say so of all in generall.

Mr. T[homa]s, the present gov[erno]r, I believe is an upright man and has the interest of the province really att heart, having done more for the good of that obstinate generation, the Quakers, than any of his predecessours have done. Neither are they so blind as not to see it, for he shares more of their respect than any of their former governours were wont to do.

There is polite conversation here among the better sort, among whom there is no scarcity of men of learning and good sense. The ladies, for the most part, keep att home and seldom appear in the streets,[85] never in publick assemblies except att the churches or meetings; therefor I cannot with certainty enlarge upon their charms, having had little or no opportunity to see them either congregated or separate, but to be sure the Philadelphian dames are as handsome as their neighbours.

The staple of this province is bread, flower, and pork. They make no tobacco but a little for their own use. The country is generally plain and levell, fruitfull in grain and fruits, pretty well watered, and abounding in woods backward. It is upon the growing hand, more than any of the provinces of America. The Germans and High Dutch are of late become very numerous here.

Wednesday, June 13. Early in the morning I set out from Philadelphia, being willing to depart that city where, upon account of the excessive heat, it was a pain to live and breath. Two gentlemen of the city, Mr. Currie and Mr. Wallace,[86] complimented me with their company 5 miles of the road. I remarked in the neighbourhood of Philadelphia some stone bridges, the first that I had seen in America. The country people whom I met asked in generall whether war had been proclaimed against France.

Shamany Ferry—Bristo'

About 9 in the morning I crossed Shamany Ferry[87] and half an hour after rested att Bristo,[88] a small town 20 miles N. East of Philadelphia situated upon Delaware River, opposite to which upon the other side of the river stands Burlington, the chief town in the East Jerseys.

I put up my horses in Bristo' and breakfasted att Malachi Walton's att the Sign of the Crown,[89] intending to tarry till the cool of the evening and then proceed to Trenton about 10 miles farther. Bristo' is pleasantly situated and consists of one street that runs upon a descent towards the river and then, making an angle or elbow, runs paralell to the river for about a quarter of a mile. Here are some wharfs, pritty commodious, for small vessels to load and unload. The houses in the town are chiefly brick, and the adjacent land pritty levell and woody.

Delaware Ferry—Jersey Goverment—Trenton

I took horse about 5 in the afternoon, crossed the ferry of

Delaware[90] about 7 a'clock, and a little after arrived att Trenton
in East Jersey. Upon the left hand near the river on the Jersey
side is a pritty box of a house, the propperty of Governour
Thomas of Pensylvania, in which Coll. Morris,[91] the present
Governour of the Jerseys, lives. Upon the right hand close
upon the town is a fine water mill belonging likewise to Collonell Thomas, with a very pritty cascade that falls over the
dam like a transparent sheet about 30 yards wide.[92]

I was treated att my entry into the town with a dish of
staring and gaping from the shop doors and windows, and I
observed two or three people laying hold of Dromo's stirrups,
enquiring, I suppose, who I was and whence I came.

I put up att one Eliah Bond's att the Sign of the Wheat
Sheaf.[93] Two gentlemen of the town came there and invited
me into their company. One was named Cadwaller,[94] a doctor in
the place and, as I understood, a fallen of[f] Quaker. We supped upon cold gammon and a sallet. Our discourse was mixed
and rambling; att first it was politicall; then Cadwaller gave
me the character of the constitution and goverment. The
House of Assembly here, he told me, was chiefly composed
of mechanicks and ignorant wretches, obstinate to the last
degree; that there were a number of proprietors in the
goverment, and a multitude of Quakers. He enlarged a little
in the praise of Governour Morris, who is now a very old man.
From politicks the discourse turned to religion and then to
physick.

Cadwaller asked me concerning severall people in Maryland, and among the rest (not yet knowing me) he came across
my self, asking me if Hamilton att Annapolis was dead or alive.
"Here he is," says I, "bodily and not spiritually." He told me the
reason why he enquired was that about a twelvemonth agoe,
one Dr. Thomson[95] from Maryland had been there and had re-

ported he was going to settle att Annapolis in place of Hamilton there who they did not expect would live. "But, sir," says he, "if you be the man, I congratulate you upon your unexpected recovery."

Thus passing from one subject to another in discourse, Cadwaller inveighed bitterly against the idle ceremonies that had been foisted into religious worship by almost all sects and perswasions—not that there was any thing materiall in these ceremonies to cavill att providing the true design of them was understood and they were esteemed only as decent decorations and ornaments to divine service in the temples and churches, but upon account that the vulgar in all ages had been misled and imposed upon by wicked, politick, and designing priests and perswaded that the strength and sinews of religion lay in such fopperies, and that there was no such thing as being a good man or attaining salvation without all this trumpery. "It is certain," added he, "that a superstitious regard and veneration to the mere ceremonials of religion has contributed very much to corrupt the manners of men, turning their thoughts from true morality and virtue (to promote which ought to be the sole aim of all religions whatsoever) to dwell upon dreams, chimeras fit only to distract the human mind and give place for mad zeal, the woefull author of persecution, murder, and cruelty."

To this I replied that priests of all sorts and sects whatsoever made a kind of trade of religion, contriving how to make it turn out to their own gain and profit; yet notwithstanding, many were of opinion that to inculcate religion into vulgar minds we must use other methods than only preaching up fine sense and morality to them. Their understanding and comprehension are too gross and thick to receive it in that shape. Men of sense of every perswasion whatsoever are sensible of the emptiness and nonsense of the mere cermonial part of religion but, att the same time, allow it to be in some degree necessary and usefull, because the ignorant vulgar are to be dealt with in this point as we manage children by showing them toys in order to perswade them to do that which all the good reasoning of the world never would. The mobile, that many headed beast, cannot be reasoned into religious and pious duties. Men are not all philosophers. The tools by which we must work upon the gross senses and rough cast minds of the vulgar are such as form and lay before their eyes, rewards and punishments whereby the passions of hope and fear are excited; and withall our doctrines must be interlaced with something amazing and misterious in order to command their attention, strengthen their belief, and raise their admiration, for was one to make religion appear to them in her genuine, simple, and plain dress, she would gain no credit and would never be so regarded—. Here Cadwaller interupted me and said all these discourses signified nothing, for he thought she was very little regarded even as it was. We dismissed att twelve att night.

Thursday, June 14. A little after 5 in the morning I departed Trenton and rid twelve miles of a very pleasant road well stored with houses of entertainment. The country round about displays variety of agreeable prospects and rurall scenes. I observed many large fields of wheat, barley, and hemp, which is a great staple and commodity now in this province, but very little maiz or Indian corn; only two or three small fields I observed in riding about 40 miles. They plant it here much thicker than in Maryland, the distance of one stalk from another not exceeding two foot and a half or three foot at most. All round you in this part of the country you observe a great many pleasant fertile meadows and pastures which diffuse, att this season of the year in the cool of the morning, a sweet and refreshing smell. The houses upon the road are many of them built with rough stone.

Princetown

I passed thro' Princetown, a small village,[96] at eight in the morning and was saluted with *How' s't ni tap*[97] by an Indian traveller. About half a mile from this village I observed upon the road a quarry of what appeared to me grey slate, the first I had seen in America.

Kingstown

Att half an hour after eight in the morning, I put up att one Leonards's[98] att the Sign of the Black Lyon in Kingstown,[99] another small village upon the road. I breakfasted there upon a dish of tea and was served by a pritty smiling girl, the landlord's daughter. After breakfast, as I sat in the porch, there arrived a waggon with some company. There were in it two Irishman, a Scotsman, and a Jew. The Jew's name was Abraham Du-bois, a French man by birth. He spoke such bad English that I could scarce understand him. He told me he had been att Conestogo to visit some relations he had there; that he left that place upon Monday last, and att that time there had arived there 40 canoes of Indians of the tribes of the Mohooks and 5 Nations going to treat with the Governours and Commissioners of the American provinces.[100]

This Jew and the company that were with him begun a dispute about sacred history. He insisted much upon the books of Moses and the authority of the Old Testament. He asked the Scotsman in particular if he believed the Old Testament. He replied that now a days there were few Old Testament people, all having become *New Light men,* "for," says he, "among the Christians, one wife is sufficient for one man, but your Old Testament fornicators were allowed a plurality of wives and as many concubines as they could afford to maintain." The Jew made no answer to this nonsensicall reply but began very wisely to settle what day of the week it was and what time of that day that God began the creation of the world. He asserted that it was upon the day that the Christians call Sunday, and that when the light first appeared, it was in the west, and therefor it was in the evening that the creation was begun. "Had that evening no morning then?" replyed the Scotsman with a sneer. To which the Jew answered that there had been no dawn or sun rising that day because the sun was not yet created to run his diurnall course, but that a glorious stream of light suddenly appeared by the mandate of God in the west. "I never heard of an evening without a morning in my life before," replied his antagonist, "and it is nonsence to suppose any such thing." "Cannot black exist," said the Jew, "without its opposite white?" "It may be so," said the Scotsman, "but why does your countryman Moses say 'and the evening and the morning was the first day?' " The Jew answered that the evening was there first mentioned because the work was begun upon the evening, att which the Scotsman swore that the words were misplaced by the translators, which pert reply put an end to the dispute.

After a deal of such stuff about the Jewish sabbath and such like subjects, the waggon and company departed. They travell here in light, convenient waggons made somewhat chaise fashion, being high behind and low before, many of them running upon 4 wheels so that the horses bear no weight but only draw, and by this means they can travell att a great rate, perhaps 40 or 50 miles a day.[101]

Betwixt twelve a'clock and three in the afternoon there came up three smart thunder gusts with which fell a deal of rain, but it did not much cool the air. In the middle of the first rain a solemn old fellow lighted att the door. He was in a homely rustick dress, and I understood his name was Morgan. "Look ye here," says the landlord to me, "here comes a famous philosopher." "Your servant, Mr. Morgan, how d'ye?" The old fellow had not settled himself long upon his seat before he entered upon a learned discourse concerning astrology and the influences of the stars, in which he seemed to put a great deal more confidence than I thought was requisite. From that he made a transition to the causes of the tides, the shape and dimensions of the earth, the laws of gravitation, and 50 other physicall subjects in which he seemed to me not to talk so much out of the way as he did upon the subject of judiciall astrology. Att every period of this old philosopher's discourse, the landlord's address to him was, "Pray, Mr. Morgan, you that are a philosopher know such and such reasons for such and such things, please inform the gentleman of your opinion." Then he fell upon physick and told us that he was a riding for his health. I found him very deficient in his knowledge that way, tho a great pretender. All this chat passed while the old fellow drank half a pint of wine, which done, the old don took to his horse and rid off in a very slow solemn pace, seemingly well satisfied with his own learning and knowledge. When he was gone, I enquired of the landlord more particularly concerning him, who told me that he was the most conspicuous and notorious philosopher in all these American parts; that he understood mademadigs [mathematics] to a hair's breadth and had almost discovered whereabouts the longitude lay and had writ home to the States of Holland and some other great folks about it a great while agoe but had as yet received no answer.

A little after two a clock we went to dinner, and att 4 I took horse, having in company a comicall old fellow named

Brown that was going to New York to examine the old records concerning some land he had a title to in the lower countys of Pensylvania goverment. This old fellow entertained me the whole way with points of law and showed himself tollerably well versed, for one of his education, in the quirps, quibbles, and the roguish part of that science. As we jogged on I observed some mountanous land about 15 or 16 miles to the northward.

Brunswick

We arived att 6 a clock att Brunswick,[102] a neat small city in East Jersey goverment, built chiefly of brick and lying upon Raretin River about 60 miles northeast of Philadelphia. I put up this night att one Miller's att the Sign of Admiral Vernon[103] and supped with some Dutchmen and a mixed company of others. I had a visit from one Dr. Farquar[104] in town who did not stay long with me, being bound that night for New York by water. Our conversation att supper was such a confused medley that I could make nothing of it. I retired to bed att eleven a'clock after having eat some very fine pickled oysters for supper.

Raretin Ferry

Friday, June 15. A little before 6 in the morning I forded Raretin River,[105] the tide being low and the skeow aground so that I could not ferry it over. I went by way of Perth Amboy, but before I came to that place I was overtaken by two men, a young man and an old, grave, sedate fellow. The young man gave me the salute which I returned and told him that if he was going to Amboy, I should be glad of company. He replied he was going that way. First of all (as it is naturall) we enquired concerning news. I gave him an account of such scraps of news as I had picked up att Philadelphia, and he gave me an account of a capture that had well nigh been made of an English sloop by a Frenchman that had the impudence to pursue her into the hook at the entrance of York Bay, but the English vessel getting into Amboy harbour, the Frenchman betook himself to sea again. "But had this French rogue known Amboy as well as I," added my newsmonger, "he would have taken her there at anchor." After discussing news, we discoursed concerning horses, by which I discovered that my chap was a jockey by trade. This topic lasted till we came to Perth Amboy, and the old don spoke not one word all the way but coughd and chawd tobacco.

Perth Amboy

At nine in the morning we stoped att the Sign of the King's Arms in Amboy where I breakfasted. As I sat in the porch I observed an antick figure pass by having an old plaid banyan, a pair of thick worsted stockings, ungartered, a greasy worsted nightcap, and no hat. "You see that originall," said the landlord. "He is an old batchellor, and it is his humour to walk the street always in that dress. Tho he makes but a pitifull appearance, yet is he proprietor of most of the houses in town. He is very rich, yet for all that, has no servant but milks his own cow, dresses his own vittles, and feeds his own poultry himself."

Amboy is a small town (it is a very old American city, being older than the city of New York)[106] being a chartered city, much less than our Annapolis,[107] and here frequently the Supream Court and Assembly sit. It has in it one Presbyterian meeting[108] and a pritty large market house, lately built. It is the principall town in New Jersey and appears to be laid out in the shape of a St. George's cross, one main street cutting the other att right angles. 'Tis a sea port, having a good harbour but small trade. They have here the best oysters I have eat in America. It lyes close upon the water, and the best houses in town are ranged along the water side.

In the Jerseys the people are chiefly Presbyterians and Quakers, and there are so many proprietors that share the lands in New Jersey, and so many doubtfull titles and rights that it creates an inexhaustible and profitable pool for the lawers.

Amboy Ferry—New York Goverment—Staten Island

Att ten a'clock I crossed the ferry[109] to Staten Island where are some miles of pritty stony, sandy, and uneven road. I took notice of one intire stone there about 10 foot high, 12 foot long, and 6 or 7 foot thick. Att one end of it grew an oak tree, the trunk of which seemed to adhere or grow to the stone. It lay close by a little cottage which it equalld pritty near in dimensions. I remarked this stone because I had not seen so large a one any where but in the Highlands of Scotland. A great many of the trees here are hung thick with long, hairy, grey moss which, if handsomly oild and powdered and tyed behind with a bag or ribbon, would make a tollerable beau-periwig. In this island are a great many poor, thatched cottages. It is about 18 miles long and 6 or 7 miles broad. It seems to abound with good pasture and is inhabited by farmers. There are in or near it some towns, the chief of which are Kathrin's Town, Cuckold's Town,[110] and Woodbridge.[111]

Narrows Ferry

I came to the Narrows att two a'clock and dined att one Corson's that keeps the ferry.[112] The landlady spoke both Dutch and English. I dined upon what I never had eat in my life before— a dish of fryed clams, of which shell fish there is abundance in these parts. As I sat down to dinner I observed a manner of saying grace quite new to me. My landlady and her two daughters put on solemn, devout faces, hanging down their heads and holding up their hands for half a minute. I, who had gracelessly fallen too without remembering that duty according to a wicked custom I had contracted, sat staring att them with my mouth choak full, but after this short meditation was over, we began to lay about us and stuff down the fryed clams with rye-bread and butter. They took such a deal of chawing that we were long att dinner, and the dish began to cool before we had eat enough. The landlady called for the bedpan. I could not guess what she intended to do with it unless it was to warm her bed to go to sleep after dinner, but I found that it was used by way of a chaffing dish to warm our dish of clams. I stared att the novelty for some time, and reaching over for a mug of beer that stood on the opposite side of the table, my bag sleeve catched hold of the handle of the bed pan and unfortunatly overset the clams, at which the landlady was a little ruffled and muttered a scrape of Dutch of which I understood not a word except mynheer, but I suppose she swore, for she uttered her speech with an emphasis.

After dinner I went on board the ferry boat and, with a pritty good breeze, crossed the Narrows in half an hour to Long Island.

Long Island

Att the entry of this bay is a little craggy island about one or two miles long called Coney Island. Before I came to New York Ferry, I rid a bye way where, in seven miles' riding, I had 24 gates to open. Dromo, being about 20 paces before me, stoped att a house where, when I came up, I found him discoursing a negroe girl who spoke Dutch to him. "Dis de way to York?"

says Dromo. "Yaw, dat is Yarikee," said the wench, pointing to the steeples. "What devil you say?" replys Dromo. "Yaw, mynheer," said the wench. "Damme you, what you say?" said Dromo again. "Yaw, yaw," said the girl. "You a damn black bitch," said Dromo and so rid on. The road here for severall miles is planted thick upon each side with rows of cherry trees, like hedges, and the lots of land are mostly inclosed with stone fences.

York Ferry

Att 5 in the afternoon I called att one Baker's that keeps the York Ferry[113] where, while I sat waiting for a passage, there came in a man and his wife that were to go over. The woman was a beauty, having a fine complexion and good features, black eyes and hair, and an elegant shape. She had an amorous look, and her eyes, methought, spoke a language which is universally understood. While she sat there her tongue never lay still, and tho' her discourse was of no great importance, yet methought her voice had musick in it, and I was fool enough to be highly pleased to see her smiles att every little impertinence she uttered. She talked of a neighbour of hers that was very ill and said she was sure she would dye, for last night she had dreamt of nothing but white horses and washing of linnen. I heard this stuff with as much pleasure as if Demosthenes or Cicero had been exerting their best talents, but mean time was not so stupid but I knew that it was the fine face and eyes and not the discourse that charmed me. Att six a'clock in the evening I landed att New York.

New York

This city makes a very fine appearance for above a mile all along the river, and here lyes a great deal of shipping. I put my horses up att one Waghorn's att the Sign of the Cart and Horse.[114] There I fell in with a company of toapers. Among the rest was an old Scotsman, by name Jameson,[115] sheriff of the city, and two aldermen whose names I know not. The Scotsman seemed to be dictator to the company; his talent lay in history, having a particular knack att telling a story. In his narratives he interspersed a particular kind of low wit well known to vulgar understandings. And having a homely carbuncle kind of a countenance with a hideous knob of a nose, he screwd it into a hundred different forms while he spoke and gave such a strong emphasis to his words that he merely spit in one's face att three or four foot's distance, his mouth being plentifully bedewed with salival juice, by the force of the liquor which he drank and the fumes of the tobacco which he smoaked. The company seemed to admire him much, but he set me a staring.

After I had sat some time with this polite company, Dr. Colchoun,[116] surgeon to the fort, called in, to whom I delivered letters, and he carried me to the taveren which is kept by one Todd,[117] an old Scotsman, to supp with the Hungarian Club of which he is a member and which meets there every night. The company were all strangers to me except Mr. Home, Secretary of New Jersey, of whom I had some knowledge, he having been att my house att Annapolis. They saluted me very civily, and I, as civilly as I could, returned their compliments in neat short speeches such as, "Your very humble servant," "I'm glad to see you," and the like commonplace phrazes used upon such occasions. We went to supper, and our landlord Todd entertained us as he stood waiting with quaint saws and jack pudding speeches. "Praised be God," said he, "as to cuikry, I defaa ony French cuik to ding me, bot a haggis is a dish I wadna tak the trouble to mak. Look ye, gentlemen, there was anes a Frenchman axed his frind to denner. His frind axed him 'What ha' ye gotten till eat?' 'Four an' twenty legs of mutton,' quo' he, 'a' sae differently cuiked that ye winna ken whilk is whilk.' Sae whan he gaed there, what deel was it, think ye, but four and twenty sheep's trotters, be God.'" He was a going on with this tale of a tub when, very sasonably for the company, the bell, hastily pulled, called him to another room, and a little after we heard him roaring att the stair head, "Dam ye bitch, wharefor winna ye bring a canle?"

After supper they set in for drinking, to which I was averse and therefor sat upon nettles. They filled up bumpers att each round, but I would drink only three which were to the King, Governour Clinton, and Governour Bladen, which last was my own.[119] Two or three toapers in the company seemed to be of opinion that a man could not have a more sociable quality or enduement than to be able to pour down seas of liquor and remain unconquered while others sunk under the table. I heard this philosophical maxim but silently dissented to it. I left the company att 10 att night pritty well flushed with my three bumpers and, ruminating on my folly, went to my lodging att Mrs. Hogg's in Broadstreet.[120]

Saturday, June 16. I breakfasted with my landlady's sister, Mrs. Boswall. In the morning Dr. Colchoun called to see me, and he and I made an appointment to dine att Todd's. In the afternoon I took a turn thro' severall of the principall streets in town, guarding against staring about me as much as possible for fear of being remarked for a stranger, gaping and staring being the true criterion or proof of rustick strangers in all places.

The following observations occurred to me: I found this city less in extent but, by the stirr and frequency upon the streets, more populous than Philadelphia; I saw more shipping in the harbour; the houses are more compact and regular and, in generall, higher built, most of them after the Dutch modell with their gavell ends fronting the street.[121] There are a few built of stone, more of wood, but the greatest number of brick, and a great many covered with pan tile and glazed tile with the year of God when built figured out with plates of iron upon the fronts of severall of them. The streets, in generall, are but narrow and not regularly disposed. The best of them run paralell to the river, for the city is built all along the water. In generall this city has more of an urban appearance than Philadelphia. Their wharfs are mostly built with logs of wood piled upon a stone foundation. In the city are severall large publick buildings. There is a spacious church belonging to the English congregation with a pritty high but heavy, clumsy steeple built of freestone fronting the street called Broadway.[122] There are two Dutch churches,[123] severall other meetings, and a pritty large Town House[124] at the head of Broadstreet. The Exchange stands near the water and is a wooden structure, going to decay.[125] From it a peer runs into the water, called the Long Bridge, about 50 paces long, covered with plank and supported with large wooden posts. The Jews have one synagogue in this city.[126] The women of fashion here appear more in publick than in Philadelphia and dress much gayer. They come abroad generally in the cool of the evening and go to the Promenade.

I returned to my lodging att 4 a'clock, being pritty much tired with my walk. I found with Mrs. Boswall a handsom young Dutch woman. We drank tea and had a deal of trifling chat, but the presence of a pritty lady, as I hinted before, makes even triffling agreeable. In the evening I writ letters to go by the post to Annapolis and att night went and supped with the Hungarian Club att Todd's, where, after the bumpers began to go round according to their laudable custom, we fell upon various conversation in which Todd, standing by, mixed a deal of his clumsy wit which, for the mere stupidity of it, sometimes drew a laugh from the company. Our conversation ended this night with a piece of criticism upon a poem in the newspaper, where one of the company, Mr. M[oor]e,[127] a lawer, showed more learning than judgement in a disquisition he made upon nomnatives and verbs, and the necessity there was for a verb to each nomnative in order to make sense. We dismissed att eleven a'clock.

Sunday, June 17th. At breakfast, I found with Mrs. Boswall some gentlemen, among whom was Mr. J[effer]ys,[128] an officer of the customs in New York. To me he seemed a man of an agreeable conversation and spirit. He had been in Maryland some years agoe and gave me an account of some of his adventures with the planters there. He shewed me a deal of civility and complaisance, carried me to church, and provided me with a pew. The minister who preached to us was a stranger. He gave us a good discourse upon the Christian virtues. There was a large congregation of above a thousand, among which was a number of dressed ladies. This church is above 100 foot long and 80 wide. Att the east end of it is a large semicircular area in which stands the altar, pritty well ornamented with painting and guilding. The gallerys are supported with wooden pillars of the Ionick order with carved work of foilage and cherubs' heads guilt betwixt the capitals. There is a pritty organ att the west end of the church consisting of a great number of pipes handsomly guilt and adorned, but I had not the satisfaction of hearing it play, they having att this time no organist, but the vocall musick of the congregation was very good.[129]

Mr. J[effer]ys carried me to Mr. Bayard's[130] to dine, and att 4 a'clock we went to the coffee house.[131] I drank tea att a gentlewoman's house, whose name I know not, being introduced there by Mr. J[effer]ys. There was an old lady and two young ones, her daughters I suppose. The old lady's discourse run upon news and politicks, but the young women sat mute, only now and then smiled att what was said, and Mr. Jeffrys enlivened the conversation with repartee.

Att six o'clock I went to see the fort and battery. The castle, or fort, is now in ruins, having been burnt down three or four years agoe by the conspirators, but they talk of repairing it again. The Leutenant Governour had here a house and a chapell, and there are fine gardens and terrass walks from which one has a very pritty view of the city. In the fort are severall guns, some of them brass and cast in a handsome mould. The new battery is raised with ramparts of turf, and the guns upon it are in size from 12 to 18 pounders. The main battery is a great half moon or semicircular rampart bluff upon the water, being turf upon a stone foundation about 100 paces in length, the platform of which is laid in some places with plank, in others with flag stone. Upon it there are 56 great iron guns, well mounted, most of them being 32 pounders. Mr. J[effery]s told me that to walk out after dusk upon this platform was a good way for a stranger to fit himself with a courtezan, for that place was the generall rendezvous of the fair sex of that profession after sun set. He told me there was a good choice of pritty lasses among them, both Dutch and English. However, I was not so abandoned as to go among them but went and supped with the Club att Todd's.

It appeared that our landlord was drunk, both by his words and actions. When we called for any thing he hastily pulled the bell rope, and when the servants came up, Todd had by that time forgot what was called for. Then he gave us a discourse upon law and gospell and swore by God that he would prove that law was founded upon gospell and gospell upon law, and that reason was depending upon both, and therefor to be a good lawer it was substituted to be a good gospeller. We asked him what such a wicked dog as he had to do with gospell. He swore by God that he had a soul to be saved as well as the King, and he would neither be hang'd nor damn'd for all the Kings in Christendome. We could not get rid of him till we put him in a passion by affirming he had no soul and offering to lay him a dozen of wine that he could not prove he had one. Att which, after some taggs of incoherent arguments, he departed the room in wrath, calling us heathens and infidels. I went home att 12 a'clock.

Monday, June 18. Most of this day proved rainy, and therefor I could not stir much abroad. I dined att Todd's with Dr. Colchoun and a young gentleman, a stranger. After dinner the doctor and I went to the coffee-house and took a hitt att backgammon. He beat me two games. Att 5 in the afternoon I drank tea with Mrs. Boswall and went to the coffee house again, where I looked on while they playd att chess. It continued to rain very hard. This night I shunned company and went to bed att nine.

Tuesday, June 19th. At breakfast with my landlady, I found two strange gentlemen that had come from Jamaica. They had just such cloudy countenances as are commonly wore the morning after a debauch in drinking. Our conversation was a medley, but the chief subject we went upon was the differences of climates in the American provinces with relation to the influence they had upon human bodies. I gave them as just an account as I could of Maryland—the air and temperature of that province, and the distempers incident to the people there.

I could not help suspecting that there were some physicians in the company by the tenor of the discourse but could not understand for certain that any one there besides myself was a professed physician. One gentleman there that came from Coraçoa told us that in a month's time he had known either 30 or 40 souls buried which, in his opinion, was a great number in the small neighbourhood where he lived. I could scarce help laughing out at this speech and was just going to tell him that I did not think it was customary to bury souls anywhere but in Ireland, but I restrained my tongue, having no mind to pick a quarrell for the sake of a joke.

We dined att Todd's, with seven in company, upon veal, beef stakes, green pease, and rasp berries for a desert. There, talking of a certain free negroe in Jamaica who was a man of estate, good sense, and education, the 'forementioned gentleman who had entertained us in the morning about burying of souls, gravely asked if that negroe's parents were not whites, for he was sure that nothing good could come of the whole generation of blacks.

Afternoon I drank tea with Mrs. Boswall, having, to pass away time, read some of the Journal of Proceedings against the conspirators att New York.[132] Att night I went to a taveren fronting the Albany coffee house along with Doctor Colchoun, where I heard a tollerable concerto of musick performed by one violin and two German flutes. The violin was by far the best I had heard playd since I came to America. It was handled by one Mr. H——d.

Wednesday, June 20. I dined this day att Todd's where I mett with one Mr. M——ls [Milne],[133] a minister att Shrewsbery in the Jerseys who had formerly been for some years minister att Albany. I made an agreement to go to Albany with him the first opportunity that offered. I enquired accordingly

THE CLUBMAN'S PROGRESS

Club Life was a prominent feature of colonial America. Especially was this so in the larger towns and cities where gentlemen resorted almost nightly to a "set club" consisting of a limited number and meeting at a stated time at their favorite tavern. "We meet," said Jonas Green, "converse, laugh, talk, smoke, drink, differ, agree, argue, Philosophize, harangue, pun, sing, dance and fiddle together, nay we are really in fact a club." The portraits by Feke, Bridges, Wollaston, Copley, and other colonial limners always show the gentry of eighteenth-century America in a pose of self-conscious dignity. When the clubs assembled, however, such stiffness vanished. Through the amateur drawings of Dr. Alexander Hamilton we are fortunately permitted a glimpse, as it were through the keyhole, of the gentlemen in a relaxed mood—and not infrequently with their wigs off.

These seven sketches, which we may properly call *The Clubman's Progress,* obviously take their cue from the great Hogarth, who was in these same years giving English pictorial satire its unity of style. The first, third, and seventh were drawn by Dr. Hamilton as embellishments for the Record of the Tuesday Club between 1747 and 1754, and it is not improbable that the fourth and sixth, representing the Royalist Club, are also his work.

The very amateurish quality of the drawings gives them a greater realism than the imaginative subleties of Hogarth. Collectively they provide a unique record of the colonial gentry at play, exhibiting their special blend of intellectualism, ribaldry and horseplay. First we see the dignified opening of the meeting with a reading of the minutes; next the installation ritual (which modern fraternities have inherited via Phi Beta Kappa); followed by inevitable dissension. The next sequence depicts conviviality and bibulousness (note the absence of glasses!), succeeded by a brawl and a temporary breakdown of fraternalism and good fellowship. All this, however, is kept within the club, and when, as in the last picture, the members sally forth into the public view all are affable and decorous.

FRONTISPIECE

The grand Ceremony of the Capation —

The Grand Clubical Battle of the Great Seal,
and the decathedration of the Lord President.

The Royalist Club

Mr Neilson's anger restrained by Philosophy.

Mr Neilson's battle with the Royalist Club

The first Grand Anniversary Procession

att the coffee house for the Albany sloops, but I found none ready to go. I got acquainted with one Mr. Weemse, a merchant of Jamaica, my countryman and fellow lodger att Mrs. Hog's. He had come here for his health, being afflicted with the rheumatism. He had much of the gentleman in him, was good natured but fickle, for he determined to go to Albany and Boston in company with me but, sleeping upon it, changed his mind. He drank too hard; whence I imagined his rheumatism proceeded more than from the intemperature of the Jamaica air. After dinner I playd backgammon with Mr. J[effer]ys, in which he beat me two games for one. I read out the Journall of Proceedings and att night prepared my baggage to go for Albany.

Thursday, June 21. I dined att Todd's with severall gentlemen and called upon Mr. M——ls [Milne] att two o'clock, with whom I intended to go by water to Albany in a sloop belonging to one Knockson. I met here with one Mr. Knox, a young man, son of David Knox late of Edinburgh, surgeon, in whose shop I had learnt pharmacy. While we talked over old storys, there passed some comic discourse betwixt Todd and four clumsy Dutchmen. These fellows asked him if they could all drink for 4 pence. "That you may," says Tod, "such liquor as 4 pence will afford." So he brought them a bottle of ship-beer and distributed it to them in a half pint tumbler, the last of which being mostly froth. The Dutchman, to whose share it came, looking angrily att Todd, said, "The Deyvill dam the carle!" "Dam the fallow," says Tod, "what wad he ha' for his 4 pennies?" After getting my baggage and some provisions ready, I went on board the Albany sloop where I found Mr. M——s [Milne] and his wife, an old jolly, fat Dutchwoman, mother to the Patroon att Albany,[134] a gentleman there of Dutch extract, the chief landed man in the place.

Nutting Island

Having a contrary wind and an ebb tide, we dropt anchor about half a mile below New York and went ashore upon Nutting Island,[135] which is about half a mile in dimension every way, containing about 60 or 70 square acres. We there took in a cask of spring water. One half of this island was made into hay, and upon the other half stood a crop of good barley, much dammaged by a worm which they have here which, so soon as their barley begins to ripen, cuts off the heads of it. There lived an old Scots-Irishman upon this island with his family in a ruinous house, a tennant of the Governour's to whom the island belongs *durante officio*. This old man treated us with a mug of ship beer and entertained us with a history of some of the adventures of the late Governour Cosby[136] upon that is-land. It is called Nutting Island from its bearing nuts in plenty, but what kind of nuts they are I know not, for I saw none there. I saw myrtle berrys growing plentifully upon it, a good deal of juniper, and some few plants of the ipecacuan. The banks of the island are stonny and steep in some places. It is a good place to erect a battery upon to prevent an enimy's approach to the town, but there is no such thing, and I believe that an enimy might land on the back of this island out of reach of the town battery and plant cannon against the city or even throw boombs from behind the island upon it.

We had on board this night 6 passengers, among whom were three women. They all could talk Dutch but muself and Dromo, and all but Mr. M——s[Milne] seemed to preferr it to English. Att eight a'clock att night, the tide serving us, we weighed anchor and turned it up to near the mouth of North River and dropt anchor again att 10 just opposite to the great church in New York.

Friday, June 22d. While we waited the tide in the morning,

Mr. M——s [Milne] and I went ashore to the house of one Mr. Van Dames[137] where we breakfasted and went from thence to see the new Dutch church, a pritty large but heavy stone building, as most of the Dutch edifices are, quite destitute of taste or elegance. The pulpit of this church is prittily wrought, being of black walnut. There is a brass supporter for the great Bible that turns upon a swivell, and the pews are in a very regular order. The church within is kept very clean, and when one speaks or hollows, there is a fine eccho. We went up into the steeple where there is one pritty large and handsom bell, cast att Amsterdam, and a publick clock. From this steeple we could have a full view of the city of New York.

Early this morning two passengers came on board of the sloop, a man and a woman, both Dutch. The man was named Marcus Van Bummill. He came on board drunk and gave us a surfet of bad English. If any body laughed when he spoke, he was angry, being jealous that they thought him a fool. He had a good deal of the bully and braggadocio in him, but when thwarted or threatened, he seemed faint hearted and cowardly. Understanding that I was a valitudinarian, he began to advise me how to manage my constitution. "You drink and whore too much," said he, "and that makes you thin and sickly. Could you abstain as I have done and drink nothing but water for 6 weeks, and have to do with no women but your own lawfull wife, your belly and cheeks would be like mine, look ye, plump and smooth and round." With that he clapt his hands upon his belly and blowd up his cheeks like a trumpeter. He brought on board with him a runlett of rum, and, taking it into his head that somebody had robed him of a part of it, he went down into the hold and fell a swearing bitterly by *Dunder Sacramentum*, and *Jesu Christus*. I, being upon deck and hearing a strange noise below, looked down and saw him expanding his hands and turning up his eyes as if he had been att prayers. He was for having us all before a magistrate about it, but att last Knockson, the master of the sloop, swore him into good humour again and perswaded him that his rum was all safe. He quoted a deal of scripture, but his favorite topics when upon that subject was about King David, and King Solomon, and the shape and size of the Tower of Babel. He pretended to have been mighty familiar with great folks when they came in his way, and this familiarity of his was so great as even to scorn and contemn them to their faces. After a deal of talk and rattle, he went down and slept for four hours and, when he waked, imagined he had slept a whole day and a night, swearing it was Saturday night when it was only Friday afternoon. There was a Dutch woman on board, remarkably ugly, upon whom this Van Bummill cast a loving eye and wanted much to be att close conference with her.

Greenwitch

Att twelve a clock we passed a little town, starboard, called Greenwitch [Greenwich Village], consisting of eight or ten neat houses, and two or three miles above that on the same shoar, a pritty box of a house with an avenue fronting the river, belonging to Oliver Dulancie.[138] On the left hand some miles above York, the land is pritty high and rockey, the west bank of the river for severall miles being a steep precipice above 100 foot high.

Mr. M——s [Milne] read a treatise upon microscopes and wanted me to sit and hear him, which I did, tho' with little relish, the piece being trite and vulgar, and tiresome to one who had seen Leewenhoek[139] and some of the best hands upon that subject. I soon found M——ls's [Milne's] ignorance of the thing, for as he read he seemed to be in a kind of surprize

att every little trite observation of the author's. I found him
an intire stranger to the mathematicks, so as that he knew not
the difference betwixt a cone and a pyramid, a cylinder and
a prysm. He had studied a year att Leyden under Boerhaave,[140]
even after he had entered into holy orders. He had once wore
a souldier's livery, was very whimsicall about affairs relating
to farming in so much that he had spent a deal of money
in projects that way but reaped as little profit as projectors
commonly do. I was told by a gentleman that knew him that
formerly he had been an immoderate drinker so as to expose
himself by it, but now he was so much reformed as to drink
no liquor but water. In some parts of learning, such as the
languages, he seemed pritty well versed. He could talk Latine
and French very well and read the Greek authors, and I was
told that he spoke the Dutch to perfection. He enquired of me
concerning Parson C——se of Maryland, but I could not find
out which of the C——ses it was. He told me he had once
given him a hearty horsewhipping for some rude language he
gave him in a theologicall dispute which they had. I was informed by him that Morgan, the philosopher and mathe-
matician whom I had seen att Kingstown, was his curate.

We passed a little country house belonging to one Philips[141]
att 4 a'clock, starboard. This house is about 20 miles above
York. We had severall learned discourses in the evening from
Van Bummill concerning doctors. "You are a doctor," says he
to me; "what signifys your knowledge? You pretend to know
inward distempers and to cure them, but to no purpose; your
art is vain. Find me out a doctor among the best of you that
can mend a man's body half so well as a joiner can help a
crazy table or stool. I myself have spent more money on doctors than I would give for the whole tribe of them if I had
it in my pocket again. Experience has taught me to shun them

as one would impostors and cheats, and now no doctor for me but the great Doctor above." This was the substance of his discourse, tho it was not so well connected as I have delivered it. After this harangue he took a dram or two and got again into his wonted raving humour. He took it in his head that Lord B——e was confined in the tower of Troy, as he called it, went down into the hold, and after he had there disgorged what was upon his stomach, he went to sleep and dreamt about it. He came upon deck a little before sunset and was so full of it that he hailed each vessel that passed us and told it as a piece of news.

We had a fresh westerly wind att night, which died away att 10 a'clock, and we dropt anchor about 40 miles above York.

Saturday, June 23. We weighed anchor about 4 in the morning, having the wind northeast and contrary, and the tide beginning to fall, we dropt anchor again att 7. Mr. Van Bummill was early upon deck and was very inquisitive with Mr. M——s [Milne] about the meaning of the word superstition, saying he had often met with that word in English books but never could understand what was meant by it. Then he read us the 26th chapter of the Ecclesiasticus concerning women, and after he had murdered the reading in the English, he read it from the Dutch Bible and lectured upon it att large to the passengers and crew, and tho he looked himself as grave as a parson, yet the company broke frequently out into fits of laughter.

We went ashore to fill water near a small log cottage on the west side of the river inhabited by one Stanespring and his family. The man was about 37 years of age, and the woman 30. They had seven children, girls and boys. The children seemed quite wild and rustick. They stared like sheep upon M——s [Milne] and I when we entered the house, being amazed att my laced hat and sword. They went out to gather black-berries for us, which was the greatest present they could make us. In return for which, we destributed among them a hand-full of copper halfpence. This cottage was very clean and neat but poorly furnished. Yet Mr. M——s [Milne] observed severall superfluous things which showed an inclination to finery in these poor people, such as a looking glass with a painted frame, half a dozen pewter spoons and as many plates, old and wore out but bright and clean, a set of stone tea dishes, and a tea pot. These, Mr. M——ls [Milne] said, were superfluous and too splendid for such a cottage, and therefor they ought to be sold to buy wool to make yarn; that a little water in a wooden pail might serve for a looking glass, and wooden plates and spoons would be as good for use and, when clean, would be almost as ornamental. As for the tea equipage it was quite un-necessary, but the man's musket, he observed, was as usefull a piece of furniture as any in the cottage. We had a pail of milk here which we brought on board, and the wind coming southerly att eleven a'clock, we weighed anchor and entered the Highlands which presented a wild, romantick scene of rocks and mountains covered with small scraggy wood, mostly oak.

Dunder Barrak—Anthony's Nose—Cook's Island

We passed Dunder Barrak, or Thunder Hill,[142] larboard, att half an hour after eleven, and another hill, starboard, called Anthony's Nose[143] from its resemblance to a man's nose, under which lyes Cook's Island, being a small rock about 10 paces long and 5 broad upon which is buried a certain cook of a man of war from whom it got its name. His sepulchre is surrounded with 10 or 12 small pine trees about 20 foot high which make a grove over him. This wild and solitary place, where nothing presents but huge precipices and inaccessible steeps where foot of man never was, infused in my mind a kind of melancholly and filled my imagination with odd thoughts which, att the same time, had something pleasant in them. It was pritty to see the springs of water run down the rocks, and what entertained me not a little was to observe some pritty large oaks growing there, and their roots to appearance fixed in nothing but the sollid stone where you see not the least grain of mould or earth. The river is so deep in these Narrows of the Highlands that a large sloop may sail close upon the shore. We kept so near that the extremity of our boom frequently rustled among the leaves of the hanging branches from the bank. In some places of the channell here there is 90 fathom water, and very near the shore in severall places 70 or 60 fathom.

Hay Ruck

We passed the Hay Ruck, a hill so called from its resemblance, upon our starboard att dinner time. There are severall cottages here, very small that a man can scarce stand upright in them, and you would think that a strong fellow would carry his wooden hut upon his back.

Deoper's Island

About three in the afternoon we cleared the Highlands and left a small island called Doeper's, or Dipper's Island,[144] to the starboard. It is so named because, they say, it has been customary to dip strangers here unless they make the sloop's crew drink, and by that they save their dipping and are made free in the river. Wherefor, as I never had been that way before, I saved my dipping with a bottle of wine which I spared them from my stores.

Butter Mountain—Murder Creek

Att 4 a'clock we passed the Butter Mountain[145] on our larboard, above which is Murder Creek,[146] so called from a massacre of the white men that was committed by the Indians at the first settlement of the part.

Dancing Hall

Att 6 a'clock we passed Dancing Hall[147] larboard, a little square and levell promontory which runs about 50 paces into the river, overgrown with bushes where, they report, about 60 or 70 years agoe, some young people from Albany, making merry and dancing, were killed by some Indians who lay in ambush in the woods.

   We had a discourse this evening from Van Bummill about the Tower of Babel, which was his constant and darling theme. He told us that in all his reading he never could be informed of the height of it, and as to its figure, he was pretty certain of that from the pictures of it which he had seen. When he had finished his argument he got to talking a medley of Dutch and English to the women, which confusion of language was a propos after he had been busy about the Tower of Babel. The learned Van Bummill and the two Dutch women left us att seven a'clock, going ashore to a place two miles below Poughcapsy where they lived.

Poughcapsy

We anchored att eight o'clock att the entry of that part of the river called Long Reach,[148] the weather being very thick and rainy, and close by us on the starboard side stood a small village called Poughcapsy[149] where the master and hands went ashore and left us to keep the sloop.

   Sunday, June 24th. At four in the morning Mr. M——s [Milne] and I went ashore to the taveren, and there we met with a justice of the peace and a New Light taylor. The justice seemed to have the greatest half or all the learning of the county in his face, but so soon as he spoke, we found that he was no more learned than other men. The taylor's phizz was screwed up to a santified pitch, and he seemed to be either under great sorrow for his sins or else a hatching some mischief in his heart, for I have heard that your hipocriticall rogues always put on their most solemn countenance or vizzard when they are contriving how to perpetrate their villanies. We soon discovered that this taylor was a Moravian. The Moravians are a wild, fanatick sect with which both this place and the Jerseys are pestered. They live in common, men and women mixed in a great house or barn where they sometimes eat and drink, sometimes sleep, and sometimes preach and howl, but are quite idle and will employ themselves in no usefull work. They think all things should be in common and say that religion is intirely corrupted by being too much blended with the laws of the country. They call their religion the true religion, or the religion of the Lamb, and they commonly term themselves the followers of the Lamb, which I believe is true in so far as some of them may be wolves in sheep's clothing. This sect was first founded by a German enthusiast, Count Zenzindorff,[150] who used to go about some years agoe and perswade the people to his opinions and drop a certain catechism which he had published upon the high way. They received a considerable strength and addition to their numbers by Whitefield's preaching in these parts but now are upon the decline since there is no opposition made to them. M———ls [Milne] and I anatomized this Moravian taylor in his own hearing, and yet he did not know of it, for we spoke Latin. He asked what language that was. The justice told him he believed it was Latin, att which the cabbager sigh'd and said it was a pagan language. We treated him, however, with a dram and went from the taveren to one Cardevitz's who, having the rheumatism in his arm, asked my advice, which I gave him. The land here is high and woody, and the air very cool.

Sopus Village

We weighed anchor att 7 a clock with the wind south west and fresh and half an hour after passed by Sopus,[151] a pleasant village situated upon the west side of the river, famous for beer and ale.

Little Sopus Island

A little above that is a small island called Little Sopus which is about half way betwixt Albany and York. Att Sopus we passed by the Governour's fleet consisting of three painted sloops. That therein Clinton was had the union flag a stern. He had been att Albany treating with the Indians.

Blue Mountains

We now had a sight of the range of mountains called the Catskill, or Blue Mountains, bearing pritty near N. W. and capd with clouds. Here the river is about 2 miles broad, and the land low, green, and pleasant. Large open fields and thickets of woods, alternatly mixed, entertains the eye with variety of landskips.

Ancrum—Ransbeck

Att 12 a'clock we sailed by Ancrum,[153] starboard, the seat of Mr. Livingston, a lawer, where he has a fine brick house standing close upon the river. The wind blew very high att south east. Att half an hour after 12 we saw the town of Ransbeck,[154] a German town, starboard, in which are two churches.

Livingston Mannor

Att one a'clock we scudded by Livingston Mannor;[155] then the Catskill Hills, bore W. by south. Att three o'clock we sailed by a Lutheran chappell larboard, where we could see the congregation dismissing, divine service being over.

Carnine Island—Musman's Island

Att 4 a'clock we passed by Carnine Island, about 3 miles in length. Att five we sailed past Musman's Island, starboard, where there is a small nation of the Mochacander Indians[156] with a king that governs them. We run aground upon a sand bank att half an hour after 5 a'clock and by hard labour got clear again in about an hour. This was a great dissappointment to us, for we expected that night to reach Albany. There came up a thunder gust as soon as we got clear which obliged us to furle our sails and fix our anchor, but it soon went over; so with a small wind we made three miles farther and passed a sloop bound for York where some fine folks were on board. Att eight a'clock there came up a hard storm with very sharp thunder so that we were obliged to let go our anchor again and there remain all night.

Monday, June 25th. We went ashore this morning upon a farm belonging to 'Cobus Ranslaer, brother to the Patroon att Albany. (James by the Dutch appellation is 'Cobus, being Jacobus contracted.) There is here a fine saw mill that goes by water.

Prec Stone

Att seven o clock, the wind being southerly, we hoised anchor, and sailing up the river we passed a large stone, larboard, called Prec Stone, or Preaching Stone, from its resemblance to a pulpit. We had not made much way before the wind changed to

north west so we resolved to go to Albany in the sloop's canoe
and went ashore to borrow another to carry our baggage. We
found the poor people there in great terror of the Indians;
they being apprehensive that they would begin their old trade
of scalping.

Albany

We set off in the canoes att nine a clock and saw Albany att
a distance. We landed upon an island belonging to Mr. M——s
[Milne], upon which there was fine grass of different sorts and
very good crops of wheat and pease, of which they bring up
great quantitys here for the use of the ships—the bug not getting
into their pease there as with us. These were the first fields of
pease I had seen since I left Brittain. We met severall Dutchmen on the island who had rented morgans of land upon
it; they call half an acre of land there a morgan.

These people were very inquisitive about the news and
told us of a French man and his wife that had been att Albany
the day before we arrived. They had come from Canada, and
it was they we saw on board the sloop that passed us last night.
The Frenchman was a fugitive, according to his own account,
and said he had been a priest and was expelled his convent for
having an intrigue with that lady who was now his wife. The
lady had been prosecuted att law and had lost the greatest
part of her estate which went among these cormorants, the
lawers. The Governour of Canada, Mons'r Bon Harnois,[157]
being her enimy, she could not expect justice, and therefor
fled with this priest to the English settlements in order to prevent her being intirely beggar'd, taking the residue of her
estate along with her. This Bonharnois is now a very old man
and, they say, behaves himself tyrranically in this goverment.
He was a courtier in Lewis XIVth's time and then went by

the name of Mons'r Bon Vit, which being an ugly name in the French language, the King changed his name to Bonharnois. This day there came some Canada Indians in two canoes to Albany to pursue this priest and his lady. 15,000 livres were laid upon each of their heads by the Governour. They said they had orders to bring back the priest dead or alive, if dead to scalp him and take the consecrated flesh from his thumb and forefinger. The lady they were to bring back alive, but they came too late to catch their game. Mr. M——s [Milne] imagined that all this story was a plausable fiction, and that the Frenchman was sent among them as a spy, but this conception of his to me seemed improbable.

Albany

Tuesday, June 26th. Early this morning I went with Mr. M——s [Milne] to Albany, being a pleasant walk of two miles from the island. We went a small mile out of town to the house of Jeremiah Ranslaer, who is dignified here with the title of Patroon. He is the principal landed man in these parts, having a large mannor, 48 miles long and 24 broad, bestowed upon his great grandfather by K. Charles the Second after his restoration. The old man, it seems, had prophesied his recovering of his kingdoms ten years before it happened. The King had been his lodger when he was in Holland, and thereby he had an opportunity to ingratiate himself and procure the royall favour. This mannor is divided into two equall halves by Hudson's River, and the city of Albany stands in the middle of it. This city pays him a good yearly rent for the liberty of cutting their fire wood. The Patroon is a young man of good mein and presence. He is a batchellor, nor can his friends perswade him to marry. By paying too much hommage to Bacchus, he has acquired a hypochondriac habit. He has a great number of tennants upon his mannor, and he told me himself that he could muster 600 men fit to bear arms. Mr. M——s [Milne] and I dined att his house and were handsomly entertained with good viands and wine. After dinner he showed us his garden and parks, and M——s [Milne] got into one of his long harangues of farming and improvement of ground.

Att 4 a'clock M——s [Milne] and I returned to town where M——s [Milne], having a generall acquaintance, for he had practised physick ten years in the city and was likewise the Church of England minister there, he introduced me into about 20 or 30 houses where I went thro' the farce of kissing most of the women, a manner of salutation which is expected (as M——s [Milne] told me) from strangers coming there. I told him it was very well, if he led the way I should follow, which he did with clericall gravity. This might almost pass for a pennance, for the generality of the women here, both old and young, are remarkably ugly.

Att night we went to the island, where we supped. While we were att supper we smelt something very strong like burnt oatmeal which they told me was an animall called a schunk, the urine of which could be smelt att a great distance, something of the nature of the polecat but not quite so dissagreeable.

Cohoos

Wednesday, June 27. I went this morning with the Patroon's brother, Stephen Renslaer,[158] to see the Cochoos,[159] a great fall of water 12 miles above Albany. The water falls over a rock almost perpendicular, 80 foot high and 900 foot broad, and the noise of it is easily heard att 4 miles' distance; but in the spring of the year when the ice breaks, it is heard like great guns all the way att Albany. There is a fine mist scattered about where it falls for above half a mile below it, upon which when the sun shines opposite, appears a pritty rainbow. Near the fall the noise is so great that you cannot discern a man's voice unless he hollows pritty loud. Below the fall the river is very narrow and very deep, running in a rockey channell about 200 foot wide, att each side of which channell there is a bank of sollid rock about 3 or 400 foot wide, as smooth and levell as a table.

In this journey we met a Mohook Indian and his family going a hunting. His name was Solomon. He had a squaw with him over whom he seemed to have an absolute authority. We travelled for two miles thro impenetrable woods, this Indian being our guide, and when we came to the banks of the river near the falls, we were obliged to leave our horses and descend frightfull precipices. One might walk across the river on foot upon the top of the rock whence the water falls was it not for fear of being carried down by the force of the water, and Solomon told us that the Indians sometimes run across it when the water is low.

Mohooks Town

We rid att a pritty hard rate 15 or 16 miles farther to the Mohooks town standing upon the same river. In it there are severall wooden and brick houses, built after the Dutch fashion, and some Indian wigwams or huts, with a church where one Barclay[160] preaches to a congregation of Indians in their own language, for the bulk of the Mohooks up this way are Christians.

Returning from here we dined att Coll. Skuyler's[161] about 4 a'clock in the afternoon, who is naturalized among the Indians, can speak severall of their languages, and has lived for years among them. We spent part of the evening att the Patroon's, and going to town att night I went to the taveren with Mr. Livingston,[162] a man of estate and interest there, where we had a mixed conversation.

Schenectady

Thursday, June 28. Early this morning I took horse and went in company with one Collins,[163] a surveyor here, to a village called Schenectady about 16 miles from Albany and pleasantly situated upon the Mohook's River. It is a trading village, the people carrying on a traffic with the Indians—their chief commoditys wampum, knives, needles, and other such pedlary ware. This village is pritty near as large as Albany and consists chiefly of brick houses, built upon a pleasant plain, inclosed all round att about a mile's distance with thick pine woods. These woods form a copse above your head almost all the way betwixt Albany and Schenectady, and you ride over a plain, levell, sandy road till, coming out of the covert of the woods, all att once the village strikes surprizingly your eye, which I can compare to nothing but the curtain rising in a play and displaying a beautifull scene.

We returned to M———s's [Milne's] island, from whence between twelve and one a'clock I went to Albany in a canoe, the day being somewhat sultry, tho in this latitude the heats are tollerable to what they are two or three degrees to the southward, the mornings and evenings all summer long being cool and pleasant, but often about noon and for three hours after the sun is very hot. I went to see the school in this city in which are about 200 schollars, boys and girls. I dined att the Patroon's; after dinner Mr. Shakesburrough, surgeon to the fort, came in, who by his conversation, seemed to have as little of the quack in him as any half hewn doctor ever I had met with. The doctors in Albany are mostly Dutch, all empyricks, having no knowledge or learning but what they have acquired by bare experience. They study chiefly the virtues of herbs, and the woods there furnish their shops with all the pharmacy they use. A great many of them take the care of a family for the value of a Dutch dollar a year, which makes the practise of physick a mean thing and unworthy of the application of a gentleman. The doctors here are all barbers. This afternoon I went a visiting with M——s [Milne] and had the other kissing bout to go thro'. We went at night to visit Stephen Renslaer's where we supped.

Friday, June 29th. After breakfast I walked out with M——s [Milne] and visited some more old women, where I had occasion to prescribe and enter into a dispute with a Dutch doctor. Mr. M——s's [Milne's] gesture in common discourse often afforded me subject of speculation. Att every the least triffling expression and common sentence in discourse, he would shrug up his shoulders and stare one in the face as if [he] had uttered some very wonderfull thing, and he would do the same while another person spoke tho he expressed nothing but common chat. By this means it was hard to tell when any thing struck his fancy, for by this odd habit he had contracted in his gesture, every thing seemed alike to raise his admiration. About this time one Kuyler,[164] the mayor of the city, was suspected of trading with the Canada Indians and selling powder to them. The people in town talked pritty openly of it, and the thing coming to Governour Clinton's ears, he made him give security for his appearance att the Generall Court to have the affair tried and canvassed.

I went before dinner with M——s [Milne] and saw the inside of the Town House.[165] The great hall where the court sits is about 40 foot long and thirty broad. This is a clumsy, heavy building both without and within. We went next and viewd the workmen putting up new palisading or stockadoes to fortify the town, and att ten a'clock we walked to the island and returned to town again att 12. Mr. M——s [Milne] and I dined upon cold gammon att one Stevenson's, a Scots gentleman of some credit there. We drank tea att Steph. Ranslaer's and supped att Widow Skuyler's where the conversation turned upon the Moravian enthusiasts and their doctrines.

Saturday, June 30. In the morning I went with M——s [Milne] to make some more visits, of which I was now almost tired. Among others we went to see Dr. Rosaboom, one of the Dutch medicasters of the place, a man of considerable practice in administering physic and shaving. He had a very voluminous Dutch Herbalist lying on the table before him, being almost a load for a London porter. The sight of this made me sick, especially when I understood it was writ in High Dutch. I imagined the contents of it were very weighty and ponderous, as well as the book itself. It was writ by one Rumpertus Dodonous. From this book Rosaboom had extracted all his learning in physick, and he could quote no other author but the great, infallable Rumpertus, as he stiled him. His discourse to us tended very much to self commendation, being an historicall account of cases in surgery where he had had surprizing success.

Att ten o'clock M——s [Milne] and I went to the island, where we dined, and M——s [Milne], being hot with walking, went to drink his cool water as usuall which brought an ague upon him, and he was obliged to go to bed. In the mean time the old woman and I conversed for a half an hour about a rurall life and good husbandry. Att three o'clock I walked abroad to view the island, and sitting under a willow near the water, I was invited to sleep, but scarce had I enjoyed half an hour's repose when I was waked by a cow that was eating up my handkercheff which I had put under my head. I pursued her for some time before I recovered it, when I supposed the snuff in it made her disgorge, but it was prittily pinked all over with holes.

I went to the house and drank tea and then walked to town with M——s [Milne]. On the way we met an old man who goes by the name of Scots Willie. He had been a souldier in the garrison but was now discharged as an invalid. He told us he had been att the battle of Killicrankie[166] in Scotland upon the side where Lord Dundee fought, and that he saw him fall in the battle. We supped by invitation att the taveren with some of the chief men in the city, it being muster day and a treat given by the officers of the fort to the muster masters. There was Messrs. Kuyller the Mayor, Tansbrook[167] the Recorder, Holland the Sherriff, Surveyor Collins, Captain Blood, Captain Haylin of the fort, and severall others. The conversation was rude and clamorous, but the viands and wine were good. We had news of the French having taken another small fort besides Cansoe.[168] I walked with M——s [Milne] to the island att 10 at night.

Sunday, July 1st. A[t] six a'clock this morning a sharp thunder gust came up with a heavy rain. I breakfasted att the island and went to town with M——s [Milne] and his wife. At 10 a'clock we went to the English Church[169] where was the meanest congregation ever I beheld, there not being above 15 or 20 in church besides the souldiers of the fort who sat in a gallery. M——s [Milne] preached and gave us an indifferent good discourse against worldly riches, the text being, "It is easier for a cable [camel] to pass thro' the eye of a needle than for a rich man to enter the kingdom of heaven." This discourse, he told me, was calculated for the naturall vice of that people, which was avarice, and particularly for Mr. Livingston, a rich but very covetous man in town who valued himself much for his riches. But unfortunately Livingston did not come to church to hear his reproof.

Att 12 a'clock another thunder gust came up. We dined at St. Renslaer's and made severall visits in the afternoon. Among the rest we went to see Captain Blood of the fort. He is nephew to the famous Blood that stole the crown.[170] This man is a downright old souldier, having in his manner an agreeable mixture of roughness and civility. He expressed a strong regard for the memory of the Duke of Berrwick, of whose death, when he heard, he could not forbear crying, for tho' he was an enimy to his master, the King of England, yet was he a brave and generous man, for when he and severall other English officers were taken prisoners in battle by the French, the duke generously gave them liberty upon their parole and lent, or indeed gave them, ten pistoles a piece to furnish their pockets when they were quite bare of money. This spirit of gratitude in the old man pleased me very much and made me conceive a good opinion of him, gratitude being a certain criterion or mark of a generous mind. After visiting him we went to Captain Haylin's house, who received us very civilly but not in such a polite manner as Captain Blood. He told us he had been a dragoon att the siege of Namur in K: William's time and was then 20 years old, which makes him an older man than Blood whose first campain was the battle of Almanza.[171] I observed the streets of this city to be most crowded upon Sunday evening, especially with women. We supped att St. Ranslaer's.

Monday, July 2d. I now began to be quite tired of this place where was no variety or choise, either of company or conversation, and one's ears perpetually invaded and molested with volleys of rough sounding Dutch, which is the language most in use here. I therefor spoke to one Wendall, master of a sloop which was to sail this evening for York, and took my passage in him. I laid in a stock of provisions for the voyage att one Miller's, a sergeant of the fort who keeps the taveren and where my landlady, happening to be a Scotswoman, was very civil and obliging to me for country's sake. She made me a present of a dryed tongue. As I talked with her a certain ragged fellow came bluntly up and took me by the hand, naming me. "Sir," says he, "there is a gentleman here in town who says he knows you and has been in your garden att Annapolis in Maryland when he lived with one Mr. Dulany[172] there. He swears by G—d he would be glad to see you to talk a little or so, as it were, about friends and aquaintances there. He bid me tell you so and, 'damme,' says I, 'if I dont,' so I hope the gentleman wont be offended." I told him no, there was no offence, but bid him give my service to my friend and tell him I was now in a hurry and could not wait upon him but some other time would do as well. So giving this orator a dram, I went and drank half a pint with Captains Blood and Haylin and walked to the island where I dined. In the afternoon I read Rollin's Belles Letters.[173] The day was hazy and threatned rain very much.

Att half an hour after two a'clock I saw Wendall's sloop falling down the river with the tide, and they having given me the signall of a gun which was agreed upon, they sent their canoe for me. Att three o'clock I took my leave of M——s [Milne] and his wife, thanking them for all their civilitys and the hospitality I had met with in their house. I followed the sloop for near two miles in the canoe before I overtook her and went on board half an hour after three. We had scarce been half an hour under sail after I came on board when we run aground upon some shoals about a mile above the Oversleigh[174] and dropt anchor till after 6. The tide rising we were afloat again and went down with the wind N. by East. Rainy.

There was a negroe fellow on board who told me he was a piece of a fiddler and played some scraping tunes to one Wilson who had come on board of us in a canoe. This was an impudent fellow. He accosted me with "How do you, countryman?" att first sight and told me he was a Scotsman, but I soon found by his howl in singing the Black Jock to the negroe fiddle that he was a genuine Teague. He told me some clever lyes and claimed kin to Arncaple in Scotland, said he had an estate of houses by heritage in Glasgow, swore he was born a gentleman for 5 generations and never intended for the plough; therefor he had come to push his fortune in these parts.

Oversleigh

Att seven o'clock we reach the Oversleigh and there run aground again. In the meantime a Dutch gentleman, one Volckert Douw, came on board a passenger, and I flattered myself I should not be quite alone but enjoy some conversation; but I was mistaken, for the devil a word but Dutch was bandied about betwixt the saylors and he, and in generall there was such a medley of Dutch and English as would have tired a horse. We heaved out our anchor and got off the shoal att half an hour after seven, so got clear of the Oversleigh, the only troublesom part in the whole voyage. We sailed four miles below it, the wind north east and the night very rainy and dark. We dropt anchor at nine at night and went to bed.

The city of Albany lyes on the west side of Hudson's River upon a rising hill about 30 or 40 miles below where the river comes out of the lake and 160 miles above New York. The hill whereon it stands faces the south east. The city consists of three pritty compact streets, two of which run paralell to the river and are pritty broad, and the third cuts the other two att right angles, running up towards the fort,[175] which is a square stone building about 200 foot square with a bastion att each corner, each bastion mounting eight or ten great guns, most of them 32 pounders. In the fort are two large, brick houses facing each other where there is lodging for the souldiers. There are three market houses in this city and three publick edifices, upon two of which are cupolos or spires, vizt., upon the Town House and the Dutch church.[176] The English church is a great, heavy stone building without any steeple, standing just below the fort. The greatest length of the streets is half a mile. In the fort is kept a garrison of 300 men under the King's pay, who now and then send reinforcements to Oswego, a frontier garrison and trading town lying about 180 miles south [north] and by west of Albany. This city is inclosed by a rampart or wall of wooden palisadoes about 10 foot high and a foot thick, being the trunks of pine trees rammed into the ground, pinned close together, and ending each in a point att top. Here they call them stockadoes. Att each 200 foot distance round this wall is a block house, and from the north gate of the city runs a thick stone wall down into the river, 200 foot long, att each end of which is a block house. In these block houses about 50 of the city militia keep guard every night, and the word all's well walks constantly round all night long from centry to centry and round the fort. There are 5 or 6 gates to this city, the chief of which are the north and the south gates. In the city are about 4,000 inhabitants, mostly Dutch or of Dutch extract.

The Dutch here keep their houses very neat and clean, both without and within. Their chamber floors are generally laid with rough plank which, in time, by constant rubbing and scrubbing becomes as smooth as if it had been plained. Their chambers and rooms are large and handsom. They have their beds generally in alcoves so that you may go thro all the rooms of a great house and see never a bed. They affect pictures much, particularly scripture history, with which they adorn their rooms. They set out their cabinets and bouffetts much with china. Their kitchens are likewise very clean, and there they hang earthen or delft plates and dishes all round the walls in manner of pictures, having a hole drilled thro the edge of the plate or dish and a loop of ribbon put into it to hang it by. But notwithstanding all this nicety and cleanliness in their houses, they are in their persons slovenly and dirty. They live here very frugally and plain, for the chief merit among them seems to be riches, which they spare no pains or trouble to acquire, but are a civil and hospitable people in their way but, att best, rustick and unpolished. I imagined when I first came there that there were some very rich people in the place. They talked of 30, 40, 50 and 100 thousand pounds as of nothing, but I soon found that their riches consisted more in large tracts of land than in cash. They trade pritty much with the Indians and have their manufactorys for wampum, a good Indian commodity. It is of two sorts—the black, which is the most valuable, and the white wampum. The first kind is a bead made out of the bluish black part of a clam shell. It is valued att 6 shillings York money per 100 beads. The white is made of a conch shell from the W. Indies and is not so valuable. They grind the beads to a shape upon a stone, and then with a well tempered needle dipt in wax and tallow, they drill a hole thro' each bead. This trade is apparently triffling but would soon make an estate to a man that could have a monopoly of it, for being in perpetuall demand among the Indians from their custome of burying quantitys of it with their dead, they are very fond of it, and they will give skins or money or any thing for it, having (tho they first taught the art of making it to the Europeans) lost the art of making it themselves.

They live in their houses in Albany as if it were in prisons, all their doors and windows being perpetually shut. But the reason of this may be the little desire they have for conversation and society, their whole thoughts being turned upon profit and gain which necessarily makes them live retired and frugall. Att least this is the common character of the Dutch every where. But indeed the excessive cold winters here obliges them in that season to keep all snug and close, and they have not summer sufficient to revive heat in their veins so as to make them uneasy or put it in their heads to air themselves. They are a healthy, long lived people, many in this city being in age near or above 100 years, and 80 is a common age. They are subject to rotten teeth and scorbutick gumms which, I suppose, is caused by the cold air and their constant diet of salt provisions in the winter, for in that season they are obliged to lay in as for a sea voyage, there being no stirring out of doors then for fear of never stirring again. As to religion they have little of it among them and of enthusiasm not a grain. The bulk of them, if any thing, are of the Lutheran church.[177] Their women in generall, both old and young, are the hardest favoured ever I beheld. Their old women wear a comicall head dress, large pendants, short petticoats, and they stare upon one like witches. They generally eat to their morning's tea raw hung beef sliced down in thin chips in the manner of parmezan cheese. Their winter here is excessive cold so as to freeze their cattle stiff in one night in the stables.

To this city belongs about 24 sloops about 50 tons burden that go and come to York. They chiefly carry plank and rafters. The country about is very productive of hay and good grain, the woods not much cleared.

The neighbouring Indians are the Mohooks to the north west, the Canada Indians to the northward, and to the southward a small scattered nation of the Mohackanders.

The young men here call their sweethearts luffees, and a young fellow of 18 is reckoned a simpleton if he has not a luffee; but their women are so homely that a man must never have seen any other luffees else they will never entrap him.

Tuesday, July 3d. We sailed for some time betwixt one and three in the morning, and then, the tide turning against us, we dropt anchor.

Musman's Island

We weighed att 6 in the morning and passed Musman's Island larboard, wind north and by east. Att half an hour after seven we met two sloops from York by whom we had news of a French privateer taken by Captain Ting, master of the Boston gally.[178]

Kenderhuick—Vanskruick

Att nine a'clock we passed the Kenderhuick,[179] larboard, and a little below on the same side, a small peninsula called Vanskruick where stood a farm house, and the fields were covered with good grain and hay. About this time two Dutch men in a batteau came on board of us and fastened the batteau to the sloop's side. The wind freshened up and was fair.

Blue Mountains

We could now observe the Catskill Mountains bearing S. W. starboard. Att half an hour after ten the wind freshened so much that the batteau broke loose from the sloop and overset, and one of the Dutchmen that was stepping down to save her was almost drowned. The fellows scampered away for blood in our canoe to recover their cargoe and loading, which was all afloat upon the water, consisting of old jackets, breeches, baggs, wallets, and buckets. This kept us back some miles, for we were obliged to drop our anchor to stay for our canoe. They picked up all their goods and chattells again excepting a small hatchet which, by its ponderosity, went to the bottom, but the rest of the cargoe being old cloths, ropes ends, and wooden tackle, floated on the surface.

My fellow passenger, Mr. Douw, was very devout all this morning. He kept poring upon Whitefield's sermons.

Kemp

Att 12 a'clock we passed a place called the Kemp larboard, where some High Germans are settled. The Catskill Mountains bore W. by S.

Hybane and Murlanin Islands

Att one a clock we passed Haybane and Murlanin Islands, larboard. The Catskill Mountains bore due west.

Sopus Creek—Little Sopus Island

Att three a clock we cleared Sopus Creek, otherwise called Murder Creek, starboard, and half an hour after four, Little Sopus Island, reckoned half way betwixt Albany and York. Catskill Mountains bore west north west.

Poughcapsy

Att half an hour after seven we passed by Poughcapsy, larboard. We sailed all night, but slowly, our wind failing us.

Wednesday, July 4th. Att two in the morning, the wind dying away and the tide being against us, we dropt anchor 5 miles to the northward of the Highlands. I got up by 5 in the morning, and going upon deck I found a scattered fog upon the water, the air cold and damp, and a small wind att south. The ebb tide began att six in the morning, so we weighed anchor and tript it down with a pritty strong southerly wind in our teeth.

Doepper's Island—Highlands

Att 10 a'clock we passed Doepper's Island, larboard, and as we entered the Highlands the wind left us. At half an hour after ten, the wind turned fair att N. east, but small, att 12 southerly again, att half an hour after 2 very variable, but settled att last in the southerly quarter.

Cammasky, or Buttermilk Island

We came opposite a little log-house, or cottage, upon the top of a high, steep precipice in view of Cammasky, or Buttermilk Island, where we dropped anchor, the tide beginning to flow. We went ashore to this house in expectation of some milk or fowls or fresh provision but could get none, for the people were extremly poor. This appeared a very wild, romantick place surrounded with huge rocks, dreadfull precipices, and scraggy broken trees. The man's name that inhabited here was James Williams, a little old man that followed fishing and cutting of timber rafters to send to Albany or York. He had four children, three sons and a daughter, whom he kept all employed about some work or other. I distributed a few copper halfpence among them for which they gave me a great many country bows and curtsies. It is surprizing how these people in the winter time live here or defend themselves in such slight houses against the violent cold. Going on board again att 4 a clock I killed a snake which I had almost trod upon as I clambered down the steep. Had it been a rattle snake I should have been entituled to a collonell's commission, for it is a common saying here that a man has no title to that dignity untill he has killed a rattlesnake.

The rock here is so steep that you may stand within twenty yards of the edge of the bank and yet not see the river altho' it is very near a mile broad in this place. The tide ebbing att half an hour after 6, we weighed anchor and found by the tiresome length of our cable that there was 90 foot water within 20 paces of the shoar.

Hay Ruck

We passed by the Hay Ruck half an hour after seven, the wind south west. We sent our canoe ashore here to a farm house and got a bucket full of butter milk and a pail of sweet milk.

Anthony's Nose—Cook's Island

Att half an hour after eight we passed Anthony's Nose, larboard, wind strong att south, att nine Cook's Island, larboard, att 10 cleared the Highlands, and anchored att 2 in the morning some miles below the Highlands.

Thursday, July 5th. We weigh'd anchor a little after 6 in the morning, wind south west, and dropt anchor again a quarter after two in the afternoon, York Island being in view att a distance. We went ashore to the house of one Kaen Buikhaut, a Dutch farmer. The old man was busy in making a slaigh, which is a travelling machine used here and att Albany in the winter time to run upon the snow. The woman told us she had eighteen children, nine boys and as many girls. Their third daughter was a handsom girl about 16 years of age. We purchased there three fat fowls for ninepence and a great bucket full of milk into the bargain.

We went on board a quarter after 6 and had hard work in weighing, our anchor having got fast hold of a rock. Dromo grinned like a pagod as he tugged att the cable, or like one of his own country idols. However, we got it up att length. Att 10 att night we had a very hard southerly wind and had almost lost our canoe. The wind came up so furious that we were obliged to drop anchor att eleven a'clock. Another sloop, running like fury before the wind, had almost been foul of us in the dark till we gave her the signall of a gun which made her bear away.

York Island—Grenwitch

Friday, July 6th. We weighed anchor before 5 in the morning, having the ebbe tide, the wind still southerly and the weather rainy. We came up with York Island and Dulancie's house att half an hour after 6, larboard. Here we were becalmed and so floated with the tide till 9 a'clock, Greenwitch larboard. The wind sprung up att north west very fresh with a heavy shower, and about half an hour after 9 we landed att New York.

New York

I never was so destitute of conversation in my life as in this voyage. I heard nothing but Dutch spoke all the way. My fellow passenger Volkert Douw could speak some English but had as little in him to enliven conversation as any young fellow ever I knew that looked like a gentleman. Whoever had the care of his education had foundered him by instilling into him enthusiastick religious notions.

A[t] ten a clock I went to my lodging att Mrs. Hog's where I first heard the melancholly news of the loss of the Philadelphia privateer.[180] I dined att Todd's where there was a mixed company, among the rest Mr. H[orsemande]n, the city recorder,[181] Oliver Dulancie,[182] and a gentleman in a green coat with a scarified face, whose name I cannot recollect, from Antegua. After dinner they went to the old trade of bumpering; therefor I retired.

In this company there was one of these despicable fellows whom we may call c[our]t spys, a man, as I understood, pritty intimate with G[overno]r C[linto]n,[183] who might perhaps share some favour for his dexterity in intelligence. This fellow, I found, made it his business to foist himself into all mixed companies to hear what was said and to enquire into the business and character of strangers. After dinner I happened to be in a room near the porch fronting the street and overheard this worthy intelligencer a pumping of Todd, the landlord. He was inquiring of him who that gentleman in the green coat was whom I just now mentioned. Todd replied, "He is a gentleman from Antegua who comes recommended to C[ommodo]re W[arre]n by Gov. G[ooc]h of Virginia," and that he had been with Lord Banff and left him upon some disgust or quarrell. Todd next informed him who I was upon his asking the question. "You mean the pock-fretten man," said he, "with the dark colourd silk coat. He is a countryman of mine, by God, one Hamilton from Maryland. They say he is a doctor and is travelling for his health." Hearing this stuff, "this is afternoon's news," thinks I, "for the G[overno]r," and just as the inquisitor was desiring Todd to speak lower, he was not deaf, I bolted out upon them and put an end to the enquiry, and the inquisitor went about his business.

I went to the inn to see my horses, and finding them in good plight, Mr. Waghorn desired me to walk into a room where were some Boston gentlemen that would be company for me in my journey there. I agreed to set out with them for Boston upon Monday morning. Their names were Messrs. Laughton and Parker,[184] by employment traders. There was in company an old grave don who, they told me, was both a parson and physitian. Being a graduate, he appeared to be in a mean attire. His wig was remarkably weather beaten, the hairs being all as streight as a rush and of an orange yellow at the extremitys, but that it had been once a fair wig you might know by the appearance of that part which is covered by the hat, for that head wear, I suppose, seldom went off unless att propper times to yield place to his night cap. The uncovered part of his wig had changed its hue by the sun beams and rain alternatly beating upon it. This old philosopher had besides, as part of his wearing aparrell, a pair of old greasy gloves not a whit less ancient than the wig, which lay carefully folded up upon the table before him. And upon his legs were a pair of old leather spatter-dashes, clouted in twenty different places and buttoned up all along the outside of his leg with brass buttons. He was consumedly grave and sparing of his talk, but every now and then a dry joke escaped him.

Att the opposite side of the table sat another piece of antiquity, one Major Spratt, a thin, tall man, very phtisicall and addicted much to a dry cough. His face was adorned and set out with very large carbuncles, and he was more than half seas over in liquor. I understood he professed poetry and often applied himself to rhiming, in which he imagined himself a very good artist. He gave us a specimen of his poetry in an epitaph which he said he had composed upon one Purcell, a neighbour of his, lately dead; asked us if we did not think it excellent and the best of that kind ever we heard. He repeated it ten times over with a ludicrous air and action. "Gentlemen," said he, "pray take notise now, give good attention. It is perhaps the concisest, wittiest, prittiest epigram or epitaph, call it what you will, that you ever heard. Shall I get you pen and ink to write it down? Perhaps you mayn't remember it else. It is highly worth your noting. Pray observe how it runs,—

> Here lyes John Purcell;
> And whether he be in heaven or in hell,
> Never a one of us all can tell."

This poet asked me very kindly how I did and took me by the hand, tho I never had seen him in my life before. He said he liked me for the sake of my name, told me he was himself nearly related to Coll. Hamilton[185] in the Jerseys, son of the late Govr. Hamilton there. Then from one digression to another he told me that the coat he had upon his back was 30 years old. I believed him, for every button was as large as an ordinary turnip, the button holes att least a quarter of a yard long, and the pocket holes just down att the skirts.

After some confused topsy turvy conversation, the landlord sung a bawdy song att which the grave parson-doctor got up, told us that was a language he did not understand, and therefor took his horse and rid away; but in little more than half an hour or three quarters returned again and told us he had forgot his gloves and had rid two miles of his way before he missed them. I was surprized at the old man's care of such a greasy bargain as these gloves. They were fit for nothing but to be wore by itchified persons under a course of sulphur, and I don't know but the doctor had lent them to some of his patients for that purpose, by which means they had imbibed such a quantity of grease. The landlord told me he was a man worth 5000 pounds sterl. and had got it by frugality. I replied that this instance of the gloves was such a demonstration of carefullness that I wondered he was not worth twice as much.

At four a'clock I came to my lodging and drank tea with Mrs. Hog, and Mr. John Watts,[186] a Scots gentleman, came to pay me a visit. Att 5 I went to the coffee house, and there meeting with Mr. Dupeyster,[187] he carried me to the taveren where in a large room was conveen'd a certain club of merry fellows. Among the rest was H———d, the same whom I extolled before for his art in touching the violin, but that indeed seemed to be his principall excellency. Other things he pretended to but fell short. He affected being a witt and dealt much in pointed satyre, but it was such base metall that the edge or point was soon turned when put to the proof. When any body spoke to him, he seemed to give ear in such a careless manner as if he thought all discourse but his own triffling and insignificant. In short he was fit to shine no where but among your good natured men and ignorant blockheads. There was a necessity for the first to bear with the stupidity of his satire and for the others to admire his pseudosophia and quaintness of his speeches and, att the same time, with their blocks, to turn the edge and acuteness of his wit. He dealt much in proverbs and made use of one which I thought pritty significant when well applied. It was *the devil to pay and no pitch hot?* An interrogatory adage metaphorically derived from the manner of sailors who pay their ship's bottoms with pitch. I back'd it with *great cry and little wool, said the devil when he shore his hogs,* applicable enough to the ostentation and clutter he made with his learning.

There was in this company one Dr. McGraa,[188] a pretended Scots-man, but by brogue a Teague. He had an affected way of curtsieing instead of bowing when he entered a room. He put on a modest look uncommon to his nation, spoke little, and when he went to speak, leaned over the table and streeched out his neck and face, goose-like, as if he had been going to whisper you in the ear. When he drank to any in the company, he would not speak but kept bowing and bowing, sometimes for the space of a minute or two, till the person complimented either observed him of his own accord or was hunched into attention by his next neighbour; but it was hard to know who he bowed to upon account of his squinting. However, when the liquor began to heat him a little, he talked at the rate of three words in a minute, and sitting next me (he was very complaisant in his cups), he told me he had heard my name mentioned by some Marylanders and asked me if I knew his unkle Grierson in Maryland. I returned his compliments in as civil a manner as possible, and for half an hour we talked of nothing but waiting upon one another at our lodgings, but after all this complimentary farce and promises of serving and waiting was over, I could not but observe that none of us took the trouble to enquire where the one or the other lodged. I never met with a man so wrapt up in himself as this fellow seemed to be, nor did I ever see a face where there was so much effronterie under a pretended mask of modesty.

There was, besides, another doctor in company named Man, a doctor of a man of war. The best thing I saw about him was that he would drink nothing but water, but he eat lustily at supper, and nothing remarkable appeared in his discourse (which indeed was copious and insipid) but only an affected way he had of swearing by Ged att every two words; and by the motion of his hands at each time of swearing that polite and elegant oath, he would seem to let the company understand that he was no mean orator, and that the little oath was a very fine ornament to his oration.

But the most remarkable person in the whole company was one Wendal, a young gentleman from Boston. He entertained us mightily by playing on the violin the quickest tunes upon the highest keys, which he accompanied with his voice so as even to drown the violin with such nice shakings and gracings that I thought his voice outdid the instrument. I sat for some time imoveable with surprize. The like I never heard, and the thing seemed to me next a miracle. The extent of his voice is impossible to describe or even to imagine unless by hearing him. The whole company were amazed that any person but a woman or eunuch could have such a pipe and began to question his virility; but he swore that if the company pleased he would show a couple of as good witnesses as any man might wear. He then imitated severall beasts, as cats, dogs, horses, and cows, with the cackling of poultry, and all to such perfection that nothing but nature could match it. When the landlord (a clumsy, tallow faced fellow in a white jacket) came to receive his reckoning, our mimick's art struck and surprized him in such a manner that it fixed him quite, like one that had seen the Gorgon's head, and he might have passed for a statue done in white marble. He was so struck that the company might have gone away without paying and carried off all his silver tankards and spoons, and he never would have observed.

After being thus entertained I returned to my lodging att 11 o'clock.

Saturday, July 7th. In the morning I waited upon Stephen Bayard to whom my letters of credit were directed. He invited me to a Sunday's dinner with him. We heard news of a coasting vessel belonging to N. England taken by a French privateer in her passage betwixt Boston and Rhode Island. I writ to Annapolis by the post. I dined att Todd's and went in the afternoon to see the French prizes in the harbour. Both of them were large ships about 300 ton burden, the one Le Jupiter and the other Le Saint Francois Xaviers. Warren, who took the St. Francis, has gained a great character. His praise is in every body's mouth, and he has made a fine estate of the business.[189] I went home at night and shunned company.

Sunday, July 8th. I spent the morning att home and att one a'clock went to dine with Mr. Bayard. Among some other gentlemen there was my old friend Dr. McGraa who to day seemed to have more talk and ostentation than usuall, but he did not shine quite bright till he had drank half a dozen glasses of wine after dinner. He spoke now in a very arbitrary tone as if his opinion was to pass for an ipse dixit. He and I unhappily engaged in a dispute which I was sorry for, it being dissonant to good manners before company, and what none but rank pedants will be guilty of. We were obliged to use hard physicall terms, very discordant and dissagreeable to ears not accustomed to them. I wanted much to drop it, but he keept teizing of me.

I found my chap to be one of those learned bullys who, by loud talking and an affected sneer, seem to outshine all other men in parts of literature where the company are by no means propper judges, where for the most part the most impudent of the disputants passes for the most knowing man. The subject of this dispute was the effect which the moon has upon all fluids, as well as the ocean, in a proportionable ratio by the law of gravitation or her attractive power, and even upon the fluids in the vessels of animals. The thing that introduced this was an action of McGraa's which exceeded every thing I had seen for nastiness, impudence, and rusticity. He told us he was troubled with the open piles and with that, from his breeches, pulled out a linnen handkercheff all stained with blood and showed it to the company just after we had eat dinner. After my astonishment att this piece of clownish impudence was over, I asked him if that evacuation att any particular times was greater or less, such as the full or change of the moon in the same manner as the cataméné in women. I intended only to play upon him. He answered with a sneer that he did not be-lieve the moon had anything to do with us or our distempers and said that such notions were only superstitious nonsense, wondering how I could give credit to any such stuff. We had a great deal of talk about attraction, condensation, gravitation, rarifaction, of all which I found he understood just as much as a goose; and when he began to show his ignorance of the mathematical and astronomical problems of the illustrious Newton and blockishly resolve all my meaning into judiciall astrology, I gave him up as an unintelligent, unintelligible, and consequently inflexible disputant. And the company, being no judges of the thing, imagined, I suppose, that he had got the victory, which did not att all make me uneasy. He pretended to have travelled most countrys in Europe, to have shared the favour and acquaintance of some foreign princes and grandees and to have been att their tables, to be master of severall European languages, tho I found he could not speak good French and he merely murdered the Latin. He said he had been very intimate with Professor Boerhaave and Dr. Astruc[190] and subjoined that he knew for certain that the majority of the Spanish bishops were Jews.

There was another doctor att dinner with us who went away before this dispute began. His name was Ascough. When he came first in he told Mr. Bayard he would dine with him provided he had no green pease for dinner. Mr. Bayard told him there were some, but that they should not come to table, upon which, with some entreaty, the doctor sat down and eat pritty heartily of bacon, chickens, and veal, but just as he had begun upon his veal, the stupid negroe wench, forgetting her orders to the contrary, produced the pease, att which the doctor began to stare and change colour in such a manner that I thought he would have been convulsed, but he started up and ran out of doors so fast that we could never throw salt on his tail again. Mr. Bayard was so angry that he had almost oversett the table, but we had a good dish of pease by the bargain which otherwise we should not have tasted. This was the oddest antipathy ever I was witness to. Att night I went to Waghorn's and found my company had delayed their setting off till Tuesday; so I returned home.

Monday, July 9th. I waited upon Mr. Bayard this morning and had letters of credit drawn upon Mr. Lechmere att Boston. I dined with Mr. M——s [Milne] and other company att Todd's and went to tarry this night att the inn where my horses were in order to set out to morrow morning by times on my journey for Boston. We heard news this day of an English vessel loaden with ammunition and bound for New England being taken on the coast. I spent the evening att Waghorn's where we had Mr. Wendall's company who entertained us as before. We had among us this night our old friend Major Spratt who now and then gave us an extempore rhime. I retired to bed att 12 o'clock.

The people of New York att the first appearance of a stranger are seemingly civil and courteous, but this civility and complaisance soon relaxes if he be not either highly recommended or a good toaper. To drink stoutly with the Hungarian Club, who are all bumper men, is the readiest way for a stranger to recommend himself, and a sett among them are very fond of making a stranger drunk. To talk bawdy and to have a knack att punning passes among some there for good sterling wit. Govr. C[linto]n himself is a jolly toaper and gives good example and, for that one quality, is esteemed among these dons.

The staple of New York is bread flower and skins. It is a very rich place, but it is not so cheap living here as att Philadelphia. They have very bad water in the city, most of it being hard and brackish. Ever since the negroe conspiracy, certain people have been appointed to sell water in the streets, which they carry on a sledge in great casks and bring it from the best springs about the city, for it was when the negroes went for tea water that they held their caballs and consultations, and therefor they have a law now that no negroe shall be seen upon the streets without a lanthorn after dark.

In this city are a mayor, recorder, aldermen, and common council. The goverment is under the English law, but the chief places are possessed by Dutchmen, they composing the best part of the House of Assembly. The Dutch were the first settlers of this province, which is very large and extensive, the States of Holland having purchased the country of one Hudson who pretended first to have discovered it, but they att last exchanged it with the English for Saranam, and ever since there have been a great number of Dutch here, tho now their language and customs begin pritty much to wear out and would very soon die were it not for a parcell of Dutch domines here who, in the education of their children, endeavour to preserve the Dutch customs as much as possible. There is as much jarring here betwixt the powers of the legislature as in any of the other American provinces.

They have a diversion here, very common, which is the barbecuing of a turtle, to which sport the chief gentry in town commonly go once or twice a week.

There are a great many handsome women in this city. They appear much more in publick than att Philadelphia. It is customary here to ride thro the street in light chairs. When the ladys walk the streets in the day time, they commonly use umbrellas, prittily adorned with feathers and painted.

There are two coffee-houses in this city, and the northeren and southeren posts go and come here once a week. I was tired of nothing here but their excessive drinking, for in this place you may have the best of company and conversation as well as att Philadelphia.

York Ferry—Long Island—Jamaica

Tuesday, July 10th. Early in the morning we got up, and after preparing all our baggage, Messrs. Parker, Laughton, and I mounted horse and crossed the ferry att seven a'clock over to Long Island. After a tedious passage and being detained sometime att Baker's, we arrived a quarter after 10 att Jamaica, a small town upon Long Island just bordering upon Hampstead Plain. It is about half a mile long, the houses sparse.[191] There are in it one Presbyterian meeting, one English, and one Dutch church.[192] The Dutch church is built in the shape of an octagon, being a wooden structure. We stopt there att the Sign of the Sun and paid dear for our breakfast, which was bread and mouldy cheese, stale beer and sower cyder.

Hampstead

We set out again and arrived att Hampstead, a very scattered town standing upon the great plain to which it gives name. We put up here att one Peter's[193] att the Sign of Guy of Warwick where we dined with a company that had come there before us and were travelling southward. There was a pritty girl here with whom Parker was mightily taken and would fain have staid that night. This girl had intermitting fevers. Parker pretended to be a doctor and swore he could cure her if she would submitt to his directions. With difficulty we perswaded Parker to mount horse.

Att 4 a'clock, going across this great plain, [194] we could see almost as good a horizon round us as when one is att sea, and in some places of the plain, the latitude might be taken by observation att noon day. It is about 16 miles long. The ground is hard and gravelly, the road very smooth but indistinct and intersected by severall other roads which makes it difficult for a stranger to find the way. There is nothing but long grass grows upon this plain, only in some particular spots small oak brush, not above a foot high. Near Hampstead there are severall pritty winding brooks that run thro' this plain. We lost our way here and blundered about a great while. Att last we spyed a woman and two men at some distance. We rid up towards them to enquire, but they were to wild to be spoke with, running over the plain as fast as wild bucks upon the mountains. Just after we came out of the plain and sunk into the woods, we found a boy lurking behind a bush. We wanted to enquire the way of him, but as soon as we spoke the game was started and away he run.

Huntington

We arrived att Huntington att eight a'clock att night, where we put up at one Flat's att the Sign of the Half Moon and Heart. This Flat is an Irishman. We had no sooner sat down when there came in a band of the town politicians in short jackets and trowsers, being probably curious to know who them strangers were who had newly arrived in town. Among the rest was a fellow with a worsted cap and great black fists. They stiled him doctor. Flat told me he had been a shoemaker in town and was a notable fellow att his trade, but happening two years agoe to cure an old woman of a pestilent mortal disease, he thereby acquired the character of a physitian, was applied to from all quarters, and finding the practise of physick a more profitable business than cobling, he laid aside his awls and leather, got himself some gallipots, and instead of cobling of soals, fell to cobling of human bodies. Att supper our landlord was very merry and very much given to rhiming. There were three buxom girls in this house who served us att supper, to whom Mr. Parker made strenuous courtship. One was an Indian girl named Phoebe, the other two were Lucretia and Betty, but Betty was the top beauty of the three.

Wednesday, July 11. We left Huntington att half an hour after six in the morning, and after riding 5 miles stonny road, we breakfasted att a house upon the road att the Sign of Bacchus. Then proceeding ten or eleven miles farther, we forded Smithtown River, otherwise called by the Indians, Missaque. We baited our horses att a taveren where there was a deaf landlady. After half an hour's rest we mounted horse again and rid some miles thro' some very barren, unequal, and stonny land. We saw the mouth of Smithtown River running into the Sound thro some broken sandy beaches about eight miles to our left hand N.N.W., and about 24 miles farther to the northward, the coast of New England or the province of Connecticut.

Brookhaven, or Setoquet

We arrived att a scattered town called Brookhaven, or by the Indians, Setoquet, about two a'clock afternoon and dined att one Buchanan's there. Brookhaven is a small scattered village standing upon barren, rocky land near the sea. In this town is a small windmill for sawing of plank, and a wooden church with a small steeple.[195] Att about 50 miles' distance from this town eastward is a settlement of Indians upon a sandy point which makes the south fork of the island and runs out a long narrow promontory into the sea almost as far as Block Island.

While we were at Buchanan's, an old fellow named Smith called att the house. He said he was a travelling to York to get a license or commission from the Governour to go a privateering and swore he would not be under any commander but would be chief man himself. He showed us severall antick tricks such as jumping half a foot high upon his bum without touching the floor with any other part of his body. Then he turned and did the same upon his belly. Then he stood upright upon his head. He told us he was 75 years of age and swore damn his old shoes if any man in America could do the like. He asked me whence I came and whither I went. I answered him I came from Calliphurnia and was going to Lanthern Land. He swore damn his old shoes again if he had not been a sailor all his life long and yet never had heard of such places. Mr. Parker made him believe that he was a captain of a privateer, and for a mug of syder made him engage to go on board of him upon Friday next, promising to make him his leutenant, for nothing else would satisfy the old fellow. The old chap was mightily elevated at this and damned his old shoes twenty times over. Att last he wanted to borrow a little advance money of Parker, which when he found he could not obtain, he drank up his cider and swore he would not go.

We took horse again att half an hour after 5 o'clock, and had scarce got a mile from Brookhaven when we lost our way but were directed right again by a man whom we met. After riding 10 miles thro' woods and marshes in which we were pestered with muscettoes, we arrived att eight o'clock att night att one Brewster's where we put up for all night, and in this house we could get nothing either to eat or drink and so were obliged to go to bed fasting or supperless. I was conducted up stairs to a large chamber. The people in this house seemed to be quite savage and rude.

Thursday, July 12. When I waked this morning I found two beds in the room besides that in which I lay, in one of which lay two great hulking fellows with long black beards, having their own hair and not so much as half a nightcap betwixt them both. I took them for weavers, not only from their greasy appearance, but because I observed a weaver's loom at each side of the room. In the other bed was a raw boned boy who, with the two lubbers, huddled on his cloths and went reeling down stairs making as much noise as three horses.

We set out from this desolate place att 6 a'clock and rid 16 miles thro very barren and waste land. Here we passed thro a plain of 6 or eight miles long where was nothing but oak brush or bushes two foot high, very thick, and replenished with acorns; and thinly scattered over the plain were severall old naked pines at about two or three hundred foot distance one from another, most of them decayed and broken. In all this way we met not one living soul nor saw any house, but one in ruins. Some of the inhabitants here call this place the Desart of Arabia. It is very much infested with muscettoes. We breakfasted att one Fanning's. Near his house stands the county court house, a decayed wooden building, and close by his door runs a small rivulett into an arm of the sea about 20 miles' distance, which makes that division of the eastren end of Long Island called the Fork.

Southhold

This day was rainy, but we took horse and rid 10 miles farther to one Hubbard's[196] where we rested half an hour, then proceeded eight miles farther to the town of Southhold,[197] near which the road is levell, firm, and pleasant, and in the neighbourhood are a great many windmills. The houses are pritty thick along the road here. We put up att one Mrs. More's in Southhold. In her house appeared nothing but industry. She and her grandaughters were busied in carding and spinning of wool. Messieurs Parker and Laughton were very much disposed to sleep. We ordered some eggs for dinner and some chickens. Mrs. More asked us if we would have bacon fried with our eggs; we told her no. After dinner we sent to enquire for a boat to cross the Sound.

Att night the house was crowded with a company of patchd coats and tattered jackets, and consequently the conversation consisted chiefly in "damne ye, Jack," and "Here's to you, Tom." A comicall old fellow among the rest asked me if I had come from the new country. His name, he told me, was Cleveland, and he was originally of Scots parentage. I told him then his genuine name must be Cleland. We asked him what entertainment we could have att the Oyster Pond where we designed to take boat to cross the Sound. "Why truly," said he, "if you would eat such things as we Gentills do, you may live very well, but as your law forbids you to eat swine's flesh, your living will be but indifferent." Parker laughed and asked him if he took us for Jews or Mahometans. He replied, "Gentlemen, I ask pardon, but the landlady informed me you were Jews." This notion proceeded from our refusing of bacon to our eggs att dinner.

While we were att supper there came in a pedlar with his pack along with one Doctor Hull, a practitioner of physick in the town. We were told that this doctor was a man of great learning and very much of a gentleman. The pedlar went to show him some linnen by candle light and told him very ingenuously that now he would be upon honour with him and recommend to him the best of his wares, and as to the price he would let him know the highest and lowest att one word and would not bate one penny of 6 shillings a yard. There passed some learned conversation betwixt this doctor and pedlar in which the doctor made it plain that the lawers, clergy, and doctors tricked the rest of mankind out of the best part of their substance and made them pay well for doing of nothing. But the pedlar stood up mightily for the honour of his own profession and affirmed that they made as good a hand of it as any cheat among them all. "But then," added he, "you have something to handle for your money, good or bad as it happens." We left this company att 9 a'clock att night and went up stairs to bed, all in one chamber.

Oyster Pond[198]

Friday, July 13. We took horse after 6 in the morning and rid 5 or 6 miles close by the Sound till we came to one Brown's who was to give us passage in his boat. Then we proceeded 7 miles farther and stopped att one King's to wait the tide, when Brown's boat was to fall down the river to take us in.

The family att King's were all busy in preparing dinner, the provision for which chiefly consisted in garden stuff. Here we saw some handsome country girls, one of whom wore a perpetuall smile in her face and prepared the chocolate for our breakfast. She presently captivated Parker, who was apt to take flame upon all occasions. After breakfast, for pastime, we read Quevedo's Visions[199] and att one a'clock dined with the family upon fat pork and green pease. Att two a'clock we observed the boat falling down the river, and having provided our selves with a store of bread and cheese and some rum and sugar in case of being detained upon the water, that part of the Sound which we had to cross being 18 miles broad, we put our horses on board 10 minutes before three and set sail with a fair wind from the Oyster Pond.

Sound

Att three a'clock we passed the Gutt, a rapid current betwixt the main of Long Island and Shelter Island caused by the tides.

Shelter Island—Gardiner's Island

Att a quarter after three we cleared Shelter Island, larboard, upon our weather bow. Gardiner's Island[200] bore east by north, starboard, about three leagues' distance. This island is in the possession of one man and takes its name from him. It had been a prey to the French privateers in Queen Anne's war, who used to land upon it and plunder the family and tennants of their stock and provisions, the island lying very bleak upon the ocean just att the eastermost entry of the Sound betwixt Long Island and the main of Connecticut.

Fisher's Isl.—Two-tree Isl.

A little to the northward of this lyes Fisher's Island, and about 3 or four leagues' distance upon our larboard we saw a small island called Two-Tree Island because they say there are only two trees upon it which are of a particular kind of wood which nobody there can give a name to, nor are such trees to be seen any where else in the country.

Connecticut Goverment—New London

We arrived in the harbour att New London att half an hour after 6 and put up att Duchand's att the Sign of the Anchor.[201] The town of New London is irregularly built along the water side, in length about a mile.[202] There is in it one Presbyterian meeting and one church. 'Tis just such another desolate expensive town as Annapolis in Maryland, the houses being mostly wood. The inhabitants were allarmed this night att a sloop that appeared to be rowing up into the harbour, they having heard a little before a firing of guns out in the Sound and seen one vessell, as they thought, give chase to another. There was a strange clamour and crowd in the street, chiefly of women. The country station sloop lay in the harbour, who, when she was within shot, sent a salute, first one gun, sharp shot, but the advancing sloop did not strike; then she bestowed upon her another, resolving next to proceed to a volley; but att the second shot, which whistled thro' her rigging, she struck and made answer that it was one Captain Trueman from Antegua. Then the people's fears were over, for they imagined it was old Morpang,[203] the French rover, who in former times used to plunder these parts when he wanted provision.

New London Ferry

Saturday, July 14th. We departed New London att seven a'clock in the morning, crossing the ferry, and rid eight miles thro a very stonny rough road where the stones upon each hand of us seemed as large as houses, and the way it self a mere rock.

Stonnington

This is propperly enough called Stonnington. We breakfasted att one Major Williams's[204] and proceeded 10 miles farther to Thomson's[205] where we baited our horses. Here we met one Captain Noise,[206] a dealer in cattle, whose name and character seemed pritty well to agree, for he talked very loud, joaked and laughed heartily att nothing. The landlady here was a queer old woman, an enormous heap of fat. She had some daughters and maids whom she called by comical names. There was Thankfull, Charity, Patience, Comfort, Hope, etc.

Rhode Island and Providence Government

Upon the road here stands a house belonging to an Indian King named George,[207] commonly called King George's house or palace. He possesses twenty or thirty 1000 acres of very fine levell land round this house, upon which he has many tennants and has, of his own, a good stock of horses and other cattle. This King lives after the English mode. His subjects have lost their own goverment policy and laws and are servants or vassals to the English here. His queen goes in a high modish dress in her silks, hoops, stays, and dresses like an English woman. He educates his children to the belles letters and is himself a very complaisant mannerly man. We pay'd him a visit, and he treated us with a glass of good wine.

We dined att one Hill's,[208] and going from thence att 4 a'clock and travelling thro 12 miles more of stonny, rough road, we passed by an old fashioned wooden house att the end of a lane, darkened and shaded over with a thick grove of tall trees. This appeared to me very romantick and brought into my mind some romantick descriptions of rural scenes in Spencer's Fairy Queen.

Sugar Loaf

About a quarter of a mile farther, att the end of a lane, is a little hill that rises up in a conicall form and is therefor called the Sugar Loaf. The fencing here is all stone. We could see to our right hand the ocean and part of the Sound, the long point of Long Island called Montaque [Montauk], Block Island,[209] and att a good distance, behind an island called Conannicut,[210] part of Rhode Island.

Att 6 o'clock we arrived att a village called Tower Hill or South-Kingstown. It lyes near the sea. All round here the country is high, hilly, and rockey, few woods and these dwarfish. You have a large extensive prospect from here, both to the sea and landward. We put up att the house of one Case[211] in Kingstown, who keeps a pritty good house, is a talkative, prating man, and would have every body know that he keeps the best publick house in the country. We heard news of some prizes brought into Newport by the Rhode Island privateers, and among the rest a large Spanish snow, with no loading but 30,000 pounds' value, New England money, in silver, which is 5000 lbs sterling.

Sunday, July 15. We tarried att Case's all this day, it being unlawfull here to travell upon Sunday or, as they term it, Sabbath Day (Sunday being a pagan name). We loitered about all the forenoon, having nothing to do and no books to read except it was a curious History of the Nine Worthys[212] (which we found in Case's library), a book worthy of that worthy author Mr. Burton, the diligent compiler and historian of Grubstreet. Case was mightily offended att Mr. Laughton for singing and whistling, telling him that he ought not so to profane the Sabbath. Laughton swore that he had forgott what day it was, but Case was still more offended a[t] his swearing and left us in bad humour.

This day was bleak and stormy, the wind being att east by north. I diverted myself by looking att the coasting sloops passing up and down Conannicut Point which runs out here much like Greenberry's near Annapolis but is quite bare, rockey, and barren. Upon it the tide beats with great violence so as to raise a white foam a great way round it. We dined att three a clock and after dinner walked out to see our horses in the pasture, where my grey, having laid himself down att full length to sleep, I imagined att a distance that he was dead; but throwing a stone at him, he started up and got to his heels. We viewed the sea from a high rock where we could see the spray beating with violence over the tops of the rocks upon the coast and below us, of three or four miles' extent, a pleasant green meadow, thro' the middle of which run a pritty winding river. Most of the country round is open, hilly, and rocky, and upon the rocks there is a great deal of spar, or substance like white marble, but in very small pieces.

We returned home att 6 o'clock and had a rambling conversation with Case and a certain traveller upon different subjects. There came to the house att night a Rhode Island collonell (for in this country there is great plenty of collonells, captains, and majors) who diverted us with some storys about the New Light men. There are a great many Seventh-day-men here who keep Saturday instead of Sunday and so go to work when others go to church. Most of the people here begin their Sunday upon Saturday night after sunset and end it upon Sunday att sunsett when they go to any kind of recreation or work upon other days lawfull. After a light supper of bread and milk, we went to bed.

Naragantset Ferry

Monday, July 16. We sett off from Case's att half an hour after six in the morning and crossed Conannicut Ferry or Naragantsett betwixt eight and nine o clock.[213]

Dutch Island—Rhode Island Ferry

There is a small island lyes betwixt the main and Conannicut called Dutch Island because the Dutch first took possession of it. We crossed the other ferry to Newport upon Rhode Island a little after 10 a'clock and had a very heavy rain all the passage.

Dumplins—Rose Island

There are some rocks there called the Dumplins, and a little above a small island called Rose Island[214] upon which there is one tree. Here you have very pritty views and prospects from the mixture of land and water. As we stept into the ferry boat, there were some stones lay in her bottom which obstructed the horses getting in. Dromo desired the skipper to "trow away his stones, de horse be better ballast." "No," says the fellow, "I cannot part with my stones yet; they will serve for a good use att another time."

Newport

We arrived att Newport att 12 o'clock. Rhode Island is a pleasant, open spot of land, being an intire garden of farms, 12 or 13 miles long and 4 or 5 miles broad att its broadest part. The town Newport is about a mile long, lying pritty near north and south. It stands upon a very levell spot of ground and consists of one street, narrow but so streight that standing att one end of it you may see to the other. It is just close upon the water. There are severall lanes going from this street on both sides. Those to the landward are some of them pritty long and broad. There is one large market house near the south end of the main street.[215] The Town House[216] stands a little above this market house away from the water and is a handsom brick edifice, lately built, having a cupola at top. There is, besides, in this town two Presbyterian meetings,[217] one large Quaker meeting,[218] one Anabaptist,[219] and one Church of England.[220] The church has a very fine organ in it, and there is a publick clock upon the steeple as also upon the front of the Town House. The fort is a square building of brick and stone, standing upon a small island which makes the harbour. This place is famous for privateering, and they had about this time brought in severall prizes, among which was a large Spanish snow near 200 ton burden which I saw in the harbour with her bowsplitt shot off.[221]

This town is as remarkable for pritty women as Albany is for ugly ones, many of whom one may see sitting in the shops in passing along the street. I dined att a taveren kept by one Nicolls att the Sign of the White Horse[222] where I had put up my horses, and in the afternoon Dr. Moffat,[223] an old acquaintance and schoolfellow of mine, led me a course thro' the town. He carried me to see one Feykes, a painter, the most extraordinary genius ever I knew, for he does pictures tollerably well by the force of genius, having never had any teaching. I saw a large table of the Judgement of Hercules copied by him from a frontispiece of the Earl of Shaftesbury's which I thought very well done. This man had exactly the phizz of a painter, having a long pale face, sharp nose, large eyes with which he looked upon you stedfastly, long curled black hair, a delicate white hand, and long fingers.[224]

I went with Moffet in the evening to Dr. Keith's,[225] another countryman and acquaintance, where we spent the evening very agreeably in the company of one Dr. Brett,[226] a very facetious old man. I soon found that Keith passed for a man of great gallantry here, being frequently visited by the young ladies in town who are generally very airy and frolicksome. He showed me a drawer full of the trophys of the fair, which he called his cabinet of curiositys. They consisted of tore fans, fragments of gloves, whims, snuff boxes, girdles, apron strings, laced shoes and shoe heels, pin cussions, hussifs, and a deal of other such trumpery. I lay this night att Dr. Moffets's lodging.

Tuesday, July 17th. I breakfasted with Dr. Moffet and had recommendatory letters of him to some of the fraternity in Boston. I went with the Doctor att 10 a'clock to see a house about half a mile out of town, built lately by one Captain Mallbone,[227] a substantiall trader there. It is the largest and most magnificent dwelling house I have seen in America. It is built intirely with hewn stone of a reddish colour; the sides of the windows and corner stones of the house being painted like white marble. It is three storys high, and the rooms are spacious and magnificent. There is a large lanthern or cupola on the roof, which is covered with sheet lead. The whole stair case, which is very spacious and large, is done with mahogany wood. This house makes a grand show att a distance but is not extraordinary for the architecture, being a clumsy Dutch modell. Round it are pritty gardens and terrasses with canals and basons for water, from whence you have a delightfull view of the town and harbour of Newport with the shipping lying there.

When Mr. Parker and Laughton came up, we proceeded on our journey, riding along the Island, a broad and even road, where our eyes were entertained with various beautifull prospects of the continent, islands, and water. From some high places we could see Block Island to the westward. We dined att Burden's,[228] a Quaker who keeps the ferry, where we had good entertainment and met with one Mr. Lee, a proprietor in some iron works near Boston. We crossed the ferry att 4 a clock and rid some miles of stonny, unequall road.

Massachusets Province—Mount Hope
As we entered the Province of the Massachusets Bay, upon the

left hand we saw a hill called Mount Hope, formerly the strong hold or refuge of an Indian king named Philip[229] who held the place a long time against the first settlers and used to be very troublesome by making excursions.

Bristol

We passed thro' Bristol,[230] a small trading town laid out in the same manner as Philadelphia, about three a'clock. We crossed another little ferry att 5 a'clock and baited att one Hunt's,[231] then riding 10 miles farther we parted with Mr. Lee and lay that night att one Slake's,[232] att the Sign of the White Horse.

Wednesday, July 18. We sett out a little after six in the morning, breakfasted att Man's,[233] and from thence went 10 miles farther to Robins's[234] where we baited. We were resolved to dine att Dedham but were scarce got upon our horses when we were met by a company of gentlemen, who being acquaintances of Parker and Laughton, they perswaded us to turn back to Robins's again. There was in this company one Coffin[235] who enquired after my brother in Maryland and told me he had once been a patient of his when att Benedict Town upon Patuxent about 16 or 17 years agoe.

In this house I and my company were taken for pedlars. There happened to be a pedlar there selling some wares who saw me open my portmanteau and sort some bundles and paquets of letters. He mistook my portmanteau for a pack, for it is not very customary here to ride with such implements, and so would have chaffer'd with me for some goods.

While we were att dinner, one Mr. Lightfoot[236] came in, to whom I had a recommendatory letter. This Lightfoot is a gentleman of a regular education, having been brought up att Oxford in England, a man of good humour and excellent sense. He had upon his head, when he entered the company, a straw hat dyed black but no wig. He told us that he always rode in this trim in hot weather, but that among the country people he had been taken for a French spy upon account of the oddity of his dress. He said he had heard a grand laugh as he passed by, and guessing that there were some Boston people in the company, he was induced to call in. Then he pulled about two pounds of black rye-bread out of his pocket and told us that he thought perhaps he might come to some places upon the road where there might be a scarcity of fine bread, and therefor had provided himself.

We had news here of the French having, along with the Cape Sable and St. John Indians, made an attack upon Annapolis Royall,[237] and that they had killed all their cattle and severall men there and burnt down all the houses in the town; so that the inhabitants, in the outmost distress, were obliged to betake themselves to the fort where they were scanty of provisions and ready to surrender when Captain Ting, master of the Boston gally, came seasonably to their assistance with a reinforcement of men and a fresh supply of provisions, and as soon as the enimy heard his guns they fled into the woods. This Ting has gained a great character here for his conduct and courage.

Dedham

We parted from Robin's a little after three and betwixt 5 and 6 arrived att Dedham, a village within eleven miles of Boston, where we rested a little and drank some punch. Lightfoot had a scolding bout here with one Betty, the landlady's daughter, for secreting one of our lemons, and was obliged to vent a deal of billingsgate and swear a string of lusty oaths before he could recover it again. He told me that this place was the most sharping country ever I was in and that this little piddling trick was only the beginning of it and nothing to what I should experience if I stayed but some weeks there. We took horse att half an hour after 6 and passed severall pritty country boxes at three or 4 miles' distance from Boston belonging to gentlemen in the town.

Blue Hills

Att 13 miles' distance from Boston is a range of hills called the Blue Hills, upon the top of one of which a gentleman has built a country house where there is a very extensive view. A quarter before eight we arrived in Boston.

Boston

There I put my horses att one Barker's[238] and took lodging att Mrs. Guneau's, a French woman, att the back of the Alms House near Beacon Hill,[239] a very pleasant part of town situated high and well aired. My landlady and I conversed about two hours. She informed that one Mr. Hughes,[240] a merchant, that lately had been in Maryland, lodged att her house, which I was glad to hear, having had some small acquaintance with him. My landlady was a Frenchwoman and had much of the humour of that nation, a deal of talk, and a deal of action. I went to bed att eleven o'clock.

Thursday, July 19th. I got up half an hour after 5 in the morning, and after breakfast I took a turn in the garden with Mr. Hughes, from whence we had a view of the whole town of Boston and the peninsula upon which it stands. The neck which joins this peninsula to the land is situated south west from the town, and att low water is not above 30 or 40 paces broad and is so flat and levell that in high tides it is sometimes overflowed. The town is built upon the south and southeast side of the peninsula and is about two miles in length, extending from

the neck of the peninsula northward to that place called North
End, as that extremity of the town next the neck is called South
End. Behind the town are severall pleasant plains, and on the
west side of the peninsula are three hills in a range, upon the
highest of which is placed a long beacon pole. To the northward
over the water is situated a pritty large town called Charlestown.
We could see a great many islands out in the bay, upon one of
which about three miles from town stands the Castle, a strong
fortification that guards the entry of the harbour. Upon the most
extreme island about 12 miles out is the light house,[241] a high
building of stone in form of a pillar, upon the top of which
every night is kept a light to guide ships into the harbour. When
a snow, brig, sloop, or schooner appears out at sea, they hoist a
pinnace upon the flag staff in the Castle; if a ship, they display
a flag.

Att 12 o clock I waited upon Mr. Hooper,[242] one of the
ministers in Boston, and from thence went to Mr. Lechmere's
the surveyor's,[243] to whom my letters of credit were directed.
From his house I went to the Change or place of publick
rendezvous. Here is a great building called the Townhouse,[244]
about 125 foot long and 40 foot broad. The lower chamber of
this house, called the Change, is all one apartment, the roof
of which is supported all along the middle with a row of wooden
pillars about 25 foot high. Upon Change I met Mr. Hutchinson[245] and Captain Wendall[246] to whom I delivered letters. I
went down to view the Long Wharf.[247] This runs in a direct
line with a broad street called King's Street and is carried into
the water pritty near a quarter of a mile. Upon one side of this
wharf, all along, there is a range of wooden houses, and close
by the wharf lyes a very numerous shipping. I dined att
Withered's,[248] a taveren att the Change, and there heard news
of the magazines att Placentia being blown up.[249]

In the afternoon about 6 a'clock, Messrs. Parker and Laughton called att my lodging, and with them I took a tower round the north end of the town and to the water side, after which we went to a club att Withered's where there was a pot bellyd doctor president. This man was as round as a ball, about 5 foot high, and pretended to be very knowing in politicks. He was a Frenchman by birth, and I understood he was by trade an usurer, letting out money att 10 per cent. I left this club att 10 o'clock and went home.

Friday, July 20. I got up pritty early and took a turn in the garden. Att eleven a clock I went abroad with Mr. Hughes, and after taking a walk to the water side we went to Change at 12 a'clock where I delivered severall letters. I saw att Change some Frenchmen, officers of the flag of truce, with prisoners for exchange from Canso and of the privateer taken by Captain Ting. They were very loquacious, after the manner of their nation, and their discourse for the most part was interlaced with oaths and smutt. Att two a clock Mr. Hughes and I dined with Mr. Hooper, where we had some agreeable conversation. I came home in the afternoon and writ some letters to go by the ships to Great Brittain.

Saturday, July 21. I rose later than usuall this morning and breakfasted with Mrs. Guneau and her daughter, the latter a passable handsom girl, nothing of the French spirit in her but rather too grave and sedate. Near twelve o'clock I walked out with Mr. Hughes and went to Change where, after attending some time and observing variety of comicall phizzes, I encountered Captain Wendall who pointed out Dr. Dowglass[250] and Mr. Arbuthnott[251] to me to whom I delivered letters.

I was invited to dine with Captain Irvin upon salt cod fish, which here is a common Saturday's dinner, being elegantly dressed with a sauce of butter and eggs. In our company here was one Captain Petty, a very hard favoured man, a Scotsman by birth, hump-back'd, and the tallest humpy ever I saw, being 6 foot high att least. There was one Perkins,[252] a little, round faced man, a trader in the place. The discourse turned chiefly upon commerce and trade, and thro' the whole of it I could discover a vein of that subtilty and acuteness so peculiar to a New England genius. Mr. Arbuthnott and I had some disputes concerning some particular High Church maxims, but as I look upon the promoters and favourers of these doctrines to be every whit as absurd and silly as the doctrines themselves and adapted only for weak people, so I thought all argumentation was thrown away upon them and therefor I dropt the dispute, for as I was a stranger, I cared not, for the sake of such damnd triffles, to procure the odium or ill will of any person in the place. After dinner I went home and slept till the evening, the weather being pritty hot and I having drank too much wine; it made me heavy.

Sunday, July 22. After breakfast I went with Mr. Hughes to Hooper's meeting[253] where we heard a very good discourse and saw a genteel congregation. The ladys were most of them in high dress. This meeting house is a handsome, new, wooden building with a huge spire or steeple att the north end of it. The pulpit is large and neat with a large sounding board supported att each side with pilasters of the Dorick order, fluted, and behind it there is a high arched door over which hangs a green curtain. The pulpit cushion is of green velvet, and all the windows in the meeting are mounted with green curtains.

After dismissing I went to Change and, returning from thence, dined with Mr. Lechmere. There was a lady att table of a very masculine make but dres'd fine a la mode. She did not appear till dinner was almost over, pretending she could not endure the smell of the vittles and was every now and then lugging out her sal volatile and Hungary water, but this I observed was only a modish air, for she made a shift betwixt times to swallow down as much beef and pudding as any body att the table; in short her teeth went as fast as her tongue, and the motion of both was perpetuall.

After dinner I went to the English chappell with Mr. Lechmere and heard a small organ play'd by an indifferent organist. A certain pedantick Irishman[254] preached to us, who had much of the brogue. He gave us rather a philosophicall lecture than a sermon and seemed to be one of those conceited priggs who are fond of spreading out to its full extent all that superficial physicall knowledge which they have acquired more by hearsay than by application or study; but of all places the pulpit is the most impropper for the ostentations of this sort; the language and phraseology of which sacred *rostrum* ought to be as plain to the ploughman as the schollar. We had a load of impertinence from him about the specific gravity of air and water, the exhalation of vapours, the expansion and condensation of clouds, the operation of distillation, and the chemistry of nature. In fine it was but a very puerile physicall lecture and no sermon att all. There sat some Indians in a pew near me who stunk so that they had almost made me turn up my dinner. They made a profound reverence to the parson when he finished; the men bowed, and the squas curtsied.

After dinner I writ a letter for Annapolis and drank tea with Mrs. Guneau and some ladys.

Monday, July 23. This morning I walked abroad with Mr. Hughes and passed over the dam[255] att the reservoir to the north end of the town. We surveyed the ships a building upon the stocks and went to see the new battery, a building of wood just att the entry of that inlett of water that runs up towards

Charlestown. This new battery mounts about 14 or 15 great guns, and facing the bay it runs out about 50 paces into the water. From thence we went and survey'd the merchants' warehouses which stand all along the water side. We next viewed the new market house, and elegant building of brick, with a cupula on the top, in length about 130 foot, in breath betwixt 40 and 50. This was built att the propper expence of one Funell,[256] a substantial merchant of this place, lately dead, and presented by him to the publick. It is called by the name of Funell-Hall and stands near a little inlett of water called the Town Dock, over which, a little below the market house, is a wooden draw bridge that turns upon hinges that small vessels may pass and lye above it. In low tides this inlett is a very stinking puddle.

At nine o'clock we finished our tour and came home sharp set for breakfast. Att eleven o'clock Mr. Vans[257] came to visit me and invited me to dine with him upon Tuesday. I went to Withered's att 12 o'clock and from thence went to dine with Captain Wendall, where were some officers that had belonged to the garrison att Canso and had been there when the place was taken by the French. They were brought to Boston by Captain Mangeau in the flag of truce.[258] After dinner Captain Mangeau himself came in who spoke such broken English that I understood his French much better. In the afternoon I called att Mr. Hooper's and agreed to go to Cambridge with him upon Wednesday.

Tuesday, July 24th. I received this day a letter from Dr. Moffet att Newport, Rhode Island, and answered the same by the opportunity of Mr. Hughes who went there this day. Dr. Dowglass payed me a short visit in the morning, and att 12 a'clock I went to Change where I saw Mr. Vans who carried me to dine with him. Mr. Vans himself and his whole family I found to be great admirers of the New Light doctrines and scheme. His wife is a strenuous Whitfieldian. The word carnal was much used in our table talk, which seems to be a favorite word of the fair sex of that perswasion. There was one att table whom Mr. Vans called brother, who spoke very little but had the most solemn puritanick countenance ever I had seen. The discourse chiefly turned upon religion, but the strain of it was so enthusiastic that I thought fit only to be a hearer.

After dinner I went with Mr. Vans to an auction of books in King's Street where the auctioneer,[259] a young fellow, was very witty in his way. "This book," says he, "gentlemen, must be valuable. Here you have every thing concerning popes, cardinals, anti-christ, and the devil. Here, gentlemen, you have Tacitus, that elegant historian. He gives you an account of that good and pious person, Nero, who loved his mother and kindred so well that he sucked their very blood." The books that sold best at this auction while I was there were Pamela, Anti-Pamela, The Fortunate Maid, Ovid's Art of Love, and The Marrow of Moderen Divinity.

We were called to the windows in the auction room by a noise in the street which was occasioned by a parade of Indian chiefs marching up the street with Collonell Wendal.[260] The fellows had all laced hats, and some of them laced matchcoats and ruffled shirts, and a multitude of the plebs of their own complexion followed them. This was one Henrique[261] and some other of the chiefs of the Mohooks who had been deputed to treat with the eastren Indians bordering upon New England. This Henrique is a bold, intrepid fellow. When he first arrived att the place of rendevous, none of the eastren chiefs were come. However, he expressed himself to the commons to this purpose: "We, the Mohooks," said he, "are your fathers, and you, our children. If you are dutifull and obedient, if you brighten the chain with the English, our friends, and take up the hatchet against the French, our enimies, we will defend and protect you; but otherwise, if you are dissobedient and rebell, you shall dye, every man, woman, and child of you, and that by our hands. We will cut you off from the earth as an ox licketh up the grass." To this some of the Indians made answer that what he said was just. As for their parts they would do their best to keep their end of the house in order, but their house was a very long house, one end of it was light and the other dark, because having no doors or windows the sun could not shine in upon them. (By the dark end they meant the St. John and Cape Sable Indians of the same nation with them but in the French interest). In the light end they knew what they were a doing, but no body could see in the dark. However, they would strike a light and, if possible, discover its most secret corners. "It is true you are our fathers, and our lives depend upon you. We will always be dutifull, as we have hitherto been, for we have cleared a road all the way to Albany betwixt us and you, having cut away every tree and bush that there might be no obstruction. You, our fathers, are like a porcupine full of prickles to wound such as offend you; we, your children, are like little babes whom you have put into cradles and rocked asleep." While they delivered this answer they appeared very much frightened, and in the mean time one Lewis, an eastren chief, came upon the field, who seemed to reprove Henrique for delivering his embassy to the common people while none of the chiefs were by, telling him it was like speaking to cattle. But Henrique, with a frown, told him that he was not obliged to wait his conveniency and time, ading that what was said was said and was not again to be repeated, "but do you or your people att your perill act contrary to our will." Att that the other Indian was silent and durst not speak.

These Mohooks are a terror to all round them and are certainly a brave warlike people, but they are divided into two nations, Protestants and Roman Catholicks, for the most of them are Christians; the first take part with the English, the latter with the French, which makes the neighbouring Indians, their tributarys, lead an unquiet life, always in fear and terrour and an uncertainty how to behave.

I went this night to visit Mr. Smibert,[262] the limner, where I saw a collection of fine pictures, among the rest that part of Scipio's history in Spain where he delivers the lady to the prince to whom she had been betrothed. The passions are all well touched in the severall faces. Scipio's face expresses a majestic generosity, that of the young prince gratitude, the young lady's gratitude and modest love, and some Roman souldiers standing under a row of pillars apart in seeming discourse, have admiration delineated in their faces. But what I admired most of the painter's fancy in this piece is an image or phantome of chastity behind the solium upon which Scipio sits, standing on tip-toe to crown him and yet appears as if she could not reach his head, which expresses a good emblem of the virtue of this action. I saw here likewise a collection of good busts and statues, most of them antiques, done in clay and paste, among the rest Homer's head and a modell of the Venus of Medicis.

Wednesday, July 25. I had appointed this day to go to Cambridge with Mr. Hooper, but the weather proved too hot. I went to Change att 12 o'clock and heard no news, only some distant hints of an intended expedition of the English against Cape Breton, which is a great eye sore to their fishing trade upon this coast.[263] I dined with Mr. Hooper and drank tea there, and went in the evening to the auction but found no books of value exposed to sale. When I came to my lodging att night, Mrs. Guneau told me she had got a new lodger, one

Monsieur de la Moinnerie, a Frenchman, who had come from Jamaica. This evening was very hot, bordering upon our Maryland temperature, and being out of order I went to bed before nine.

Thursday, July 26. This day att Withered's I met with Dr. Clerk[264] to whom I delivered a letter. He invited me to the Physicall Club at the Sun Taveren [265] upon Friday evening. I promised to attend there in case the weather should prevent my journey eastward, which I intended as far as Portsmouth or Pitscataquay. I dined att Withered's with some gentlemen. While we were att dinner there came up a thunder shower which cooled the air very much, it having been for some days very hot.

After dinner one Captain Tasker[266] came in who had been att Canso when the French took it. He had a vessel there laden with provisions for which he had contracted with the French before the war broke out. When they carried him to Cape Breton, they were so generous as to pay him for his cargo of provisions and dismiss him. In the payment it was supposed they had given him some brandy and other counterband goods which he attempted to run here, but being discovered, was called to account by the goverment, not only for running these goods but for supplying the enimy with provision. As to the latter accusation he was acquitted because the contract or bargain with the French had been made before the declaration of war, and as he was taken prisoner att Canso, it was in the power of the French to seize his vessel and cargoe without paying him for them. He had lost likewise considerably by his bills being protested by the Board of Admirality in France. He told me his losses amounted to above 20,000 pounds New England currency. I imagined that he might be related to Mr. T[aske]r att Annapolis[267] because I had known but few of that name. I asked him if he knew that gentleman. He replied that he had never seen him, but he believed he was a kinsman of his.

I went in the afternoon to Mr. Lechmere's and thence to Mr. Fletcher's, a young gentleman, son to Captain Fletcher[268] so well known in Annapolis. He and I went to the auction together, but the books sold so dear that I could not procure such as I wanted. We had only a good deal of auctioneer wit. I supped att Fletcher's, and the night being very dark and rainy, I had much adoe to find my way home to my lodging, but calling in accidentaly att Lechmere's without knowing where I went, he was so civil as to send a boy and lanthorn along with me. The streets of this town are very quiet and still a'nights; yet there is a constant watch kept in the town.

Friday, July 27th. This day proving very rainy I was prevented in my intention to travel eastward. Att breakfast with Mrs. Guneau, Mons. de la Moinnerie chattered like a magpie in his own language, having Mrs. Guneau to talk with, who speaks very good French. Their conversation run upon the rate of the markets att Boston and the price of beef, mutton, and other provisions. I dined att Withered's and, in the afternoon, went to the auction where I bought a copy of Clerk's Homer[269] very cheap. Att night I went to the Physicall Club att the Sun Taveren according to appointment, where we drank punch, smoaked tobacco, and talked of sundry physicall matters.

D[ouglas]s, the physitian here, is a man of good learning but mischievously given to criticism and the most compleat snarler ever I knew. He is loath to allow learning, merit, or a character to any body. He is of the clinical class of physicians and laughs att all theory and practise founded upon it, looking upon empyricism or bare experience as the only firm basis upon which practise ought to be founded. He has got here about him a set of disciples who greedily draw in his doctrines and, being but half learned themselves, have not wit enough to discover the foibles and mistakes of their preceptor. This man I esteem a notorious physicall heretick, capable to corrupt and vitiate the practise of the place by spreading his erroneous doctrines among his shallow bretheren.

This night we heard news of Morpang's being upon the coast. I went home att eleven o'clock att night and prepared for my journey to morrow.

Charlestown Ferry

Saturday, July 28th. I departed Boston this morning betwixt seven and eight o'clock, and crossing the upper ferry[270] I came to Charlestown, a pritty large and compact town consisting of one street about half a mile long.[271] I breakfasted there att the Sign of the Swan. Our conversation att breakfast run upon the extravagancies of the New-light-men and particularly one Gilman,[272] a noted preacher among them. One day this fellow being in his pulpit, he exerted himself to the outmost to move the passions in his audience by using such pathetick expressions as his dull, costive fancy could frame. "What!" said he, "Not shed one tear for poor Christ who shed his blood for you; not one tear, Christians! Not one single tear! Tears for blood is but a poor recompence. O fy! Fy! This is but cold comfort." Att that an old woman bolted up in pious fury and, mounting the pulpit steps, bestowed such a load of close huggs and kisses upon the preacher that she stopped his mouth for some time and had almost suffocated him with kindness.

Mistick—Linn

Departing Charlestown I passed thro' Mistick[273] att 10 o'clock, a pritty large village about 4 miles north east from Boston. A little after 12 I passed thro Linn,[274] another village, but very scattered and standing upon a large compass of ground, the situation very open and pleasant. Here I could have a view of the sea upon my right hand and upon my left, a large open hilly and rocky country with some skirts of woods which seemed to be but low and of a small growth.

Marblehead

Att one o'clock I arrived att Marblehead,[275] a large fishing town, lying upon the sea coast, built upon a rock and standing pritty bleak to the easterly winds from the sea. It lyes 18 miles N.E. from Boston and is somewhat larger than Albany but not so neatly or compactly built, the houses being all of wood, and the streets very uneven, narrow, and irregular. It contains about 5000 inhabitants, and their commodity is fish. There is round the town above 200 acres of land covered with fish flakes, upon which they dry their cod. There are 90 fishing sloops always employed, and they deal for 34,000£ sterling prime cost value in fish yearly, bringing in 30,000 quintalls, a quintall being 100 weight dryed fish, which is 3,000,000 pound weight, a great quantity of that commodity.

I put up here att one Reid's att the Sign of the Dragon,[276] and while I was att dinner, Mr. Malcolm,[277] the Church of England minister to whom I was recommended, came in. After I had dined he carried me round the town and showed me the fish flakes and the town battery, which is built upon a rock, naturally well fortified, and mounts about 12 large guns. We had a great deal of talk about affairs at home. I went to his house and drank tea with him. He showed me some pritty pieces of musick and played some tunes on the flute and violin. He is author of a very good book upon musick which shows his judgement and knowledge in that part of science.

Sunday, July 29th. This morning enquiring for my portmanteau, I was told by my man Dromo that it was in his room. I had the curiosity to go and see what kind of a room his room was and, upon a reconoitre, found it a most spacious one, furnished alamode de cabaret with tables, chairs, a fine feather bed with quilted counterpine, white callicoe canopy or tester, and curtains, every way adapted for a gentleman of his degree and complexion.

I went to church to hear Mr. Malcolim in the forenoon, who gave us a pritty discourse. This church is a building of wood about 80 foot square, supported in the inside with eight large octagonal wooden pillars of the Dorick order. Upon this church stands a steeple in which there is a publick clock. The floor of the church is raised 6 or 7 foot above the ground, and under it is a burying place. The pulpit and altar are neat enough, the first being set out with a cushion of red velvet, and the other painted and adorned with the King's arms at top. There is one large gallery facing the pulpit, opposite to which at the south entry of the church hangs a pritty large gilt candle branch. The congregation consisted of about 400 people. I dined with Mr. Malcolm and went to church again with him in the afternoon and spent the evening agreeably in his company. In this town are likewise two great Presbyterian meetings.

Salem

Monday, July 30. Mr. Malcolim and I set out att eleven o'clock in the morning for Salem,[278] which is a pritty town about 5 miles from Marblehead going round a creek, but not above two if you cross the creek. We arrived there betwixt 12 and one o'clock and called att Justice Sewell's, who invited us to dine with him. We put up our horses att the Ship Taveren[279] and went to Mr. Sewell's.[280]

Our conversation run upon the enthusiasm now prevalent

in these parts and the strange madness that had possessed some people att Ipswitch occasioned by one Woodberry,[281] a mad enthusiast, who, pretending to inspiration, uttered severall blasphemous and absurb speeches, asserting that he was the same to day, yesterday, and for ever, saying he had it in his power to save or damn whom he pleased, falling down upon the ground, licking the dust, and condemning all to hell who would not do the like, drinking healths to King Jesus, the self existing Being, and prosperity to the kingdom of heaven, and a thousand other such mad and ridiculous frolicks. I was quite shoked att these relations, both when I heard them mentioned in conversation and saw them published in the news paper, being surprized that some of the chief clergy there had been so weak as to be drawn away by these follies. This is a remarkable instance to what lengths of madness enthusiasm will carry men once they give it a loose [rein], and tho' excursions may appear shoking to people in their senses, yet so much good may follow them as that the interest and influence of these fanatick preachers will be thereby depressed among all such people as are not quite fools or mad. These extravagancies take all their first root from the labours of that righteous apostle Whitefield who, only for the sake of private lucre and gain, sowed the first seeds of distraction in these unhappy, ignorant parts.

In the afternoon Mr. Malcolm and I rid to the country seat of one Brown, a gentleman who married a daughter of the late Governour Burnet's, a grandaughter of the bishop's. His house[282] stands upon the top of a high hill and is not yet quite finished. It is built in the form of an H with a middle body and two wings. The porch is supported by pillars of the Ionick order about 15 foot high, and betwixt the windows of the front are pilasters of the same. The great hall or parlour is about 40 foot long and 25 wide, with a gallery over the first row of windows, and there is two large roms upon a floor in each of the wings, about 25 foot square. From this hill you have a most extensive view. To the southwest you see the Blue Hills about 36 miles' distance, to the east the sea and severall islands, to the northwest the top of a mountain called Machuset[283] Mountain, like a cloud, about 90 miles' distance towards Albany, and all round you a fine landskip covered with woods, a mixture of hills and valleys, land and water, upon which variety the eye dwells with pleasure. This hill Mr. Brown calls Mount Burnett in compliment to his wife.

In the hall I saw a piece of tapestry, or arras of scripture history, done by Vanderbank,[284] a Dutch artist. For elegance and design it is like painting, the passions in the faces being well expressed. It is the best of the kind ever I saw.

This gentleman has a fine estate but, withall, has the character of being narrow and avaritious, a vice uncommon to young men. He has a strange taste for theologicall controversy. While we were there the conversation turned chiefly upon nice metaphysicall distinctions relating to original sin, imputed righteousness, reprobation, effectual calling, and absolute decrees, which stuff, as I esteem it to be no more than the monstruous and deformed ofspring of scholastick, theologicall heads, I should choose to hear it at no other times but when I took a cathartick or emetick in order to promote the operation if it proved too sluggish.[285]

Mr. Malcolm and I returned to Salem a little before eight o'clock and went to the Ship Taveren where we drank punch and smoked tobacco with severall collonells; for collonells, captains, and majors are so plenty here that they are to be met with in all companys, and yet me thinks they look no more like souldiers than they look like divines, but they are gentlemen of the place, and that is sufficient. We went to Mr. Sewell's lodging betwixt nine and ten at night and, after some chat with him, went to bed.

The town of Salem is a pritty place,[286] being the first settled place in New England. In it there is one Church of England, one Quaker meeting, and 5 Presbyterian meetings.[287] It consists of one very long street running nearly east and west. Upon the watch house is a grenadeer carved in wood, shouldering his piece.[288]

Salem Ferry—Ipswitch

Tuesday, July 31. At eleven o'clock this morning Mr. Malcolm accompanied me to Salem Ferry[289] where I crossed and rid a pleasant levell road all the way to Ipswitch,[290] where the houses are so thick planted that it looks like one continued village. I put up at one Howel's[291] in Ipswitch att the Sign of the Armed Knight. I waited upon Mr. John Rogers,[292] the minister there, and delivered him a paquet of letters from his son att Annapolis. I returned again to the taveren and there met a talkative old fellow who was very inquisitive about my place of abode and occupation, as he called it. He frequently accosted me with *please your honour,* with which grand title, like some fools whom I know, I seemed highly pleased tho I was conscious it did not belong to me. When I told him I came from Maryland, he said he had frequently read of that place but never had seen it. This old fellow, by his own account, had read of every thing but had seen nothing. He affected being a schollar, or a man much given to reading or study, and used a great many hard words in discourse, which he generally missapplied.

There was likewise a young man in company who rid with me some miles on my way to Newberry. He valued himself much upon the goodness of his horse and said that he was a prime beast as ever went upon 4 legs or wore hoofs. He told me he had a curiosity to ride to Maryland but was afraid of the terrible woods in the way and asked me if there were not a great many dangerous wild beasts in these woods. I told him that the most dangerous wild beasts in these woods were shaped exactly like men, and they went by the name of buckskins, or bucks, tho they were not bucks neither but something, as it were, betwixt a man and a beast. "Bless us! You don't say so," says he; "then surely you had needs ride with guns" (meaning my pistols). I parted with this wiseacre when I had got about half way to Newburry.

A little farther I met a fat sheep driving in a chaise, a negroe sitting upon the box. I asked the negroe if that was his master. He told me no, but that it was a weather belonging to Mr. Jones, who had strayed and would not come home without being carried. Passing by this prodigy I met another, which was two great fat women riding upon one horse.

Newburry

I arrived att Newburry att seven o'clock and put up att one Choat's[293] att the Sign of the Crown, which is a good house. Newburry is a pritty large village lying close upon the water.[294] The houses are chiefly wood. In this town there is one handsom meeting built in a square form with a spire or steeple upon which is a little neat publick clock.[295]

Newburry Ferry—Hampton

Wednesday, August 1. This morning proved very rainy, and therefor I did not set out till eleven o'clock. I crossed Newburry Ferry[296] and rid a pleasant even road, only somewhat stonny, and in a perpetual drizzle so that I could not have an advantageous view of the country round me. Att half an hour after one I passed thro Hampton, a very long, scattered town.

Having proceeded some miles farther I was overtaken by a man who bore me company all the way to Portsmouth. He was very inquisitive about where I was going, whence I came, and who I was. His questions were all stated in the rustick civil stile. "Pray sir, if I may be so bold, where are you going?" "Prithee, friend," says I, "where are you going?" "Why, I go along the road here a little way." "So do I, friend," replied I. "But may I presume, sir, whence do you come?" "And from whence do you come, friend?" says I." "Pardon me, from John Singleton's farm," replied he, "with a bag of oats." "And I come from Maryland," said I, "with a portmanteau and baggage." "Maryland!" said my companion, "where the devil is that there place? I have never heard of it. But pray, sir, may I be so free as to ask your name?" "And may I be so bold as to ask yours, friend?" said I. "Mine is Jerry Jacobs, att your service," replied he. I told him that mine was Bombast Huynhym van Helmont, att his service. "A strange name indeed; belike your a Dutchman, sir,—a captain of a ship, belike." "No, friend," says I, "I am a High German alchymist." "Bless us! You don't say so; that's a trade I never heard of; what may you deal in sir?" "I sell air," said I. "Air," said he, "damn it, a strange commodity. I'd thank you for some wholesom air to cure my fevers which have held me these two months." I have noted down this dialogue as a specimen of many of the same tenour I had in my journey when I met with these inquisitive rusticks.

New Hampshire Goverment

Having now entered New Hampshire Goverment, I stopped att a house within 5 miles of Portsmouth to bait my horses, where I had some billingsgate with a sawcy fellow that made free in handling my pistols. I found a sett of low, rascally company in the house and, for that reason, took no notice of what the fellow said to me, not being over fond of quarrelling with such trash. I therefor mounted horse again at half an hour after three and, having rid about two miles, saw a steeple in a skirt of woods which I imagined was Portsmouth; but when I came up to it, found it was a decayed wooden meeting house standing in a small hamlet within two miles of Portsmouth. In this part of the country one would think there was a great many towns by the number of steeples you see round you, every country meeting having one, which by reason of their slenderness and tapering form appear att a distance pritty high.

Portsmouth

I arrived in Portsmouth att 4 in the afternoon, which is a seaport town very pleasantly situated close upon the water and nearly as large as Marblehead.[297] It contains betwixt 4 and 5 thousand inhabitants. There are in it two Presbyterian meetings[298] and one Church of England, of which last one Brown, an Irishman, is minister, to whom I had a letter recommendatory from Mr. Malcolm. I put up here at Slater's,[299] a widow woman, who keeps a very good house and convenient lodging. After I had dined I waited upon Mr. Brown, and he invited me to breakfast with him to morrow. I returned to my lodging att eight o'clock, and the post being arrived, I found a numerous company att Slater's reading the news. Their chit-chat and noise kept me awake 3 hours after I went to bed.

Thursday, August 2d. I went and breakfasted with Mr. Brown, and after breakfast we waited upon Governour Wentworth[300] who received me very civily and invited me to take a souldier's dinner with him, as he called it, att the fort.

Newcastle—Kitterick

Att 10 o'clock we went by water in the Governour's barge to

Newcastle, a small town two miles from Portsmouth, where the fort[301] stands upon a little island. Opposite to Newcastle upon the other side of the water, there is a village called Kitterick.[302] The tide in these narrows runs with great rapidity and violence, and we having it in our favour and six oars in the barge, we were down att the fort in about 10 minutes. This fort is almost a triangle, standing on a rock facing the bay. That side next the town is about 200 foot long, built of stone, having a small bastion att each end. The other two sides next the water are each about 300 foot long and consist of turf ramparts erected upon a stone foundation about 7 foot high and ten foot thick, so that the largest bullets may lodge in it. This fort mounts about 30 guns, most of them 32 pounders, besides 15 or 20 small ones or twelve pounders. In the guard room where we dined are small arms for about 60 men, but kept in very bad order, being eat up with rust. After dinner, the sky turning clear, we took a view to the eastward towards the ocean and could see severall islands and Cape Anne att a distance, like a cloud, with about 24 sail of small coasting vessels.

York

Mr. Brown and I crossed the water att three a clock and rid nine miles up the country to a place called York.[303] In our way we had a variety of agreeable prospects of a rocky and woody country and the ocean upon our right hand. We returned to the fort again a little after 7 o'clock.

This province of New Hamshire is very well peopled and is a small colony or goverment, being inclosed on all hands by the Massachusets province to which it once belonged but has lately, for some state reasons, been made a separate goverment from New England. The provinces here are divided into townships instead of shires or countys. The trade of this place is fish and masting for ships, the navy att home being supplied from here with very good masts.

I observed a good many geese in the fort. The Governour took notice that they were good to give an alarm in case of a nocturnal surprize, mentioning the known story of the Roman capitol. We rowed back to town against the tide betwixt 8 and 9 att night. I took my leave of Gov. Wentworth att 9 o'clock att night and went to my lodging.

Hampton

Friday, August 3. I departed Portsmouth att half an hour after 5 in the morning and had a pleasant route to Hampton. This town is about 7 or eight miles long but so disjoined that some of the houses are half a mile's distance one from another. About the middle of it is a pritty large plain about half a mile broad and 4 or 5 miles long which is marshy and overgrown with salt water hay. On my left hand here I could see the sea and Cape Anne where the plain opened. I breakfasted att one Griffin's att Hampton. I had some discourse with the landlord who seemed to be very fond of speculative points of religion and was for spiritualizing of everything.

Newburry Ferry

Near Newburry Ferry I met an old man who was very inquisitive about news. He rid above a mile with me. I crossed the ferry att 12 o'clock and dined att Choat's with two Boston gentlemen, and after dinner they would have had me go to the Presbyterian meeting to hear a sermon, but I declined it and, getting upon horseback, departed Newburry att 3 in the afternoon, the day being pritty hot. Some miles from this town I passed thro a pleasant, small plain about a quarter of a mile broad thro the middle of which runs a pritty winding river. On the way I met a young sailor on foot who kept pace with my horse, and he told me he was bound for Salem that night. He entertained me with his adventures and voyages and dealt much in the miraculous according to the custom of most travellers and sailors.

Ipswitch

I arrived att Ipswitch att 6 o'clock and put up att Howell's. I went to see Mr. Rogers, the minister there, and att night drank punch with his son, the doctor.

Salem Ferry

Saturday, August 4. I left Ipswitch early in the morning and had a solitary ride to Salem. I put up my horses there att the Ship Taveren and called att Messrs. Sewell's and Brown's, but they were both gone out of town.

Att Salem there is a fort with two demibastions, but they stand less in need of it than any of the other maritim towns here, for the entry to this harbour is so difficult and rocky that even those who have been for years used to the place will not venture in without a good pilot; so that it would be a hard task for an enimy to enter. Portsmouth harbour is easy enough, but the current of the tides there are so violent that there is no getting in or out but att particular seasons, and besides, they are locked in on all hands by islands and promontorys. Att Marblehead the entry is very easy and open.

Att 12 a clock I thought of going to Marblehead again to pay another visit to Mr. Malcolm, whose company and conversation had much pleased me, but meeting here with a gentleman going to Boston, I took the opportunity for the sake of company to go along with him.

Lower Ferry

We rid hard to the lower ferry,[304] having made 15 miles in two hours. We had a tollerable good passage over the ferry, which here is two miles broad.

Boston

I left my horses att Barker's stables and drank tea with my landlady, Mrs. Guneau. There was in the company a pritty young lady. The character of a certain Church of England clergiman in Boston was canvassed, he having lost his living for being too sweet upon his landlady's daughter, a great belly being the consequence. I pitied him only for his imprudence and want of policy. As for the crime, considdered in a certain light it is but a peccadillo, and he might have escaped unobserved had he had the same cunning as some others of his bretheren who doubtless are as deep in the dirt as he in the mire. I shall not mention the unfortunate man's name (absit foeda calumnia), but I much commiserated his calamity and regretted the loss, for he was an execellent preacher; but the wisest men have been led into silly scrapes by the attractions of that vain sex, which, I think, explains a certain enigmatic verse.

> Diceti grammatici, cur mascula nomina cunnus
> Et cur Famineum mentula nomen habet

The first is masculine, because it attracts the male, the latter feminine, because it is an effeminate follower of the other.

I had the opportunity this night of seeing Mons. la Moinnerie, my fellow lodger. He was obliged to keep the house close for fear of being made a prisoner of war. He was the strangest mortal for eating ever I knew. He would not eat with the family but always in his own chamber, and he made a table of his trunk. He was always a chawing except some little intervalls of time in which he applied to the study of the English language.

Sunday, August 5. I went this morning into Monsieur's chamber and asked him how he did. He made answer in French but asked me in maimd English if I had made un bon voyage, what news, and many other little questions culled out of his grammar. I was shy of letting him know I understood French, being loath to speak that language as knowing my faultiness in the pronounciation. He told me that hier a soir he had de mos' excellen' soupé and wished I had been to eat along with him. His chamber was strangely set out: here a bason with the relicts of some soup, there a fragment of bread, here a paper of salt, there a bundle of garlick, here a spoon with some pepper in it, and upon a chair a saucer of butter. The same individual bason served him to eat his soup out of and to shave in, and in the water, where a little before he had washed his hands and face, he washed likewise his cabbages. This, too, served him for a punch-bowl. He was fond of giving directions how to dress his vittles and told Nanny, the cook maid, "Ma foy, I be de good cock, Madame Nannie," said he. The maid put on an air of modest anger and said she did not understand him. "Why, here you see," says he, "my cock be good, can dress de fine viandes."

This morning I went and heard Mr. Hooper and dined with Mr. Grey. I went to meeting again in the afternoon. He (Mr. Hooper) is one of the best preachers I have heard in America, his discourse being sollid sense, strong connected reasoning, and good language. I drank tea with Mrs. Guneau in the afternoon and staid at home this night reading a little of Homer's first Iliad.

Monday, August 6. I was visited this morning by Mons.

de la Moinnerie, who spoke bad English and I indifferent
French; so we had recourse to Latin and did somewhat better.
He gave me an account of his own country, their manners and
goverment, and a detail of his own adventures since he came
abroad. He told me that he had studied the law and showed
me a deploma granted him by the University of Paris. He had
practised as a chamber councel in Jamaica for two months
and was coming into pritty business, but intermeddling in
some political matters procured the ill will of the grandees
there and, being obliged to go away, took to merchandizing;
but his vessel being cast away att sea, he took passage for Bost-
ton in a sloop before the French war was declared, intending
from thence to old France.

I dined this day att Withered's and spent the evening with
Dr. Clerk, a gentleman of a fine naturall genius, who, had his
education been equivalent, would have outshone all the other
physitians in Boston. Dr. D[ouglass] was there, and Mr. Lightfoot, and another gentleman, a lawer, a professed connoiseur.

Dr. D[ouglass] talked very slightingly of Boerhaave and
upon all occasions, I find, sets himself up as an enimy to his plan
of theory and laughs att all practise founded upon it. He called
him a mere helluo librorum, an indefatigable compiler that
dealt more in books than in observation or αὐτοψια. I asked
his pardon and told him that I thought he was by far the greatest genius that ever appeared in that way since the days of
Hippocrates. He said his character was quite eclipsed in England. "Pardon me, sir," said I, "you are mistaken. Many of
the English physitians who have studied and understand his
system admire him. Such as have not, indeed, never understood
him, and in England they have not as yet taught from his books,
but till once they embrace his doctrines they will always, like the
French, be lagging behind a century or two in the improve-

ments of physick." I could not learn his reasons for so vilify-
ing this great man, and most of the physitians here (the young
ones I mean) seem to be awkward imitators of him in this
railing faculty. They are all mighty nice and mighty hard to
please, and yet are mighty raw and uninstructed (excepting
D[ouglass] himself and Clerk) in even the very elements of
physick. I must say it raised my spleen to hear the character
of such a man as Boerhaave picked att by a parcell of pigmies,
mere homuncios in physick, who shine no where but in the
dark corner allotted them like a lamp in a monk's cell, obscure
and unknown to all the world excepting only their silly hearers
and imitators, while the splendour of the great character which
they pretend to canvass eclipses all their smaller lights like the
sun, enlightens all equally, is ever admired when looked upon,
and is known by every one who has any regard for learning
or truth; so that all their censure was like the fable of the dog
barking att the moon. I found, however, that Dr. D[ouglass]
had been a disciple of Pitcairn's,[305] and as some warm disputes
had subsisted betwixt Pitcairn and Boerhave at his leaving
the professional chair of Leyden when turned out by the interest of K: William (for Pitcairn was a strenuous Jacobite) he
bore Boerhaave a mortall grudge afterwards and endeavoured
all he could to lessen his interest and deminish his character. I
left the company att eleven a'clock and went home.

Tuesday, August 7th. I was visited this morning by Monsieur, whose address was, "Eh bien, Monsieur, comment se porte,
monsieur, votre vit, a't'il erigé ou Badiné ce matin?" "Oui monsieur," repartis je, "et comment se porte, monsieur, le votre?"
"Perfaitment bien, monsieur. Il vous rendit graces."

I dined att Withered's and called att Mr. Hooper's after
dinner to know when he intended to go for Cambridge; we
agreed upon to morrow afternoon. Coming home again I had

the other volley of French from Monsieur, accompanied with a deal of action.

Att night I went to the Scots' Quarterly Society[306] which met att the Sun Taveren. This is a charitable society and act for the relief of the poor of their nation, having a considerable summ of money att interest which they give out in small pensions to needy people. I contributed for that purpose 3 pounds New England currency and was presented with a copy of their laws. When the bulk of the company were gone I sat sometime with Dr. Dowglass, the president, and two or three others and had some chat on news and politicks. Att half an hour after ten I went home and had some more French from Monsieur who was applying strenuously to learn English.

Wednesday, August 8. This proving a very rainy day, I was frustrated in my design of going to Cambridge and was obliged to stay att home most of the day. I had severall dialogues with La Moinnerie relating to the English language. Mr. Hughes and I eat some of his soup. By way of whet he made us some punch, and rinsing the bowl with water, tossed it out upon the floor without any ceremony. The French are generally the reverse of the Dutch in this respect. They care not how dirty their chambers and houses are but affect neatness much in their dress when they appear abroad. I cannot say cleanliness, for they are dirty in their linnen wear. Mr. Hughes and I dined with Mrs. Guneau and went to Withered's. After dinner we walked out upon the Long Wharf. The rain still continuing, I went home att 4 o'clock and stayed att home all that evening.

Thursday, August 9th. I went with Mr. Hughes before dinner to see my countrywoman Mrs. Blackater (here Blackadore, for our Scots names generally degenerate when transplanted to England or English America, loseing their propper orthography and pronounciation). She is a jolly woman with a great, round, red face. I bought of her a pound of chocolate and saw one of her daughters, a pritty buxom girl in a gay tawdry deshabille, having on a robe de chambre of cherry coloured silk laced with silver round the sleeves and skirts and neither hoop nor stays. By this girl's phisiognomy, I judged she was one of that illustrious class of the sex commonly called coquetts. She seemed very handsom in every respect and, indeed, needed neither stays nor hoop to set out her shapes which were naturally elegant and good. But she had a vile cross in her eyes which spoilt in some measure the beauty and symmetry of her features. Before we went away the old woman invited Hughes and I to drink tea any afternoon when att leisure.

I dined with Mr. Fletcher in the company of two Philadelphians, who could not be easy because forsooth they were in their night-caps seeing every body else in full dress with powdered wigs; it not being customary in Boston to go to dine or appear upon Change in caps as they do in other parts of America. What strange creatures we are, and what triffles make us uneasy! It is no mean jest that such worthless things as caps and wigs should disturb our tranqulity and disorder our thoughts when we imagin they are wore out of season. I was my self much in the same state of uneasiness with these Philadelphians, for I had got a great hole in the lappet of my coat, to hide which employed so much of my thoughts in company that, for want of attention, I could not give a pertinent answer when I was spoke to.

I visited Mr. Smibert in the afternoon and entertained my self an hour or two with his paintings. Att night I was visited by Messrs. Parker and Laughton, who did not tarry long. Dr. Clerk came and spent the evening with me, and as we were a discussing points of philosophy and physick, our enquirys were interrupted by La Moinnerie who entered the room with a dish of roasted mutton in his hand. "Messieurs, votre serviteur," says he. "Voila de mouton rotie. Voulez vous manger une peu avec moi?" Dr. Clerk could not refrain laughing, but I payed a civil compliment or two to Monsieur, and he retired, bowing, carrying his mutton with him.

I had occasion to see a particular diversion this day which they call *hawling the fox*. It is practised upon simple clowns. Near the town there is a pond of about half a quarter of a mile broad. Across this they lay a rope, and two or three strong fellows, concealed in the bushes, hold one end of it. To a stump in view, there is tied a large fox. When they can lay hold of an ignorant clown on the opposite side of the pond, they inviegle him by degrees into the scrape—two people pretending to wager, one upon the fox's head and the other upon the clown's, twenty shillings or some such matter that the fox shall not or shall pull him thro' the water in spight of his teeth. The clown easily imagines himself stronger than the fox and, for a small reward, allows the rope to be put around his waste. Which done, the sturdy fellows on the other side behind the bush pull lustily for their friend the fox who sits tied to his stump all the time of the operation, being only a mere spectator, and haul poor pill-garlick with great rapidity thro' the pond, while the water hisses and foams on each side of him as he ploughs the surface, and his coat is well wet. I saw a poor country fellow treated in this manner. He run thro the water upon his back like a log of wood, making a frothy line across the pond, and when he came out he shook himself and swore he could not have believed the fox had so much strength. They gave him 20 shillings to help to dry his coat. He was pleased with the reward and said that for so much a time he would allow the fox to drag him thro' the pond as often as he pleased.

Friday, August 10th. This morning proving very rainy, I could not go abroad till 12 o'clock. Att that hour I went to Withered's where I dined and from thence walked down the Long Wharf with Mr. Hughes, Mr. Peach and his brother.

We saw a French prize brought in which was taken by Waterhouse,[307] a Boston privateer. She was laden with wine, brandy, and some bail goods to the value of 4000£ sterling. They expected in two more (fishing vessels) taken by the same privateer. This Waterhouse has a well fitted vessel and a great many stout hands, but by some misbehaviour in letting go a small privateer and a large merchant ship, he has acquired the character of cowardice. He was tryed upon the affair before the Governour and Council but acquitted himself tollerably tho his character must for ever suffer by it.

We went on board of Mr. Peach's schooner in the harbour where we drank some Bristo' bottled syder. From thence we went to Close Street to visit Mrs. Blackater, where we saw the two young ladys, her daughters. They are both pritty ladys, gay and airy. They appear generally att home in a loose deshabille which, in a manner, half hides and half displays their charms, notwithstanding which they are clean and neat. Their fine complexion and shapes are good, but they both squint and look two ways with their eyes. When they go abroad they dress in a theatricall manner and seem to study the art of catching. There passed some flashes of wit and vivacity of expression in the conversation, heightened no doubt by the influencing smiles of the young ladys. The old lady, after having understood something of my history, gave me a kind invitation to come and practise physick in Boston and proffered me her business and that of the friends she could make, expressing a great regard for her countrymen, and particularly for physitians of that nation who, she said, had the best character of any. She entertained us much with the history of a brother of hers, one Philips,[308] Governour of St. Martin's, a small Dutch settlement, and had got seven or eight copies of his picture done in graving hung up in her room. Peach passed her a compliment and said the pictures were exceeding like, for he knew her brother; but he told us afterwards that they were only words of course, for there was no more likeness betwixt the man and his picture than betwixt a horse and a cow. This old woman is rich, and her daughters are reputed fortunes. They are both beautys, and were it not for the squinting part, they would be of the first rate.

After a very gay conversation of three hours we went away, and I repaired to Withered's to the Physicall Club, where Dr. D[ouglass] gave us a physicall harangue upon a late book of surgery published by Heyster,[309] in which he tore the poor author all to pieces and represented him as intirely ignorant of the affair. Heister is a man of such known learning and such an established character in Europe as sets him above any criticism from such a man as D[ouglass] who is only a cynicall mortall, so full of his own learning that any other man's is not current with him. I have not as yet seen Heister's book of surgery, but D[ouglass]'s criticism, instead of depreciating it in my opinion, adds rather to its character. I saw it recommended in the Physicall News from Edinburg and the judgement of the literati in physick of that place preponderats with me all that D[ouglass] can say against it. D[ouglass] is of the clynicall class of physitians, crys up empyricism, and practises upon grounds which neither he himself nor any body for him can reduce to so much as a semblance of reason. He braggs often of his having called Boerhaave a *helluo librorum* in a thesis which he published att Leyden and takes care to inform us how much Boerhaave was nettled att it; just as much, I believe, as a mastiff is att the snarling of a little lap-dog. There are in this town a set of half learned physicall priggs to whom he is an oracle (Dr. Clerk only excepted, who thinks for himself). Leaving this company, quite sick of criticism, I went home att eleven o'clock.

Saturday, August 11. I went this morning with Mr. Peach and breakfasted upon chocolate att the house of one Monsieur Bodineau,[310] a Frenchman, living in School Street. This house was well furnished with women of all sorts and sizes. There were old and young, tall and short, fat and lean, ugly and pritty dames to be seen here. Among the rest was a girl of small stature, no beauty, but there was life and sense in her conversation; her witt was mixed with judgement and sollidity; her thoughts were quick, lively, and well expressed. She was, in fine, a propper mixture of the French mercury and English phlegm.

I went to Change att 12 o'clock and dined with Mr. Arbuthnott. I had a tune on the spinett from his daughter after dinner, who is a pritty, agreeable lady and sings well. I told her that she playd the best spinett that I had heard since I came to America. The old man, who is a blunt, honest fellow, asked me if I could pay her no other compliment but that, which dashed me a little, but I soon replied that the young lady was every way so deserving and accomplished that nothing that was spoke in her commendation could in a strick sense be called a compliment. I breathed a little after this speech, there being something romantick in it and, considdering human nature in the propper light, could not be true. The young lady blushed; the old man was pleased and picked his teeth, and I was conscious that I had talked nonsense.

I was dissappointed in my intention of going to the Castle with Messieurs Parker and Laughton. They called before I came home and left me, expecting that I would follow with Dr. Clerk, who did not keep the appointment. I rid out in the evening with Messrs. Peach and Hughes to one Jervise's[311] who keeps publick house 4 miles out of town. This house is the rendevous of many of the gentry of both sexes, who make an evening's promenade in the summer time. There was a great deal of company that came in chairs and on horseback. I saw there my old friend Captain Noise. We drank punch and returned to town att eight o'clock att night. After some comicall chat with La Moinnerie I went and supped att Withered's with Messrs. Peach and Hughes.

Sunday, August 12. I went this day with Mr. Hughes and Peach to Hooper's meeting, dined att Laughton's, and went again to meeting in the afternoon, where I saw Mrs. Blackater and her two daughters in a glaring dress.

This day I was taken notice of in passing the street by a lady who enquired of Mr. Hughes concerning me. "Lord!" said she, "what strange mortall is that?" "'T is the flower of the Maryland beaux," said Hughes. "Good God!" said the belle, "does that figure come from Maryland?" "Madam," said Hughes, "he is a Maryland physitian." "O Jesus! A physitian! Deuce take such odd looking physicians." I desired Hughes, when he told me of this conference, to give my humble service to the lady and tell her that it gave me vast pleasure to think that any thing particular about my person could so attract her resplendent eyes as to make her take notice of me in such a singular manner, and that I intended to wait upon her that she might entertain her opticks with my oddity, and I mine with her unparallelled charms.

I took a walk on the Long Wharf after sermon and spent the evening very agreeably with Mr. Lightfoot and some other gentlemen att his lodging. Our discourse began upon philosophy and concluded in a smutty strain.

Monday, August 13. I made a tour thro the town in the forenoon with Mr. Hughes and, att a certain lady's house, saw a white monkey. It was one of those that are brought from the Muscetto shore[312] and seemed a very strange creature. It was about a foot long in its body and, in visage, exceeding like an old man, there being no hair upon its face except a little white, downy beard. It laugh'd and grinned like any Christian (as people say), and was exceeding fond of his mistress, bussing her and handling her bubbies just like an old rake. One might well envy the brute, for the lady was very handsome; so that it would have been no dissagreeable thing for a man to have been in this monkey's place. It is strange to see how fond these brutes are of women, and, on the other hand, how much the female monkeys affect men. The progress of nature is surprizing in many such instances. She seems by one connected gradation to pass from one species of creatures to another without any visible gap, intervall, or *discontinuum* in her works; but an infinity of her operations are yet unknown to us.

I allotted this afternoon to go to the Castle with Messrs. Brazier and Hughes. Before dinner I called att Hooper's and agree'd to go to Cambridge with him to morrow afternoon. Brazier, Hughes, and I took horse after dinner and rid round to the point on purpose to go to the Castle but were disappointed, no boat coming for us. It rained, and as we returned home again, we called in att the Grey Hound and drank some punch. Some children in the street took me for an Indian king upon account of my laced hat and sun burnt vissage.

Tuesday, August 14th. I went with La Moinnerie to dine at Witherhead's, he having now got a permission from the Governour to go abroad. We had there a good jolly company.

Mr. Hooper put off our going to Cambridge till to morrow; so I went in the afternoon with Hughes to the house of Mr.

Harding and had some conversation with a very agreeable lady there, Mr. Withered's sister. This lady cannot be deemed handsom, but to supply the want of that naturall accomplishment which the sex are so very fond of, she had a great deal of good sense and acquired knowledge which appeared to the best advantage in every turn of her discourse. The conversation was lively, entertaining, and solid, neither tainted with false or triffling wit nor ill natured satire or reflexion, of late so much the topic of tea tables. I was glad to find that in most of the politer caballs of ladys in this town the odious theme of scandal and detraction over their tea had become quite unfashionable and unpolite and was banished intirely to the assemblies of the meaner sort, where may it dwell for ever, quite disregarded and forgott, retireing to that obscure place Billingsgate where the monster first took its origine.

Going from this house we went and survey'd a ship upon the stocks that was intended for a privateer. I spent the evening with Mr. Parker where I drank good port wine and heard news of six prizes carried into New York by the company of privateers there. There was in our company one Hill who told us a long insipid story concerning a squint eyed parson, a cat, and the devil. I had a letter from Miss Withered to her brother in Maryland, who lives upon Sassafrass River.

Wednesday, August 15. I went this morning with Messrs. Hooper and Hughes to Cambridge. Upon the road we met two of the French Mohooks on horseback, dressed *a la mode Francois* with laced hats, full trimmed coats, and ruffled shirts. One of them was an old fellow, the other a young man with a squaw mounted behind him. The squaw seemed to be a pritty woman all bedaubed with wampum. They were upon little roan horses and had a journey of above 700 miles to make by land. Upon the road to Cambridge the lands are inclosed with fine stone fences, and some of the gates have posts of one intire stone set right up upon end about eight or 10 foot high. The country all round is open and pleasant, and there is a great number of pritty country houses scattered up and down.

Cambridge

When we came to Cambridge we waited upon Mr. Hollyhoak,[313] the president, who sent the librarian[314] to show us the college [Harvard] and the library. Cambridge is a scattered town[315] about the largeness of Annapolis and is delightfully situated upon a pleasant plain near a pritty river of the same name, over which is a wooden bridge. The college[316] is a square building or quadrangle about 150 foot every way. The building upon the left hand as you enter the court is the largest and handsomest and most ancient, being about 100 years old; but the middle or front building is indifferent and of no taste. That upon the right hand has a little clock upon it which has a very good bell. In the library are 3 or 4 thousand volumes with some curious editions of the classicks presented to the college by Dean Barklay. There are some curiositys, the best of which is the cut of a tree about 10 inches thick and eight long, entirely petrified and turned into stone.

Charlestown Ferry—Castle of Boston—Lighthouse

We returned from Cambridge by the way of Charlestown. Crossing that ferry to Boston, we dined att Withered's with a pritty large company and, in the afternoon, had a pleasant sail to the Castle where the Governour and Assembly were met to consult about fortifying of Governour's Island,[317] which is situated just opposite to that whereon the Castle stands. This Castle[318] consists of a large half moon with two bastions defended with a glassee of earth and wood which is cannon proof. Upon these are mounted about 40 great iron guns, each 32 pounders. Upon the higher works or walls of this Castle are mounted above 100 smaller guns, most of them 12 or 18 pounders. Upon the most eminent place is a look out where stands the flag-staff, and where a centry is always posted. From here you can see pritty plainly with a spy glass, about 9 miles farther out upon a small island, the light-house, which is a high stone building in form of a sugar loaf, upon the top of which every night they burn oil to direct and guide the vessels att sea into the harbour. There is a draw well in the Castle which is covered with an arch of brick and stone in fashion of a vault. In the most eminent place is a square court upon one side of which is a chappell and state room, upon the other some dwelling houses.

We went to see Mr. Philips,[319] the chaplain there, and returned to town at 9 o'clock att night. I supped with Hughes att Withered's and saw one Mr. Simmonds there, a gentleman residing att Charlestown in South Carolina, who was going there by land and proposed to go in company with me to Maryland.

Thursday, August 16. I stayed att home most of the forenoon and had a deal of chat with La Moinnerie. I regretted much that I should be obliged to leave this facetious companion so soon, upon the account of losing his diverting conversation and the opportunity of learning to speak good French, for he used to come to my room every morning and hold forth an hour before breakfast.

I intended to begin my journey homeward to morrow. I dined with Hughes att Dr. Gardiner's,[320] and our table talk was agreeable and instructing, divested of these triffles with which it is commonly loaded. We visited att Mrs. Blackater's in the afternoon and had the pleasure of drinking tea with one of her fair daughters, the old woman and the other daughter being gone to their country farm.

I went in the evening with Mr. Hughes to a club att Withered's where we had a deal of discourse in the disputatory way. One Mr. Clackenbridge (very propperly so named upon account of the volubility of his tongue) was the chief disputant as to verbosity and noise but not as to sense or argument. This was a little dapper fellow full of the opinion of his own learning. He pretended to argue against all the company, but like a confused logician, he could not hold an argument long but wandered from one topic to another, leading us all into confusion and loud talking. He set up for a woman hater and, preferring what he called liberty before every other enjoyment in life, he therefor decryed marriage as a politicall institution destructive of human liberty.

My head being quite turned this night with this confused dispute and the thoughts of my journey to morrow, I got into a strange fit of absence, for having occasion to go out of the company two or three times to talk with Mr. Withered, I heedlessly every time went into a room where there was a strange company as I returned and twice sat down in the midst of them, nor did I discover I was in the wrong box till I found them all staring att me. For the first slip I was obliged to form the best apology I could, but att the second hitt I was so confused and saw them so inclinable to laugh that I run out at the door precipitatly without saying any thing and betook me to the right company. I went to my lodging att 12 o'clock.

I need scarce take notice that Boston is the largest town in North America, being much about the same extent as the city of Glasgow in Scotland and having much the same number of inhabitants, which is between 20 and 30 thousand.[321] It is

considerably larger than either Philadelphia or New York, but
the streets are irregularly disposed and, in generall, too narrow.
The best street in the town is that which runs down towards
the Long Wharff which goes by the name of King's Street.
This town is a considerable place for shipping and carrys on
a great trade in time of peace. There were now above 100 ships
in the harbour besides a great number of small craft tho now,
upon account of the war, the times are very dead. The people
of this province chiefly follow farming and merchandise. Their
staples are shipping, lumber, and fish. The goverment is so far
democratic as that the election of the Governour's Council
and the great officers is made by the members of the Lower
House, or representatives of the people. Mr. Shirly,[322] the present Governour, is a man of excellent sense and understanding
and is very well respected there. He understands how to humour
the people and, att the same time, acts for the interest of the
Goverment. Boston is better fortified against an enimy than
any port in North America, not only upon account of the
strength of the Castle but the narrow passage up into the
harbour which is not above 160 foot wide in the channell att
high water.

There are many different religions and perswasions here,
but the chief sect is that of the Presbyterians.[323] There are above
25 churches, chapells, and meetings in the town, but the
Quakers here have but a small remnant, having been banished
the province att the first settlement upon account of some dis-
turbances they raised. The people here have latlely been, and indeed are now, in great confusion and much infested with enthusiasm from the preaching of some fanaticks and New Light
teachers, but now this humour begins to lessen. The people are
generally more captivated with speculative than with practicall
religion. It is not by half such a flagrant sin to cheat and cozen

one's neighbour as it is to ride about for pleasure on the sabbath day or to neglect going to church and singing of psalms.

The middling sort of people here are to a degree dis-singenuous and dissembling, which appears even in their common conversation in which their indirect and dubious answers to the plainest and fairest questions show their suspicions of one another. The better sort are polite, mannerly, and hospitable to strangers, such strangers, I mean, as come not to trade among them (for of them they are jealous). There is more hospitality and frankness showed here to strangers than either att York or at Philadelphia. And in the place there is abundance of men of learning and parts; so that one is att no loss for agreeable conversation nor for any sett of company he pleases. Assemblys of the gayer sort are frequent here; the gentlemen and ladys meeting almost every week att consorts of musick and balls. I was present att two or three such and saw as fine a ring of ladys, as good dancing, and heard musick as elegant as I had been witness to any where. I must take notice that this place abounds with pritty women who appear rather more abroad than they do att York and dress elegantly. They are, for the most part, free and affable as well as pritty. I saw not one prude while I was here.

The paper currency of these provinces is now very much depreciated, and the price or value of silver rises every day, their money being now 6 for one upon sterling. They have a variety of paper currencys in the provinces; viz., that of New Hampshire, the Massachusets, Rhode Island, and Connecticut, all of different value, divided and subdivided into old and new tenors so that it is a science to know the nature and value of their moneys, and what will cost a stranger some study and application. Dr. Dowglass has writ a compleat treatise upon all the different kinds of paper currencys in America, which I was att the pains to read.[324] It was the expense of the Canada expedition that first brought this province in debt and put them upon the project of issuing bills of credit.[325] Their money is chiefly founded upon land security, but the reason of its falling so much in value is their issuing from time to time such large summs of it and their taking no care to make payments att the expiration of the stated terms. They are notoriously guilty of this in Rhode Island colony so that now it is dangerous to pass their new moneys in the other parts of New England, it being a high penalty to be found so doing. This fraud must light heavy upon posterity. This is the only part ever I knew where gold and silver coin is not commonly current.

Friday, August 17. I left Boston this morning att half an hour after nine o'clock, and nothing I regretted so much as parting with La Moinnerie, the most livily and merry companion ever I had met with, always gay and chearfull, now dancing and then singing tho every day in danger of being made a prisoner. This is the peculiar humour of the French in prosperity and adversity. Their temper is always alike, far different from the English who, upon the least misfortune, are for the most part cloggd and overclouded with melancholly and vapours and, giving way to hard fortune, shun all gaiety and mirth. La Moinnerie was much concerned att my going away and wished me again and again *une bon voyage* and *bon santé*, keeping fast hold of my stirrup for about a quarter of an hour.

Dedham

I had a solitary ride to Dedham where I breakfasted att Fisher's[326] and had some comicall chat with Betty, the landlady's daughter, a jolly, buxom girl. The country people here are full of salutations. Even the country girls that are scarce old enough to walk will curtsy to one passing by. A great lubberly boy with short cut hair, having no cap, put his hand to his forehead as I past him in fashion as if he had been pulling off his cap.

Wrentham

I dined att Man's in the town of Wrentham and was served by a fat Irish girl, very pert and forward but not very engaging. I proceeded this night to Slake's where I lay. There was here a large company, and among the rest a doctor, a tall, thin man, about whom nothing appeared remarkable but his dress. He had a weather beaten black wig, an old stripd collimancoe banian, and an antique brass spur upon his right ankle, and a pair of thick soald shoes tied with points. They told me he was the learnedest physician of these parts. I went up stairs att 9 o'clock and heard my landlady att prayers for an hour after I went to bed. The partition was thin, and I could distinctly hear what she said. She abounded with tautologys and groaned very much in the spirit, praying again and again for the *fullness of grace* and the blessing of regeneration and the new birth.

Providence

Saturday, August 18. I set out from Slake's betwixt seven and eight in the morning, the weather being cloudy and close. I went by the way of Providence, which is a small but long town situated close upon the water upon rocky ground, much like Marblehead but not a sixth part so large. It is the seat of goverment in Providence Colony, there being an assembly of the delegates sometimes held here.

Nantucket Fall

About 4 miles N.E. of this town there runs a small river which falls down a rock about 3 fathom high, over which fall there is a wooden bridge.[327] The noise of the fall so scared my horses that I was obliged to light and lead them over the bridge. At this place there are iron works. I breakfasted in Providence att one Angel's[328] at the Sign of the White Horse, a queer pragmaticall old fellow, pretending to great correctness of stile in his common discourse. I found this fellow att the door and asked him if the house was not kept by one Angel. He answered in a surly manner, "no." "Pardon me," says I, "they recommended me to such a house." So as I turned away; being loath to lose his customer, he called me back. "Hark ye, friend," says he in the same blunt manner, "Angell don't keep the house, but the house keeps Angell." I hesitated for some time if I should give this surly chap my custome but resolved att last to reap some entertainment from the oddity of the fellow. While I waited for the chocolate which I had ordered for breakfast, Angell gave me an account of his religion and opinions, which I found were as much out of the common road as the man himself. I observed a paper pasted upon the wall which was a rabble of dull controversy betwixt two learned divines, of as great consequence to the publick as The Story of the King and the Cobler or The Celebrated History of the Wise Men of Gotham. This controversy was intituled *Cannons to batter the Tower of Babel.* Among the rest of the chamber furniture were severall elegant pictures, finely illuminated and coulered, being the famous piece of The Battle for the Breeches, The 12 Golden Rules taken from King Charles I's study, of blessed memory (as he is very judiciously stiled), The Christian Coat of Arms, etc., etc., etc., in which pieces are set forth divine attitudes and elegant passions, all sold by Overton,[329] that inimitable ale house designer att the White Horse without Newgate. I left this town att 10 o'clock and was taken by some children in the street for a trooper upon account of my pistols.

Providence Ferry—Ferry Bristo'—Ferry Rhode Island
I crossed Providence Ferry[330] betwixt 10 and eleven o'clock,
and after some difficulty in finding my way, I crossed another
ferry[331] about 4 miles eastward of Bristo'. I arrived in Bristo'
att one o'clock and a little after crossed the ferry to Rhode
Island and dined att Burden's. I departed thence att 4 o'clock
but was obliged to stop twice before I got to Newport upon
the account of rain. I went into a house for shelter where were
severall young girls, the daughters of the good woman of the
house. They were as simple and awkward as sheep, and so wild
that they would not appear in open view but kept peeping att
me from behind doors, chests, and benches. The country people
in this island, in generall, are very unpolished and rude.

Newport
I entered Newport betwixt seven and eight att night, a thick
fog having risen so that I could scarce find the town when
within a quarter of a mile of it. My man, upon account of the
portmanteau, was in the dark taken for a pedlar by some people
in the street who I heard coming about him and enquiring what
he had got to sell. I put up att Niccoll's att the Sign of the White
Horse and, lying there that night, was almost eat up alive with
buggs.

Sunday, August 19. I called upon Dr. Moffat in the
morning and went with him to a windmill near the town to
look out for vessels but could spy none. The mill was a going,
and the miller in it grinding of corn, which is an instance of
their not being so observant of Sunday here as in the other parts
of New England.

I dined att Dr. Moffat's lodging and in the afternoon went
to a Baptist meeting to hear sermon. A middle aged man
preached and gave us a pritty good tho trite discourse upon

morality. I took lodging att one Mrs. Leech's, a Quaker, who keeps an apothecary's shop, a sensible, discreet, and industrious old woman. Dr. Moffat took me out this evening to walk near the town where are a great many pleasant walks amidst avenues of trees. We viewed Mr. Malbone's house and gardens, and as we returned home met Malbone himself with whom we had some talk about news. We were met by a handsom bona roba in a flaunting dress, who laughed us full in the face. Malbone and I supposed she was a paramour of Moffat's, for none of us knew her. We bantered him upon it and discovered the truth of our conjecture by raising a blush in his face.

Monday, August 20. I made a tour round the town this morning with Dr. Moffat. I dined with him and, in the afternoon, went to the coffee house, and after drinking a dish of coffee we went with Mr. Grant,[332] a Scotch gentleman in town, and took a walk across one end of the island where we had severall delightful views to the water. There is one cliff here, just bluff upon the ocean, called Hog's hole, out of which filtres some springs of very fine fresh water. It affords a cool pleasant shade in the summer time, for which reason the ladys go there to drink tea in a summer's afternoon. We encountered some fair dames there and had abundance of gallantry and romping.

Att 7 o'clock I went with one Mr. Scot[333] to a club which sits once a week upon Mondays called the Philosophical Club;[334] but I was surprized to find that no matters of philosophy were brought upon the carpet. They talked of privateering and building of vessels; then we had the history of some old familys in Scotland where, by the bye, Grant told us a comic piece of history relating to Generall Wade and Lord Loveat.[335] The latter had some how or other incurred Wade's displeasure who, therefor, made it his business to gett him turned out of a collonell's commission which he then possessed. What he accused him of was his keeping a raggamuffin company of cowherds and other such trash to make the number of his regiment compleat while he put the pay in his own pocket. Wade upon a time comes to review this regiment. Loveat, being advertised before hand of this review, laid his scheme so that he procured a parcell of likely fellows to come upon the field who made a tollerable appearance. When the Generall had review'd them, my Lord asked him what he thought of his men. "Very good cowherds, in faith, my Lord," replied the Generall. Loveat asked what his Excellency meant by that reply. The Generall answered that he was ordered to signify his Majesty's pleasure to him that he should serve no longer as collonell of that regiment. "Look ye, sir," says Loveat, "his Majesty may do in that affair as he pleases; it is his gift, and he may take it again, but one thing he cannot without just reason take from me which makes a wide difference betwixt you and I." Wade desired him to explain himself. "Why, thus it is," says Loveat, "When the King takes away my commission I am still Lord Loveat; when he takes yours away, pray observe, sir, that your name is George Wade." This unconcerned behaviour nettled Wade very much and blunted the edge of his revenge. After this history was given, the company fell upon the disputes and controversys of the fanaticks of these parts, their declarations, recantations, letters, advices, remonstrances, and other such damnd stuff of so little consequence to the benifit of mankind or the publick that I look upon all time spent in either talking concerning them or reading their works as eternally lost and thrown away, and therefor disgusted with such a stupid subject of discourse, I left this club and went home.

Tuesday, August 21. I stayed att home most of the forenoon and read Murcius,[336] which I had of Dr. Moffat, a most lucious piece from whom all our moderen sallacious poets have borrowd their thoughts. I did not read this book upon account of its liquorice contents, but only because I knew it to be a piece of excellent good Latin, and I wanted to inform my self of the propper idiom of the language upon that subject.

I walked out betwixt 12 and one with Dr. Moffat an[d] viewed Malbone's house and gardens. We went to the lanthern, or cupola att top, from which we had a pritty view of the town of Newport and of the sea towards Block Island, and behind the house, of a pleasant mount gradually ascending to a great height from which we can have a view of almost the whole island. Returning from thence we went to the coffee house where, after drinking some punch, the doctor and I went to dine with Mr. Grant. After dinner I rid out of town in a chaise with Dr. Keith, one Captain Williams accompanying us on horseback.

Whitehall

We called att a publick house which goes by the name of White-hall, kept by one Anthony, about three miles out of town, once the dwelling house of the famous Dean Barclay[337] when in this island and built by him. As we went along the road we had a number of agreeable prospects. Att Anthony's[338] we drank punch and tea and had the company of a handsom girl, his daughter, to whom Captain Williams expressed a deal of gallantry. She was the most unaffected and best behaved country girl ever I met with. Her modesty had nothing of the prude in it nor had her frolicksome freeness any dash of impudence.

We returned to town att seven a clock and spent the rest of the night att the coffee-house where our ears were not only frequently regaled with the sound of "very welcome, sir," and "very welcome, gentlemen," pronounced solemnly, slowly, and with an audible voice to such as came in and went out by Hassey,[339] a queer old dog, the keeper of the coffee-house, but we were likewise allarmed (not charmed) for half an hour by a man who sung with such a trumpet note that I was afraid he would shake down the walls of the house about us. I went home betwixt 9 and 10 o'clock.

Wednesday, August 22. I stayed att home all this morning, and betwixt twelve and one, going to the coffee house, I met Dr. Keith and Captain Williams. We tossed the news about for some time. Hassey, who keeps this coffee house, is a comicall old whimsical fellow. He imagines that he can discover the longitude and affirms that it is no way to be done but by an instrument made of whalebone and cartilage or gristle. He carried his notion so far as to send proposals to the Provinciall Assembly about it, who having called him before them, he was asked if he was a proficient in the mathematicks. "Why, lookee, gentlemen," says he, "suppose a great stone lyes in the street, and you want to move it; unless there be some moving cause, how the devil shall it move?" The Assembly finding him talk thus in parables dismissed him as a crazy gentleman whom too little learning had made mad. He gives this as his opinion of Sir Isaac Newton and Lord Verulam,[340] that they were both very great men, but still they both had certain foibles by which they made it known that they were mortall men, whereas had he been blissed with such a genius, he would have made the world believe that he was immortal, as both Enos and Elias had done long agoe. He talks much of cutting the American isthmus in two so to make a short passage to the south seas, and if the powers of Europe cannot agree about it he says he knows how to make a machine with little expence by the help of which ships may be dragged over that narrow neck of land with all the ease imaginable, it being but a triffle of 100 miles, and so we may go to the East Indies a much easier and shorter way than doubling the Cape of Good Hope. He has a familiar phraze which is, "very welcome, sir," and "very welcome, gentlemen," which he pronounces with a solemn sound as often as people come in or go out.

I dined with Captain Williams and att 6 o'clock went again to the coffee house. Att seven we called upon some ladies in town and made an appointment for a promenade. In the mean time Dr. Keith and I went to the prison and there had some conversation with a French gentleman, a prisoner, and with one Judge Pemberton,[341] a man of good learning and sense. While we were there one Captain Bull[342] called in, who seemed to be a droll old man. He entertained us for half an hour with comicall stories and dry jokes. Att eight o'clock we waited on the ladies and with them walked a little way out of town to a place called the Little Rock. Our promenade continued two hours, and they entertained us with severall songs. We enjoyed all the pleasures of gallantry without transgressing the rules of modesty or good manners. There were 6 in company att this promenade; vizt., 3 dames and 3 gallants. The belle who fell to my lot pleased me exceedingly both in looks and conversation. Her name was Miss Clerk, daughter to a merchant in town. After a parting salute according to the mode of the place, I, with reluctance, bid the ladies farewell, expressing some regrett that, being a stranger in their town and obliged soon to leave it, I should perhaps never have the happy opportunity of their agreeable company again. They returned their good wishes for my compliment; so I went to my lodging and after some learned chat with my landlady concerning the apothecary's craft, I went to bed.

Thursday, August 23. It rained hard all this morning, and therefor I stayed att home till 12 o'clock. Dr. Moffat came to breakfast with me, and he and I went to the coffee-house betwixt twelve and one. We saw there some Spainiards that had been taken in the snow prize. One of them was a very handsom man and well behaved, none of that stiffness and solemnity about him commonly ascribed to their nation but perfectly free and easy in his behaviour, rather bordering upon the French vivacity. His name was Don Manuel (I don't know what). He spoke good French and Latin and run out very much in praise of the place, the civility and humanity of the people, and the charms of the ladies.

I dined att Mr. Grant's and went with Dr. Moffat in the afternoon to visit Dr. Brett, where we had a deal of learned discourse about microscopicall experiments, and the order, elegance, and uniformity of Nature in the texture of all bodies, both animate and inanimate. I spent the evening att Dr. Moffat's lodging along with Mr. Wanthon, the collector,[343] and Mr. Grant, a young gentleman of the place, and Dr. Brett, and returned to my lodging att 10 o'clock.

I found the people in Newport very civil and courteous in their way. I had severall invitations to houses in town, all of which, because of my short stay, I could not accept of. They carry on a good trade in this place in time of peace and build a great many vessels. The island is famous for making of good cheeses, but I think those made in the Jerseys as good if not preferable. In time of war this place is noted for privateering, which business they carry on with great vigour and alacrity. The island has fitted out now 13 or 14 privateers and is dayly equipping more. While I stayed in this place they sent in severall valuable prizes. But notwithstanding this warlike apparatus abroad, they are but very sorrily fortified att home. The rocks in their harbour are the best security, for the fort[344] which stands upon an island about a mile from the town is the futiest thing of that nature ever I saw. It is a building of near 200 foot square of stone and brick, the wall being about 15 foot high with a bastion and watch tower on each corner, but so exposed to cannon shot that it could be battered about their ears in ten minutes. A little distance from this fort is a battery of 17 or 18 great guns.

They are not so strait laced in religion here as in the other parts of New England.[345] They have among them a great number of Quakers. The island is the most delightfull spot of ground I have seen in America. I can compare it to nothing but one intire garden. For rural scenes and pritty, frank girls, I found it the most agreeable place I had been in thro' all my peregrinations. I am sorry to say that the people in their dealings one with another, and even with strangers, in matters of truck or bargain have as bad a character for chicane and disingenuity as any of our American colonys. Their goverment is somewhat democratick, the people choosing their governour from among their own number every year by pole votes. One Mr. Green[346] is now governour; the House of Assembly chooses the Council. They have but little regard to the laws of England, their mother country, tho they pretend to take that constitution for a precedent. Collectors and naval officers here are a kind of cyphers. They dare not exercise their office for fear of the fury and unruliness of the people, but their places are profitable upon account of the presents they receive for every cargoe of run goods. This colony separated it self from New England and was formed into a different goverment thro' some religious quarrells that happened betwixt them.

It is customary here to adorn their chimney pannells with birds' wings, peacock feathers and butterflys.

Friday, August 24. Going to breakfast this morning I found a stranger with Mrs. Leech, who in sixteen days had come from

Maryland and had been there about some business relating to iron works. When I came into the room he asked Mrs. Leech if this was the gentleman that came from Maryland. She replyed yes; then turning to me he acquainted me that he had lately been there and had seen severall people whom he supposed I knew, but he was fain to leave the place in a hurry, the agues and fevers beginning to be very frequent. He gave me an account of his having seen some of my acquaintances well att Joppa. I was glad to hear good news from home, it being now above three months since I had had any intelligence from there.

I called att Dr. Moffat's after breakfast, who entertained me for half an hour with his sun microscope which is a very curious apparatus and not only magnifys the object incredibly upon the moveable screen but affords a beautifull variety and surprizing intermixture of colours. He showed me a small spider, the down of a moth's wing, the down of feathers, and a fly's eye, in all which objects, Nature's uniformity and beautifull design, in the most minute parts of her work, appeared. The doctor walked to the ferry landing with me, and there we took leave of one another.

Connanicut Ferry—Naragantzet Ferry—Kingstown

I had a tedious passage to Connanicut.[347] It being quite calm we were obliged to row most of the way. Our passage was more expeditious over Naragantzet Ferry, and there I had the company of a Rhode Islander all the way to Kingstown, where I dined att Case's in the company of some majors and captains, it being a training day.

Betwixt Case's and Hill's I was overtaken by a gentleman of considable fortune here. He has a large house close upon the road and is possessor of a very large farm where he milks dayly 104 cows and has, besides, a vast stock of other cattle.[348] He invited me into his house, but I thanked him and proceeded, the sun being low. I put up att Hill's about sunset and enquired there att the landlord concerning this gentleman. Hill informed me that he was a man of great estate, but of base character, for being constituted one of the comittee for signing the publick bills of credit, he had counterfieted 50,000 pound of false bills and made his bretheren of the comittee sign them, and then counterfeited their names to 50,000 pound of genuine bills which the Goverment had then issued. This piece of villany being detected, the whole 100,000 pound was called in by the Goverment and he fined in 30,000 pound to save his ears.[349] But I think the fate of such a wealthy villain should have been the gallows, and his whole estate should have gone to repair the publick dammage.

As one rides along the road in this part of the country there are whole hedges of barberries.

Saturday, August 25th. I set off att seven o'clock from Hill's, and it being a thick mist, I had a dull, solitary ride to Thomson's where I breakfasted, being overtaken by a Seventh Day man going to meeting. Thankfull, a jolly, buxom girl, the landlady's daughter, made me some chocolate for which I did not thank her, it being sorry stuff. I departed from thence a little after 10 in the company of some Seventh Day men going to meeting.

Connecticut Goverment—Stonnington

In this goverment of Rhode Island and Providence you may travell without molestation upon Sunday, which you cannot do in Connecticut or the Massachusets province without a pass, because here they are not agreed what day of the week the sabbath is to be kept, some observing it upon Saturday and others upon Sunday.

I dined att Williams's att Stonington with a Boston merchant named Gardiner and one Boyd, a Scotch Irish pedlar. The pedlar seemed to understand his business to a hair. He sold some dear bargains to Mrs. Williams, and while he smoothed her up with palaber, the Bostoner amused her with religious cant. This pedlar told me he had been some time agoe att Annapolis att some horse races and enquired after some people there. He gave me a description of B——ie M——t, whose lodger he had been, and gave me a piece of secret history concerning P[au]l R[ui]z,[350] the Portuguese, and N——y H——y, how they passed for man and wife when they were in Philadelphia and the neighbourhood of that city. Our conversation att dinner was a medley; Gardiner affected much learning and the pedlar talked of trade.

N: London Ferry—N: London

I left Williams's about half an hour after 3, and crossing the ferry a little after 5 o'clock, I arrived att New London and put up att Duchand's att the Sign of the Anchor. I did not know till now that I had any relations in this town; a parcell of children, as I rid up the lane, saluted me with "How d'ye, unkle? Welcome to town, uncle."

Sunday, August 26. I stayed att home most of the forenoon and was invited to dine with Collector Lechmere,[351] son to the surveyor att Boston. There was att table there one Dr. Goddard[352] and an old maid whom they called Miss Katy, being a great fat woman with a red face, as much like an old maid as a frying pan. There sat by her a young, modest looking lady dressed in black whom Mr. Lechmere called Miss Nansy, and next her, a walnut coloured, thin woman, sluttishly dressed and very hard favoured. These ladys went to meeting after dinner, and we three sat drinking of punch and telling of droll storys.

I went home att 6 o'clock, and Deacon Green's[353] son came to see me. He entertained me with the history of the behaviour of one Davenport,[354] a fanatick preacher there who told his flock in one of his enthusiastic rhapsodies that in order to be saved they ought to burn all their idols. They began this conflagration with a pile of books in the public street, among which were Tillotson's Sermons, Beveridge's Thoughts, Drillincourt on Death, Sherlock and many other excellent authors, and sung psalms and hymns over the pile while it was a burning. They did not stop here, but the women made up a lofty pile of hoop petticoats, silk gowns, short cloaks, cambrick caps, red heeld shoes, fans, necklaces, gloves and other such aparrell, and what was merry enough, Davenport's own idol with which he topped the pile, was a pair of old, wore out, plush breaches. But this bone fire was happily prevented by one more moderate than the rest, who found means to perswade them that making such a sacrifice was not necessary for their salvation, and so every one carried of[f] their idols again, which was lucky for Davenport who, had fire been put to the pile, would have been obliged to strutt about bare-arsed, for the devil another pair of breeches had he but these same old plush ones which were going to be offered up as an expiatory sacrifise. Mr. Green took his leave of me att 10 o'clock, and I went to bed.

Monday, August 27. After visiting Deacon Green this morning and drinking tea with him and wife, he gave me a paquet for his son Jonas att Annapolis. The old man was very inquisitive about the state of religion with us, what kind of ministers we had, and if the people were much addicted to godliness. I told him that the ministers minded hogsheads of tobacco more than points of doctrine, either orthodox or hetrodox, and that the people were very prone to a certain religion called *self interest*.

Hantick Ferry

I left New London betwixt eight and 9 o'clock in the morning and crossed Hantick [Niantic] Ferry, or the Gutt, a little before ten. This is an odd kind of a ferry, the passage across it not being above 50 paces wide, and yet the inlett of water here from the Sound is near three quarters of a mile broad. This is occasioned by a long narrow point or promontory of hard sand and rock, att its broadest part not above 12 paces over, which runs out from the westeren towards the eastren shore of this inlett and is above half a mile long, so leaves but a small gutt where the tide runs very rapid and fierce. The skeow that crosses here goes by a rope which is fixed to a stake att each side of the Gutt, and this skeow is fastened to the main rope by an iron ring which slides upon it, else the rapidity of the tide would carry skeow and passengers and all away.

Nantique, an Indian Town

A little after I passed this ferry I rid close by an Indian town upon the left hand situated upon the brow of a hill. This town is called Nantique and consists of 13 or 14 hutts or wig-wams made of bark.

Toll-Bridge—Connecticut River

I passed over a bridge in very bad repair for which I payed eight pence toll, which here is something more than a penny farthing sterling, and coming down to Seabrook Ferry upon Connecticut River, I waited there 3 or 4 hours att the house of one Mather before I could get passage. The wind blew so hard att north-west with an ebb tide which, the ferrymen told me, would have carried us out into the Sound had we attempted to pass.

Mather and I had some talk about the opinions lately broached here in religion. He seemed a man of some solidity and sense and condemnd Whitefield's conduct in these parts very much. After dinner there came in a rabble of clowns who fell to disputing upon points of divinity as learnedly as if they had been professed theologues. 'Tis strange to see how this humour prevails, even among the lower class of the people here. They will talk so pointedly about justification, santification, adoption, regeneration, repentance, free grace, reprobation, original sin, and a thousand other such pritty, chimerical knick knacks as if they had done nothing but studied divinity all their life time and perused all the lumber of the scholastic divines, and yet the fellows look as much, or rather more, like clowns than the very riff-raff of our Maryland planters. To talk in this dialect in our parts would be like Greek, Hebrew, or Arabick.

I met with an old paralytic man in this house named Henderson who let me know that he had travelled the world in his youthfull days and had been in Scotland and lived some years in Edinburgh. He condemned much the conduct of the late enthusiasts here, by which he put some of our clowns in company in a frett, but the old man regarded them not, going on with his discourse, smoking his pipe, and shaking his grey locks. I was very much taken with his conversation, and he, seemingly, with mine, for he gave me many a hearty shake by the hand att parting and wished me much prosperity, health, and a safe return home.

Seabrook Ferry—Seabrook

I crossed the ferry att 5 o'clock. This river of Connecticut is navigable for 50 miles up the country. Upon it are a good many large trading towns, but the branches of the river run up above 200 miles. We could see the town of Seabrook [Saybrook] below us on the westeren side of the river. I lodged this night att one Mrs. Lay's, a widow woman, who keeps a good house upon the road about 6 miles from Seabrook. I had much difficulty to find the roads upon this side Connecticut River. They wind and turn so much and are divided into such a number of small paths.

I find they are not quite so scrupulous about bestowing titles here as in Maryland. My landlady goes here by the name of Madam Lay. I cannot tell for what, for she is the homliest piece both as to mein, make, and dress that ever I saw, being a little round shouldered woman, pale faced and wrinkly, clothed in the coarsest home spun cloth; but it is needless to dispute her right to the title since we know many upon whom it is bestowed who have as little right as she.

Tuesday, August 28. I departed Lay's att seven in the morning and rid some miles thro' a rockey high land, the wind blowing pritty sharp and cool att northwest.

Killingworth

A little after eight o'clock I passed thro' Killingsworth, a small town pleasantly situated. I breakfasted att one Scran's about half way betwixt Killingsworth and Gilfoord. This is a jolly old man, very fat and pursy, and very talkative and full of history. He had been an American soldier in Q. Anne's War and had travelled thro' most of the continent of North America. He enquired of me if poor Dick of Noye was alive, which question I had frequently put to me in my travells.

Gilfoord

Going from this house I passed thro' Gilfoord[355] att eleven o'clock in company of an old man whom I overtook upon the road. He showed me a curious stone bridge within a quarter of a mile of this town. It lay over a small brook and was one intire stone about 10 foot long, six broad, and 8 or 10 inches thick, being naturally bent in the form of an arch without the help of a chisell to cut it into that shape. "Observe here, sir," says the old man, "you may ride 1000 miles and not meet with such a stone." Gilford is a pritty town built upon a pleasant plain. In it there is a meeting, upon the steeple of which is a publick clock.

Branfoord

I came to Branfoord, another scattered town built upon high rocky ground, a little after one o'clock, where I dined att the house of one Frazer. Going from thence I passed thro' a pleasant, delightfull part of the country, being a medley of fine green plains, and little rockey and woody hills, caped over, as it were, with bushes.

Newhaven Ferry—Newhaven

I crossed Newhaven Ferry betwixt 4 and 5 o'clock in the afternoon. This is a pleasant navigable river than runs thro a spacious green plain into the Sound. I arrived in Newhaven att 5 o'clock, where I put up att one Monson's[356] att the Sign of the Half Moon. There is but little good liquor to be had in the publick houses upon this road. A man's horses are better provided for than himself, but he pays dear for it. The publick house keepers seem to be somewhat wild and shy when a stranger calls. It is with difficulty you can get them to speak to you, show you a room, or ask you what you would have, but they will gape and stare when you speak as if they were quite astonished.

Newhaven is a pritty large, scattered town laid out in squares, much in the same manner as Philadelphia, but the houses are sparse and thin sowed.[357] It stands on a large plain, and upon all sides (excepting the south which faces the Sound) it is inclosed with ranges of little hills as old Jerusalem was according to the topographicall descriptions of that city. The burying place is in the center of the town just faceing the college [Yale], which is a wooden building about 200 foot long and three stories high, in the middle front of which is a little cupula with a clock upon it. It is not so good a building as that att Cambridge, nor are there such a number of students. It was the gift of a private gentleman to this place.

Millford

Wednesday, August 29th. I set out from Monson's a little after 7 o'clock and rid a tollerable good road to Millford. Before I came there I was overtaken by a young man who asked me severall questions according to country custom, such as where I was going and whence I came, and the like, to all which I gave answers just as impertinent as the questions were themselves. I breakfasted in Millford att one Gibbs's, and while I was there the post arrived so that there came great crowds of the politicians of the town to read the news, and we had plenty of orthographi- call blunders. We heard of some prizes taken by the Phila- delphia privateers. Millford is a large scattered town situated upon a large pleasant plain.

Stratfoord Ferry—Stratfoord

I went from here in company of a young man and crossed Stratford Ferry[358] att eleven o'clock and was obliged to call att Stratfoord, my grey horse having lost a shoe. I stayed there sometime att one Benjamin's who keeps a taveren in the town. There I met a deal of company and had many questions asked me. Stratfoord is a pleasant little town prittily situated upon a rising ground within half a mile of a navigable river that runs into the Sound. In this town is one Presbyterian meeting and one church, both new buildings. The church[359] is built with some taste and elegance, having large arched sash windows and a handom spire or steeple att the west end of it.

Fairfield

My young man rid with me till I came within 5 miles of Fairfield, which is another town in which is an octogonall church[360] or meeting built of wood like that of Jamaica upon Long Island, upon the cupolo of which is a publick clock. The roads between this town and Norwalk are exceeding rough and stonny, and the stones are very full of a glittering isinglass. There is a river on the west side of this town which runs into the Sound. I forded it att high water when pritty deep.

Sagatick River

Within three miles and a half of Norwalk is another river called by the Indian name of Sagatick.[361] This I forded att low tide. I dined att one Taylor's here. My landlord was an old man of 70. He understanding from my boy that I was a doctor from Maryland and having heard that some of the doctors there were wonder workers in practice, he asked my advice about a cancer which he had in his lip. I told him there was one Bouchelle in Maryland who pretended to cure every disease by the help of a certain water which he made, but as for my part, I knew of no way of curing a cancer but by extirpation or cutting it out.

Norwalk

I arrived att Norwalk att seven o clock att night. This town is situated in a bottom midst a grove of trees. You see the steeple shoot up among the trees about half a mile before you enter the town and before you can see any of the houses. While I was att Taylor's the children were frightened att my negroe, for here negroe slaves are not so much in use as with us, their servants being chiefly bound or indentured Indians. The child asked if that negroe was a coming to eat them up. Dromo indeed wore a voracious phiz, for having rid 20 miles without eating, he grinned like a crocodile and showed his teeth most hideously.

Betwixt Taylor's and Norwalk I met a caravan of 18 or 20 Indians. I put up att Norwalk att one Beelding's,[362] and as my boy was taking off the saddles, I could see one half of the town standing about him making enquiry about his master.

I was disturbed this night by a parcell of roaring fellows that came rumbling up stairs to go to bed in the next room. They beat the walls with their elbows as if they had had a mind to batter down the house, being inspired, I suppose, by the great god Bacchus. A certain horse jockey in the company had a voice as strong as a trumpet, and Stentor like, he made the house ring. "Damme," says he, "if you or any man shall have the jade for 100 poeaunds. The jade is as good a jade as ever wore curb." (It is customary here to call both horses and mares by the name of jades.) I wished he and his jade both once and again at the devil for disturbing my rest, for just as I was a dropping asleep again he uttered some impertinence with his Stentorian voice which made me start and waked me. My rest was broken all that night, and waking suddenly from a confused dream about my horse dropping dead under me in the road, I imagined I heard somebody breath very high in the bed by me. I thought perhaps that my friend Stentor had thought fit to come there and felt about with my arms but could discover nothing but the bed cloths tho the sound continued very distinct in my ears for about a minute after I was broad awake, and then it dyed away by degrees. This, with some people, would have procured the house a bad name of its being haunted with spirits.

Stanford

Thursday, August 30. I left Norwalk att 7 in the morning and rid 10 miles of stonny road, crossing severall brooks and rivulets that run into the Sound, till I came to Stanford [Stamford]. A little before I reached this town, from the top of a stonny hill, I had a large open view or prospect of the country westward. The greatest part of it seemed as it were covered with a white crust of stone, for the country here is exceeding rockey, and the roads very rough, rather worse than Stonnington. I breakfasted att Stanford att one Ebenezar Weak's. In this town I saw a new church, which is now a building, the steeple of which was no sooner finished than it was all tore to pieces by lightning in a terrible thunder storm that happened here upon the first day of August in the afternoon. I observed the rafters of the steeple split from top to bottom, and the wooden pins or trunells that fastened the joints half drawn out.

While I was att breakfast att Weak's, there came in a crazy old man who complained much of the hardness of the times and of pains in his back and belly. "Lack a day for poor old Joseph!" said the landlady. A little after him came in one Captain Lyon, living att Rye Bridge. He wore an affected air of wisdom in his phiz and pretended to be a very knowing man in the affairs of the world. He said he had travelled the whole world over in his fancy and would fain have perswaded us that he understood the history of mankind completly. Most of his knowledge was pedantry, being made up of common place sentences and trite proverbs. I asked him if I should have his company down the road. He replied that he would be glad to wait on me, but had an appointment to eat some roast pigg with a neighbour of his which would detain him till the afternoon. So I departed the town without him.

I rode a stonny and hilly road to Horseneck and overtook

an old man who rid a sorrell mare with a colt following her. He told me he was obliged to ride slow for fear of losing the colt, for sometimes the creature strayed behind, meeting with jades upon the way. He said he had been traveling the country for 3 weeks visiting his children and grandchildren who were settled for 50 miles round him. He told me he had had 21 sons and daughters of which 19 were now alive, and 15 of them married and had children; and yet he did not marry himself till 27 years of age and was now only 72 years old. This old man called in att a house about 2 miles from Horseneck where he said there lived a friend of his. An old fellow with a mealy hat came to the door and received him with a "How d'ye, old friend Jervis?" So I parted with my company.

Horseneck

I passed thro Horseneck, a scattered town, att half an hour after eleven a clock and passed over Rye Bridge[363] att 12, the boundary of Connecticut and York goverment, after having rid 155 miles in Connecticut goverment.

"Farewell, Connecticut," said I, as I passed along the bridge. "I have had a surfeit of your ragged money, rough roads, and enthusiastick people." The countrys of Connecticut and New England are very large and well peopled, and back in the country here upon the navigable rivers as well as in the maritim parts are a great many fine large towns. The people here are chiefly husbandmen and farmers. The staples are the same as in the Massachusets province. They transport a good many horses to the West Indies, and there is one town in this province that is famous for plantations of onions, of which they send quantitys all over the continent and to the islands, loading sloops with them. Many of these onions I have seen nearly as large as a child's head.

It is reported that in Connecticut alone they can raise 50 or 60,000 men able to bear arms. One Mr. Law[364] is present governour of the province. It is but a deputy goverment under that of New England or the Massachusets.[365]

York Goverment

Coming into York goverment I found better roads but not such a complaisant people for saluting upon the road, tho' in their houses they are neither so wild nor so awkward. It is to no purpose here to ask how many miles it is to such a place. They are not att all determined in the measure of their miles. Some will tell you that you are two miles from your stage. Ride half a mile farther, they'll tell you it is 4; a mile farther, you'll be told it is 6 miles, and three miles farther they'll say it is seven, and so on.

Newrochell

I had a long ride before I arrived att Newrochell where I dined att the house of one Le Compte, a Frenchman, who has a daughter that is a sprightly, sensible girl.

Kingsbridge

Coming from thence att 4 o'clock I put up this night att Doughty's who keeps house att Kingsbridge,[366] a fat man much troubled with the rheumatism and of a hasty, passionate temper. I supped upon roasted oysters, while my landlord eat roasted ears of corn att another table. He kept the whole house in a stirr to serve him and yet could not be pleased.

This night proved very stormy and threatened rain. I was disturbed again in my rest by the noise of a heavy tread of a foot in the room above. That wherein I lay was so large and lofty that any noise echoed as if it had been in a church.

Friday, August 31. I breakfasted att Doughty's. My landlord put himself in a passion because his daughter was tardy
in getting up to make my chocolate. He spoke so thick in his
anger and in so sharp a key that I did not comprehend what
he said.

I saw about 10 Indians fishing for oysters in the gutt before
the door. The wretches waded about stark naked and threw the
oysters, as they picked them up with their hands, into baskets
that hung upon their left shoulder. They are a lazy, indolent
generation and would rather starve than work att any time,
but being unaquainted with our luxury, nature in them has
few demands, which are easily satisfied.

York Island

I passed over Kingsbridge at 9 o'clock and had a pleasant ride
to York. This small island is called York Island from the City
of York which stands upon the south west end of it. It is a
pleasant spot of ground covered with severall small groves
of trees.

Turtle Bay

About three miles before I reached York I saw the man of
war commanded by Commodore Warren lying in Turtle Bay.[367]
This was a festival day with the crew. They were a roasting
an entire ox upon a wooden spit and getting drunk as fast as
they could, Warren having given them a treat. I was overtaken
here by a young gentleman who gave me a whole paquet of news
about prizes and privateering, which is now the whole subject
of discourse. I met one Dutchman on the road who addressed
me, "May I be so bold, where do you come from, sir?"

New York

I arrived in New York about eleven o clock and put up my horses at Waghorn's. After calling att Mrs. Hog's I went to see my old friend Todd, expecting there to dine but accidentally I encountered Stephen Bayard who carried me to dine att his brother's. There was there a great company of gentlemen, among the rest Mr. D[elan]cie,[368] the Chief Justice; Mr. H[orsemande]n, the City Recorder; and one Mr. More, a lawer. There was one gentleman there whom they stiled captain who squinted the most abominably of any body ever I saw. His eyes were not matched, for one was of a lighter colour than the other. Another gentleman there wore so much of a haughty frown in his countenance, that even when he smiled it did not dissappear. There were 13 gentlemen att table but not so much as one lady. We had an elegant, sumptuous dinner with a fine desert of sweetmeats and fruits, among which last there were some of the best white grapes I have seen in America.

The table chat run upon privateering and such discourse as has now become so common that it is tiresome and flat. One there, who set up for a dictator, talked very much to the discredit of Old England, preferring New York to it in every respect whatsoever relating to good living. Most of his propositions were gratis dicta, and it seemed as if he either would not, or did not, know much of that fine country England. He said that the grapes there were good for nothing but to set a man's teeth on edge; but to my knowledge I have seen grapes in gentlemen's gardens there far preferable to any ever I saw in these northeren parts of America. He asserted also that no good apple could be brought up there without a glass and artificiall heat, which assertion was palpably false and glaringly ignorant, for almost every fool knows that apples grow best in northeren climates betwixt the latitudes of 35 and 50, and that in the southern hot climes, within the tropics, they don't grow att all, and therefor the best apples in the world grow in England and in the north of France. He went even so far as to say that the beef in New York was preferable to that of England. When he came there I gave him up as a triffler, and giving no more attention to his discourse, he lost himself, the Lord knows how or where, in a thicket of erroneous and ignorant dogmas which any the most exaggerating traveler would have been ashamed of. But he was a great person in the place, and therefor none in the company was imprudent enough to contradict him tho some were there that knew better. I have known in my time some of these great dons take upon them to talk in an extravagant and absurd manner: "What a fine temperate climate this is!" says a certain dictating fop, while every body that hears him is conscious that it is fit for none but the devil to live in. "Don't you think them fine oysters," says another exalted prigg, while every body knows he is eating of eggs. This we cannot conceive proceeds from ignorance but from a certain odd pleasure they have in talking nonsense without being contradicted. This disposition may arise from the naturall perverseness of human nature, which is always most absurd and unreasonable when free from curb or restraint. This company after dinner set in for bumpers so I left them att three o'clock.

I heard this day that Mr. H[ase]ll was in town, and that Ting, master of the Boston galley, had taken Morpang, the French cruizer, after a desperate battle and the loss of many men; but to this I gave little credit. By letters from Lisbon we had an account of Admiral Mathews[369] having taken 80 French trading ships up the straits.

Saturday, September 1. I breakfasted with Mrs. Hog this morning, and att breakfast there was a good number of gentlemen, among the rest one Mr. Griffith from Rhode Island in 5 days, who informed us that the news of Morpang's being taken was a fiction. I called att Mr. Bayard's in the morning but found him not at home. I met my old friend Dr. McGraa att the door who told me he had seen Mr. H[ase]ll, and that he had expressed a desire of seeing me. I dined att Todd's with a mixed company and, in the afternoon, crossed the river to Baker's in company with Dr. Colchoun and another gentleman. We stayed and drank some punch there and viewed the French prizes in the harbour.

We returned to town att seven o'clock. We went to the Hungarian Club att night where were present the Chief Justice, the City Recorder, Mr. [Adolph] Philips, the Speaker of the House of Assembly, and severall others. We had a deal of news by the Boston papers and some private letters, and among other news, that of the Dutch having declared war against France and the capture of some of the barrier towns in Flanders by the French, as also the taking of some tobacco ships near the capes of Virginia, which furnished matter for conversation all night. We had an elegant supper, and among other things an excellent dish of young green pease. I wanted much to have met with H[ase]ll this day but heard that he was gone over to Long Island.

Sunday, September 2. I stayed att home the forenoon and dined with Stephen Bayard. Just as we had done dinner we heard two raps at the door solemnly laid on with a knocker. A gentleman in the company was going to see who it was, but Mr. Bayard desired him not to trouble himself, for it was only the domper. I asked who that was. He told me it was a fellow that made a course thro' one quarter of the town giving two raps att each door as he passed to lett the people in the houses know that the second bell had rung out. This man has a gratuity from each family for so doing every new year. His address when he comes to ask for his perquisite is, "Sir" or "Madam, you know what I mean." So he receives a piece of money more or less according to pleasure. This custom first began in New York when they had but one bell to warn the people to church, and that bell happened to be cracked, so, for the sake of lucre, the sextons have kept it up ever since. Such a triffling office as this perhaps is worth about 40 pounds a year York currency, tho the poor fellow sometimes is drubbed for his trouble by new comers who do not understand the custom.

After dinner Mr. Jeffrys came in, and we had some very comicall jaw. He spoke of going to Maryland along with me. I went home att 4 o'clock and supped this night with Mr. Hog, there being a Scots gentleman in company. Just before supper Mr. Bourdillion[370] came in, att the sight of whom we were all surprized, he having been a pritty while gone from these parts. He gave us an account of his adventures and the misfortunes he had met with since his departure, of his narrowly escaping a drowning in his voyage to Coraçoa, his being taken by the Spainards in his passage from Jamaica to New York, and the difficultys and hardships he went thro in making his escape, being obliged to live for 4 days upon nothing but a quart of water, and being driven out to the open ocean in a small undecked boat till he was providentially taken up by a Philadelphia sloop bound homewards to Philadelphia.

Monday, September 3. I stayed att home all this forenoon and dined att Todd's where was a very large company, and among the rest Mr. Bourdillion who told me that he had seen our quondam acquaintance Paul Ruiz among his countrymen the Spainards. In the afternoon I went to the coffee house and read the news papers, and coming home att six o'clock

I drank some punch with Mr. Hog and one Heath, a dry old chap.

Tuesday, September 4. This day proving very rainy I kept my room the greatest part of it. I dined with Mr. Hog and family, and after dinner the discourse turned upon hystericks and vapours in women, when Mr. Hog, pretending to discover to me an infallible cure for these distempers, spoke good neat bawdy before his wife, who did not seem to be much surprized att it. He told me that a good mowing was a cure for such complaints. I concluded that this kind of talk was what his wife had been used to, but it is an inexcusable piece of rudeness and rusticity in the company of women to speak in this manner, especially when it is practised before wives and daughters whose ears should never receive any thing from husbands and fathers but what is quite modest and clean.

In the afternoon I sauntered about sometime in the coffee house where were some rattling fellows playing att backgammon, and some deeper headed politicians att the game of chess. Att 6 I went home, and, meeting with Mr. Bourdillion, he and I went to Todd's together expecting to sup and have some chat snugly by ourselves, but we were interrupted by three young rakes who bounced in upon us, and then the conversation turned from a grave to a wanton strain. There was nothing talked of but ladys and lovers, and a good deal of polite smutt. We drank two remarkable toasts which I never before heard mentioned: the first was to our dear selves, and the tenour of the other was my own health. I told them that if such rediculous toasts should be heard of out of doors, we should procure the name of the Selfish Club. We supped and dismissed att 9 o'clock. Mr. Bourdillion and I went home like two philosophers, and the others went a whoreing like three rakes.

Wednesday, September 5th. It threatned rain all day, and

I did not go much abroad. I went in the morning with Mr. Hog to the Jews' sinagogue[371] where was an assembly of about 50 of the seed of Abraham chanting and singing their dolefull hymns, (they had 4 great wax candles lighted, as large as a man's arm, round the sanctuary where was contained the ark of the covenant and Aaron's rod), dressed in robes of white silk. Before the rabbi, who was elevated above the rest, in a kind of desk, stood the seven golden candlesticks transformed into silver gilt. They were all slip shod. The men wore their hats in the synagogue and had a veil of some white stuff which they sometimes threw over their heads in their devotion; the women, of whom some were very pritty, stood up in a gallery like a hen coop. They sometimes paused or rested a little from singing and talked about business. My ears were so filled with their lugubrous songs that I could not get the sound out of my head all day.

I dined att Todd's with severall gentlemen, and att night after playing a hitt att backgammon with Mr. Hog, I went to Todd's again with Mr. Bourdillion where we supped by ourselves. It rained very hard, and we returned home att eleven o'clock att night.

Thursday, September 6th. This day, the weather being somewhat more serene, I went more abroad, but it passed away as many of our days do, unremarked and triffling. I did little more than breakfast, dine, and sup. I read some of Homer's 12th Iliad and went to the coffee house in the afternoon where I met my old friend Mr. Knockson in whose vessel I had made my voyage to Albany. I also saw there the learned Dr. MaGraa who told me for news that the Indians had already begun their hostilitys by murdering some familys of the back inhabitants. I played att backgammon with Mr. Hog att night and supped with him.

Friday, September 7. This morning I had a visit from my taylor who fitted me with a new coat and breeches, my cloths with which I set out being quite wore to a cobweb. Going to the coffee house with Mr. Bourdillion att eleven o'clock, I played att backgammon with him and lost one hit. Just as we had done playing Mr. H[ase]ll came in who saluted me and I him very cordially, and enquired of one another's wellfare. He told me he had been upon Long Island and was very well, but only had got a broken head. "I hope," replyed I, "you have not been a fighting." "No," says he, "but I tumbled out of my chair as I rid along the road." There was another tall, thin gentleman with him who, by his visage jaune, I took to be a West Indian, and I guessed right.

I dined att Todd's with Bourdillion and Dr. Colchoun. The doctor and I smoked a pipe after dinner and chopt politicks. I went to Waghorn's att night to enquire of the state of my horses, and after having sat some time in a mixed company, Major Spratt came in, and he and I retired into a room by ourselves. He showed me a picture of a hermit in his cell contemplating upon mortality with a death's head in his hand. It was done in oil colours upon wood, and according to my judgement it was a very nice piece of painting.

About 10 o'clock there came to us a drunken doctor who was so intoxicated with liquor that he could scarce speak one connected sentence. He was much chagrined with some people for calling him a quack.[372] "But God damn 'em," says he, "I have a case of pistols and sword; I'll make every blood of them own before long what it is to abuse a man of liberall education." I asked him what university he had studied att, Cambridge or Oxford. "Damn me, neither," said he. "Did you study att Leyden under Boerhaave, sir?" said I. "Boerhaave may go to hell for a fool and a blockhead as he was," said he. "That fellow was admired by all the world, and, damn his soul, I know not for what. For my part I always had a mean opinion of him, only because he was one of them rascally Dutchmen, damn their souls." He went on att this rate for about half an hour. I, being tired of this kind of eloquence, left him to himself and went home.

Saturday, September 8th. I called this morning att Mr. Bayard's, but he was not in town. I kept my room most of the forenoon and read Homer's XIII Illiad. I dined att Tod's with a country man of mine who had come from Virginia. He was a little, dapper young fellow with a gaudy laced jacket, his name Rhae,[373] by trade a merchant, and he had travelled most of the continent of English America. He mistook me for the doctor of the man of war, and, asking me when we should sail, l replyed that I did not expect to sail any where till such time as I should cross the ferry.

We expected great news this night from Boston, having heard that some London ships had lately arrived there; but we were dissappointed, for none had come. I supped att Todd's with Bourdillion and some French gentlemen. We heard news that Commodore Haynson[374] in his way home had taken the Acapulco ship, a very rich prize, and that some ships from New York had been taken in their way home; but there are so many lyes now stirring that I gave little credit to these nouvelles. This night was very sharp and cold. Bourdillion and I went home att 11 o'clock.

Sunday, September 9. I went this morning to the French church [375] with Monsr. Bourdillion and heard one Mons. Rue preach. He is reckoned a man of good learning and sense; but, being foolishly sarcasticall, he has an unlucky knack att dissobliging the best of his parishioners so that the congregation has now dwindled to nothing.

I dined att Todd's with a mixed company and had two letters: one from Dr. Moffat att Rhode Island in which I had the first news of the death of our great poet Pope,[376] full of glory tho not of days; the other letter came from Boston and came from the hand of La Moinnerie, which, for a specimen of the French compliment, I shall here transcribe:—

A Boston, le 28me aoust—1744

Monsieur, "Je recois dans le moment, par Monsieur Hughes, la lettre que vous avez pris la pienne de m'escrire, le 24 du courant, de Rhode Island, laquelle m'a fait une sensible plaisir apprenans votre heureuse arrivé en ce pais la. Je desire que vous conservies votre santé, et je redouble mes voeux a ciel, pour que la fatigue du voyage ne vous soit point incommode.

"Vos nouvelles me prouvent entierment la bonté que vous avez pour moi, et m'assurent aussi que j'avois tort de penser que mes entretiens vous incommodoient, car en veritié j'etois timide de vous arreter si souvent et meme dans des temps que vous eties si souhaitté dans ce qu'il y avoit de plus aimable compagnies, mais a vous parler franchement, je me trouvois si content avec vous, que je fus aussy fort chagrin de votre depart, ainsy que tous vos amis l'ont eté, et si mes affairs eussent pu finir, j'aurois eté de votre compagnie jusque dans votre pais. Je tremble quand je fais reflection sur l'hyver, si je suis obligé de rester dans les pais froids.

"J' espere que vous me donneres la satisfaction de m'escrire. Je tacherai a la premiere de vous escrire en anglois, estant bien persuadé que vous voudres bien excuser mon ignorance. Je me suis tant appliqué que je conçu tous le mottes de votre lettre, que sont fort clairs et poetique, et pour ne laisser aucune doutte Monsieur le docteur Douglass m'a fait le plaisir de la lire.

"Je n'ai pas encore pris ma medecine, mais je vas m'y deter-miner.

"Tous vos amis vous salluent et vous souhaittant bien de la santé. Je vous escris la present par une docteur medicin de la Barbade, qui va a Rhode Island. Je souhaitte qu'il vous y trouvé en bonne joye. Je suis parfaitment, monsieur et amy, votre tres humble et tres obeisant serviteur."

D. la Moinnerie,
de St. Domingue fond de l'Isle de vasche
lois [?] St. Louis

[Sir,—I have just received, by Mr. Hughes, the letter which you took the trouble to write me on the 24th of this month from Rhode Island, which has made me truly happy to learn of your safe arrival in that country. I hope that you will safeguard your health, and I redouble my pleas to heaven that the fatigue of the journey shall not incommode you in any way.

Your writing to me proved to my entire satisfaction the kind regard you have for me and assured me that I was wrong in thinking that my conversations interrupted you, for in truth I was timid about visiting you so often and at times when you were so sought after by the most distinguished society. To speak honestly I was so happy with you that I was extremely grieved at your departure, just as all your friends were, and if my affairs had been in order, I should like to have accompanied you to your own country. I shudder when I think of winter if I am obliged to remain in this cold country.

I am in hopes that you will give me the pleasure of hearing from you. I shall attempt for the first time to write in English, being quite certain that you will fully excuse my mistakes. I have studied very hard and I understand all the words in your letter, which were very clear and poetical, but so as to allow no doubt, Dr. Douglass did me the kindness to read it.

I have not yet taken my medicine, but am determined to do so.

All your friends salute you and wish for the best of health for you. I am writing you by a medical doctor from Barbados who is going to Rhode Island. I trust that he will find you enjoying it there. I am assuredly, sir and friend, your very humble and obedient servant.

D. La Moinnerie]

I went this afternoon with Mr. Hog to the Presbyterian meeting and heard there a good puritanick sermon preached by one Pemberton.[377] I supped att Todd's with two or three of my countrymen, among whom was Mr. Knox.

Monday, September 10th. I dined this day with Mr. Bayard's brother, and after dinner we tossed about the bumpers so furiously that I was obliged to go home and sleep for three hours and be worse than my word to Mr. H[ase]ll, with whom I had promised to spend the evening. I writ to Dr. Moffat att Newport and to La Moinnerie att Boston, of which letter follows the copie:

A New York, le 10me de Settembre

Monsieur,—L'honneur de la votre, en datte du 28me aoust, m'est bien parvenue. Je suis bien charmé que vous joussiez d'une bonne santé, et vous remercie de la faveur que vous m'avez fait en m'escrivant. Pour ce qui me regarde, je jouis d'une parfaite santé depuis que j'ais laisse Boston. La seule chose que je regrette est de me voire separée (et peutetre pour toujours) des agreable personnes avec qui je me suis rencontré et lie connoisance lors que j'etois a Boston, et en particulier de vous, monsieur, de qui l'humeur facetieuse, gaie, et la conversation agreable, me plaisoit beaucoup; mais helas! notre joyes ne sont pas durables. Ils sont comme les nouages d'une belle soirée, le soleil couchant, de differents formes et de diverses couleurs charmantes; mais sitost que ce lumiere glorieuse s'eloignera de notre horizon, et se couchera dans le sien de Thetis, sa belle maitresse, ce spectacle brillant se dissipera, nous sommes dans le crepuscle, le nuit s'approche, il fait sombre! Eh bien, que pense vous, monsieur? Sans doute que j'ay devenue fou ou poet, escrivant telles bagatelles en une langue dont je n'entend pas la propre idiome, mais je me flatte que vous voudres bien excuser mon ignorance.

J'ay veu differents climats et differents visage depuis que je vous ay quitté. A l'egard du pais, il est quelquefois montagneux et plien de roches, quelquefois c'est une terrain egal, et asses agreable. J'ay veu bien des hommes que l'on peut bien apeller fous, d'autre gens d'esprit, mais j'en ais peu rencontre de sages. A legarde du sexe, j'ay veu dont le charmes seroient capables d'eschauffer les roches, ou de fondre des montagnes de glace. Vraiment, monsieur, vous ne devez pas craindre l'hiver a Boston, puis que le sexe y est si plien de charmes et de chaleurs benignes, mais je nen dis pas d'avantage, laissent a cieux qui en sont les spectateurs, et qui sont du sang plus chaud que la mienne, le soins de les captiver.

You'll pardon me, sir, for writing you in bad French. To make amends I subjoin a scrap of English, tho' not much better, yet I hope more properly expressed. I expect still to hear from you, and wish you all the health and tranquillity which a mortal man can possibly enjoy.

[New York, September 10.
Sir,—Your letter dated August 28th has just arrived. I am most happy that you are enjoying good health and appreciate the honor you have done me in writing to me. Concerning myself, I have been in perfect health since I left Boston. The only thing I regret is being separated (and perhaps forever) from the agreeable persons I met and whose acquaintance I made when I was in Boston, and particularly you, sir, whose gay, facetious humor and pleasant conversation delighted me so much. But alas! Our joys are fleeting. They are like the clouds of a lovely evening at sunset, with their various shapes and diverse and enchanting colors, but as soon as the glorious luminary disappears over our horizon and lies down in the bosom of Thetis, his beautiful mistress, this brilliant spectacle vanishes, we are in shadow, it grows dark! Ah, well, what must you think, sir, without a doubt that I am a fool or a poet, writing such bagatelles in a language in which I do not even know the proper idioms. But I flatter myself that you will pardon my mistakes.

I have known different climates and different faces since I last saw you. In respect to the country, sometimes it has been hilly and rocky and other times a level plain and rather pleasant. I have seen some men whom you might call fools, other men of ingenuity, but I have not yet met any learned men. As for the sex, I have seen some whose charms could warm rocks and melt mountains of ice. Truly, sir, you ought not to fear the winter in Boston, for the sex there is so full of charm and friendly warmth, but I shall speak no more of it, leaving it to those who are their beholders and who are more warm blooded than I am, the cares of captivating them.]

I supped att Todd's this night with a mixed company where we had a deal of triffling chat.

Tuesday, September 11. This morning att the coffee house I took my leave of Mr. H[ase]ll who gave me his good wishes and promised to write to me from Barbadoes.

Ferry—Eliz. Town Point

I dined with my countryman, Mr. Rhea, att Mr. Bayard's, and taking my leave of Mrs. Hog and her sister after dinner, I took boat along with Mr. Rhea from York to Elizabeth Town Point and had a pleasant passage making 15 miles by water in three hours.

Jersey Goverment—Eliz. Town—Woodbridge

Mr. Rhea and I mounted horse and rid 12 miles farther after sun down. We passed thro' Elizabeth Town att 7 o'clock att night and arrived att Woodbridge[378] att half an hour after eight. The country here is pleasant and pritty clear with a beautifull intermixture of woods. The roads are very good in dry weather. We put up att one Heard's[379] where we supped with a simple fellow that had been bred up among the reeds and sedges and did not seem as if ever he had conversed with men. His name was Mason, a Quaker by profession. Our land-lady was a jolly, fat woman, weighing about 200 weight of fat.

I was sorry to leave New York upon account of being separated from some agreeable acquaintance I had contracted there, and att the same time I cannot but own that I was glad to remove from a place where the temptation of drinking (a thing so incompatable with my limber constitution) threw it self so often in my way. I knew here severall men of sense, ingenuity, and learning, and a much greater number of fops whom I chuse not to name, not so much for fear of giving offence as because I think their names are not worthy to be recorded either in manuscript or printed journals. These dons commonly held their heads higher than the rest of mankind and imagined few or none were their equals. But this I found always proceeded from their narrow notions, ignorance of the world, and low extraction, which indeed is the case with most of our aggrandized upstarts in these infant countrys of America who never had an opportunity to see, or if they had, the capacity to observe the different ranks of men in polite nations or to know what it is that really constitutes that difference of degrees.

Wednesday, September 12. I was waked this morning before sunrise with a strange bawling and hollowing without doors. It was the landlord ordering his negroes with an imperious and exalted voice. In his orders the known term or epithet, son of a bitch, was often repeated.

I came down stairs and found one Mr. White,[380] a Philadelphian, and the loggerheaded fellow that supped with us last night ordering some tea for breakfast. Mr. Mason, among other judicious questions, asked me how cheeses sold in Maryland. I told him I understood nothing of that kind of merchandize but if he wanted to know the price of catharticks and emeticks there, I could inform him. He asked me what sort of commoditys these were. I replied that it was a particular kind of truck which I dealt in. When our tea was made it was such abominable stuff that I could not drink of it but drank a porringer of milk.

Pitscatuay

We set off att seven o'clock and before nine passed thro' a place called Pitscatuay[381] about 3 miles from Brunswick. I have observed that severall places upon the American main go by that name. The country here is pleasant and levell, intermixed with skirts of woods and meadow ground, the road in generall good but stonny in some places.

Raretin Ferry—Brunswick

We crossed Raretin River and arrived in Brunswick att 9 o'clock. We baited our horses and drank some chocolate att Miller's.

Kingston

We mounted again att 10, and after riding 15 miles of a pleasant road, the day being somewhat sultry, we put up att Leonard's att Kingstown a little before one, where we dined. Here we met with an old chattering fellow who imagined that Mr. Rhea was an officer of Warren's man of war and wanted to list himself. He told us he had served in Queen Anne's wars and that he was born under the Crown of England, and that 18 years agoe he had left the service and lived with his wife. We asked him where his wife was now. He answered he supposed in hell, "asking your honour's pardon, for she was such a pleague that she was fit for no body's company but the devil's." We could scarcely get rid of this fellow till we made him so drunk with rum that he could not walk. He drank to Captain Warren's health, and subjoined, "not forgetting King George." We took horse again att three o clock, and White and the Quaker kept in close conversation upon the road about 20 paces before, while Rhea and I held a conference by ourselves.

Maidenhead—Trenton

Att 5 o'clock we passed thro' a town called Maidenhead and att six arrived att Bond's in Trenton where we put up for all night. Here Mason, the Quaker, left us, little regretted, because his company was but insipid. Just as Rhea and I lighted att the door, there came up a storm att north west which we were thankfull we had so narrowly escaped, for it blowed and rained vehemently. We had Dr. Cadwaller's company att supper and that of another gentleman in town whose name I cannot remember. There passed a great deal of physicall discourse betwixt the doctor and I, of which Rhea and White being tired, went to bed, and I followed att eleven o'clock.

Delaware Ferry

Thursday, September 13. This morning proved very sharp and cold. We set out from Trenton att 7 o'clock, and riding thro' a pleasant road we crossed Delaware Ferry a little before eight, where the tide and wind being both strong against us, we were carried a great way down the river before we could land.

Bristo'—Shammany Ferry

We arrived att Bristo' betwixt 9 and 10 a clock and breakfasted att Walton's. Setting out from thence we crossed Shammany Ferry att eleven a'clock. The sun growing somewhat warmer we travelled with ease and pleasure. We stoped some time att a house within 13 miles of Philadelphia where there was an overgrown landlady much of the size of B——y M——t att Annapolis who gave us bread and cheese and some cold apple pye, but we payed dear for it. Before we went into town we stopped to see the works[382] where they were casting of cannon, where I thought they made but bungling work of it, spoiling ten where they made one.

Philadelphia

We entered Philadelphia att 4 o'clock, and Rhea and I put up att Cockburn's. I went att six o clock and spent the evening with Collector Alexander.

Friday, September 14. I stayed att home most of the forenoon, the air being somewhat sharp and cold. I dined with Mr. Currie and Mr. Weemse att a private house and going home after dinner, read one of Shakespear's plays. I drank tea with my landlady Mrs. Cume and att 5 a clock went to the coffee house where I saw Dr. Spencer[383] who for some time had held a course of physicall lectures of the experimentall kind here and att York. I delivered him a letter from Dr. Moffat att Newport. I met here likewise one Mitchell,[384] a practitioner of physick in Virginia who was travelling, as he told me, upon account of his health. He was a man much of my own make, and his complaints were near a kin to mine. Here I met Dr. Phineas Bond and others of my old acquaintances.

Att Philadelphia I heard news of some conturbations and fermentations of partys att Annapolis concerning the election of certain parliament members for that wretched city and was sorry to find that these triffles still contributed so much to set them att variance, but I pray that the Lord may pity them and not leave them intirely to themselves and the devil. I went home att eight att night, the air being cold and raw, and was sorry to hear that my fellow traveller Mr. Rhea was taken with an ague, the effect of our night's ride upon Tuesday.

Saturday, September 15. This morning proving rainy I stayed att home till eleven o'clock att which time my barber came to shave me and gave me a harangue of politicks and news. I payed a visit to Dr. Thomas Bond and went and dined att Cockburn's in company with two stanch Quakers, who sat att table with their broad hats upon their heads. They eat a great deal more than they spoke, and their conversation was only yea and nay. In the afternoon I had a visit of Mr. Rhea who had expelled his ague by the force of a vomite. Att 6 o'clock I went to the coffee house and thence with Mr. Alexander to the Governour's Club, where the Governour himself was present and severall other gentlemen of note in the place. The conversation was agreeable and instructing, only now and then some persons there showed a particular fondness for introducing gross, smutty expressions which I thought did not altogether become a company of philosophers and men of sense.

Sunday, September 16. This morning proved very sharp, and it seemed to freeze a little. I breakfasted att Neilson's with Messrs. Home and Watts and went to the Presbyterian meeting in the morning with Mr. Wallace. There I heard a very Calvinisticall sermon preached by an old holder forth whose voice was somewhat rusty, and his countenance a little upon the 4 square. The pulpit appeared to me somewhat in shape like a tub, and att each side of it aloft was hung an old fashioned brass sconce. In this assembly was a collection of the most curious old fashioned screwed up faces, both of men and women, that ever I saw. There were a great many men in the meeting with linnen nightcaps, and indecent and unbecoming dress which is too much wore in all the churches and meetings in America that I have been in, unless it be those of Boston where they are more decent and polite in their dress tho more fantasticall in their doctrines and much alike in their honesty and morals.

I dined with Collector Alexander and, in the afternoon, went with Mr. Weemse to the Roman Chapell where I heard some fine musick and saw some pritty ladys. The priest, after saying mass, catechised some children in English and insisted much upon our submitting our reason to religion and believing of every thing that God said (or, propperly speaking, every thing that the priest says, who often has the impudence to quote the divine authority to support his absuritys) however contradictory or repugnant it seemed to our natural reason. I was taken with a sick qualm in this chapell which I attributed to the gross nonsense proceeding from the mouth of the priest, which, I suppose, being indigestible, bred cruditys in my intellectual stomach and confused my animal spirits. I spent the evening att the taveren with some Scotsmen.

Monday, September 17. This day was very sharp and cold for the season, and a fire was very gratefull. I did little but stay att home all day and employed my time in reading of Homer's Iliads. I dined att the taveren and walked out to the country after dinner to reap the benefit of the sharp air. When I returned I drank tea with Mrs. Cume, and there being some ladys there, the conversation run still upon the old topic, religion. I had a letter from my brother in Maryland where there was an account of some changes that had happened there since I left the place. Att the coffee house I could observe no new faces, nor could I learn any news.

Tuesday, September 18th. This forenoon I spent in reading of Shakespear's Timon of Athens, or Manhater, a play which, tho not written according to Aristotle's rules,[385] yet abounding with inimitable beauties peculiar to this excellent author.

I dined att Cockburn's where was a sett of very comical phizzes and a very vulgar unfurbished conversation which I did not join in but eat my dinner and was a hearer, reaping as much instruction from it as it would yield. I payed a visit to Collector Alexander in the afternoon and att night going to the coffee house. I went from thence along with Messieurs Wallace and Currie to the Musick Club[386] where I heard a tollerable concerto performed by a harpsicord and three violins. One Levy there played a very good violine, one Quin bore another pritty good part; Tench Francis playd a very indifferent finger upon an excellent violin that once belonged to the late Ch: Calvert, Govr. of Maryland. We dismissed att eleven o'clock after having regaled ourselves with musick and good viands and liquor.

191

Wednesday, September 19. To day I resolved to take my departure from this town. In the morning my barber came to shave me and almost made me sick with his Irish brogue and stinking breath. He told me that he was very glad to see that I was after being of the right religion. I asked him how he came to know what religion I was of. "Ohon! and sweet Jesus now!" said he, "as if I had not seen your Honour at the Roman Catholic chapell coming upon Sunday last." Then he run out upon a blundering encomium concerning the Catholicks and their principles. I dined with Mr. Alexander, and taking my leave of him and his wife, I went to Mr. Strider's in Front Street where I had some commissions to deliver to Mr. Tasker att Annapolis, and taking horse att half an hour after three o'clock, I left Philadelphia and crossed Skuilkill Ferry att a quarter after four. I passed thro the town of Darby about an hour before sunsett.

Chester

About the time of the sun's going down, the air turned very sharp, it being a degree of frost. I arrived in Chester about half an hour after seven, riding into town in company with an Irish teague who overtook me on the road. Here I put up att one Mather's,[387] an Irishmann att the Sign of the Ship.

Att my seeing of the city of Philadelphia I conceived a quite different notion of both city and inhabitants from that which I had before from the account or description of others. I could not apprehend this city to be so very elegant or pritty as it is commonly represented. In its present situation it is much like one of our country market towns in England. When you are in it the majority of the buildings appear low and mean, the streets unpaved, and therefor full of rubbish and mire. It makes but an indifferent appearance att a distance,

there being no turrets or steeples to set it of[f] to advantage,
but I believe that in a few years hence it will be a great and
a flourishing place and the chief city in North America. The
people are much more polite, generally speaking, than I appre-
hended them to be from the common account of travellers.
They have that accomplishment peculiar to all our American
colonys, viz., subtilty and craft in their dealings. They apply
themselves strenuously to business, having little or no turn
towards gaiety (and I know not indeed how they should since
there are few people here of independent fortunes or of high
luxurious taste.) Drinking here is not att all in vogue, and in the
place there is pritty good company and conversation to be had.
It is a degree politer than New York tho in its fabrick not so
urban, but Boston excells both for politeness and urbanity
tho only a town.

Thursday, September 20th. I set out att nine o'clock
from Mather's and about two miles from Chester was overtaken
by a Quaker, one of the politest and best behaved of that
kidney ever I had met with. We had a deal of discourse about
news and politicks, and after riding 4 miles together we parted.
I now entered the confines of the three notched road by which
I knew I was near Maryland. Immediately upon this some-
something ominous happened, which was my man's tumbling
down, flump, two or three times, horse and baggage and all, in
the middle of a plain road. I likewise could not help thinking that my state of health was changed for the worse upon it.

Willmington

Within a mile of Willmington I met Mr. Neilson of Philadelphia who told me some little scraps of news from Annapolis.

Christin Ferry—Newcastle

I crossed Christin Ferry att 12 o'clock, and att two o clock I dined att Griffith's in New Castle and had some chat with a certain virtuoso of the town who came in after dinner. I departed thence att half an hour after three, and about a mile from town I met a monstruous appearance, by much the greatest wonder and prodigy I had seen in my travells, and every whit as strange a sight by land as a mermaid is att sea. It was a carter driving his cart along the road who seemed to be half man, half woman. All above from the crown of his head to the girdle seemed quite masculine, the creature having a great, hideous, unshorn black beard and strong course features, a slouch hat, cloth jacket, and great brawny fists, but below the girdle there was nothing to be seen but petticoats, a white apron, and the exact shape of a woman with relation to broad, round buttocks. I would have given something to have seen this creature turned topsy turvy, to have known whether or not it was an hermaphrodite, having often heard of such animals but never having seen any to my knowledge; but I thought it most prudent to pass by peaceably, asking no questions lest it should prove the devil in disguise. Some miles farther I met two handsome country girls and enquired the road of them. One seemed fearfull, and the other was very forward and brisk. I liked the humour and vivacity of the latter and lighted from my horse as if I had been going to salute her, but they both set up a scream and run off like wild bucks into the woods.

I stopped this night att one Van Bibber's, a house 12 miles from New Castle. The landlady here affected to be a great wit, but the landlord was a heavy lubber of Dutch pedigree. The woman pretended to be jealous of her husband with two ugly old maids that were there; one of whom was named Margaret who told me she was born in Dundee in Scotland

and asked me if ever I had drank any Dundee swats out of twa lugged bickers (ale out of two eard cups.) These two old maids would sit, one att each side of Van Bibber, and teize him while his wife pretended to scold all the time as if she was jealous, and he would look like a goose.

There were in this house a certain Irish teague and one Gilpin, a dweller in Maryland. This teague and Gilpin lay in one bed upon the floor, and I in a lofty bedstead by my self. Gilpin and I talked over politicks and news relating to Maryland while we were in bed before we went to sleep, and our discourse was interlaced with hideous yawnings, like two tired and weary travellers, till att last the nodding diety took hold of us in the middle of half uttered words and broken sentences. My rest was broken and interrupted, for the teague made a hideous noise in coming to bed, and as he tossed and turned, kept still ejaculating either an ohon or sweet Jesus.

Friday, September 21. I was waked early this morning by the groanings, ohons, and yawnings of our Teague who every now and then gaped fearfully, bawling out, "O sweet Jesus!" in a mournfull melodious accent; in short he made as much noise between sleeping and waking as half a dozen hogs in a little penn could have done; but Mr. Gilpin, his bedfellow, was started and gone.

Maryland—Bohemia

I took horse att 9 o clock and arrived att Bohemia att twelve. I called att the mannor house and dined there with Miss Coursey.[388] She and I went in the afternoon to visit Coll. Colville[389] and returned home betwixt eight and 9 att night.

Saturday, September 22. I rid this morning with Miss Coursey to visit Bouchelle,[390] the famous yaw doctor, who desired me to come and prescribe for his wife who had got an hysterick palpitation, or as they called it, a wolf in her heart. I stayed and dined with him, and there passed a deal of conversation between us. I found the man much more knowing than I expected from the common character I had heard of him. He seemed to me a modest young fellow, not insensible of his depth in physicall literature, neither quite deficient in naturall sense and parts. His wife having desired my advice, I gave it and was thanked by the husband and herself for the favour of my visit.

There was there an old comicall fellow named Millner who went by the name of doctor. He was busy making a pan of melilot plaister and seemed to have a great conceit of his own learning. He gave us the history of one Du Witt,[391] a doctor att Philadelphia, who he said had begun the world in the honourable station of a porter and used to drive a turnip cart or wheel barrow thro' the streets. This old fellow was very inquisitive with me, but I did not incline much to satisfy his curiosity. He asked me if Miss Coursey was my wife. After dinner we returned homewards.

Sunday, September 23. There came up a furious north west wind this morning which prevented my setting off as I intended, knowing that I could not cross the ferrys. I was shaved by an Irish barber whose hand was so heavy that he had almost flead my chin and head. Miss Coursey and I dined by ourselves, and att 4 o'clock we walked to Collonell Collvill's where we spent the evening agreeably and returned home att eight o'clock, the night being cold and blustering and the wind in our teeth.

Monday, September 24. It seemed to threaten to blow hard this morning, but the wind changing to the south before 12 o'clock, it began to moderate, and I had hopes of getting over Elk Ferry. I dined with Miss Coursey att Coll. Colvill's and set out from there att three o'clock, intending att night for North East.

On the road here, att one Altum's who keeps publick house att Elk Ferry I met with my Irish barber who had operated upon my chin att Bohemia who had almost surfeited me with his palaber. I had some learned conversation with my ingenious friend Terence, the ferry man, and as we went along the road, the barber would fain have perswaded me to go to Parson Wye's to stay that night, which I refused, and so we took leave of one another.

I went the rest of the way in the company of a man who told me he was a carter, a horse jockey, a farmer, all three. He asked me if I had heard any thing of the wars in my travells and told me he heard that the Queen of Sheba, or some such other queen, had sent a great asistance to the King of England, and that if all was true that was said of it, they would certainly kill all the French and Spainards befor Christen mass next.

North East

Talking of these matters with this unfinished politician, I arrived att North East[392] att seven o'clock att night and put up att one Smith's there. After supper I overheard a parcell of superficiall philosophers in the kitchin talking of knotty points in religion over a mug of syder. One chap among the rest seemed to confound the whole company with a show of learning which was nothing but a puff of clownish pedantry. I went to bed att 10 a'clock.

Susquehanna Ferry

Tuesday, September 25. I departed North East this morning att nine a clock. The sky was dark and cloudy, threatning rain. I had a solitary ride over an unequall gravelly road till I came to Susquehanna Ferry, where I baited my horses, and had a ready passage but was taken with a vapourish qualm in the ferry boat which went off after two or three miles' riding.

I dined att my old friend Tradaway's, whom I found very much indisposed with fevers. He told me it had been a very unhealthy time and a hot summer. I should have known the time had been unhealthy without his telling me so by only observing the washed countenances of the people standing att their doors and looking out att their windows, for they looked like so many staring ghosts. In short I was sensible I had got into Maryland, for every house was an infirmary, according to ancient custome.

Joppa

I arrived att Joppa att half an hour after 5 o'clock, and, putting up att Brown's, I went and payed a visit to the parson and his wife, who were both complaining, or grunting as the country phraze is, and had undergone the pennance of this blissed climate, having been harrassed with fevers ever since the beginning of August. I took my leave of them att eight o'clock and supped with my landlord.

Gunpowder Ferry—Newtown

Wednesday, September 26. This morning proved very sharp and cool. I got over Gunpowder Ferry by ten a'clock and rid solitary to Newtown upon Patapscoe where I dined att Roger's[393] and saw some of my acquaintances.

Patapscoe Ferry

I crossed Patapscoe Ferry att 4 o'clock and went to Mr. Hart's where I stayed that night. We talked over old storys and held a conference some time with a certain old midwife there, one

Mrs. Harrison, and having finished our consultations, we went to bed att 10 o'clock.

Thursday, September 27. I set off from Mr. Hart's a little after nine o clock and baited att More's[394] where I met with some patients that welcomed me on my return.

Annapolis

I arrived att Annapolis att two o'clock afternoon and so ended my perigrinations.

In these my northeren travells I compassed my design in obtaining a better state of health, which was the purpose of my journey. I found but little difference in the manners and character of the people in the different provinces I passed thro', but as to constitutions and complexions, air and goverment, I found some variety. Their forms of goverment in the northeren provinces I look upon to be much better and happier than ours, which is a poor, sickly, convulsed state. Their air and living to the northward is likewise much preferable, and the people of a more gygantick size and make. Att Albany, indeed, they are intirely Dutch and have a method of living something differing from the English.

In this itineration I compleated, by land and water together, a course of 1624 miles. The northeren parts I found in generall much better settled than the southeren. As to politeness and humanity, they are much alike except in the great towns where the inhabitants are more civilized, especially att Boston.

FINIS

Notes: INTRODUCTION

1. Very little is known about the life of Dr. Alexander Hamilton; some details, not always accurate, may be found in Hester D. Richardson's sketch in the *Dictionary of American Biography,* VIII, 174.

2. After serving as minister of the church at Crammond, the Reverend William Hamilton was appointed Professor of Divinity at the University of Edinburgh in 1709. On the death of William Wishart in 1729, he became Principal, serving until 1732. He was said to be "distinguished for piety, learning, and moderation." Alexander Grant, *The Story of the University of Edinburgh* (Edinburgh, 1884), II, 264, 386-87.

3. See below, p. xvi and n. 25.

4. The *Itinerarium* shows a knowledge of both Latin and French literature as well as the languages themselves. *List of the Graduates in Medicine in the University of Edinburgh* (Edinburgh, 1867), 3.

5. Jared Sparks, ed., *The Works of Benjamin Franklin* (Boston, 1836-40), VII, 238.

6. Although John Hamilton was a clergyman, he occasionally performed the duties of a physician—"the angelic conjunction," as Cotton Mather once called it. He lived in Calvert County and was an honorary member of the Tuesday Club. Record of the Tuesday Club, Annapolis, 1744-55, pp. 5, 19, Maryland Historical Society; Mary Hamilton to her son, Alexander, July 23, Sept. 8, Nov. 15, 1739, Dulany Papers, Maryland Historical Society.

7. Stephen Bordley to M. H., Sept. 12, 1739, Stephen Bordley Letter Book, 1738-40, Maryland Historical Society.

8. Dr. Thomson, an old Edinburgh fellow-student, spoke of settling in Annapolis and taking over Hamilton's practice in event of his death. See below, p. xix; Alexander Hamilton, *A Defence of Dr. Thomson's Discourse* (Philadelphia, 1751), 4; Alexander to Gilbert Hamilton, Oct. 20, 1743, Hamilton Letter Book, 1739-43, Dulany Papers.

9. Broadside, Dulany Papers; Mary to Alexander Hamilton, Nov. 15, 1739, Dulany Papers.

10. Quoted by Charles C. Sellers, *Artist of the Revolution: The Early Life of Charles Willson Peale* (Hebron, Conn., 1939), 37.

11. Alexander to Gilbert Hamilton, Oct. 20, 1743, Hamilton Letter Book, 1739-43, Dulany Papers.

12. Alexander Hamilton to J—n B—n, Nov. 6, 1743; Alexander to Gilbert Hamilton, Nov. 20, 1743, Hamilton Letter Book, 1739-43, Dulany Papers.

13. See below, p. 199.

14. *Maryland Gazette,* May 3, 10, 17, 24, 1745.

15. "Remember me to all the Members of the whin-bush Club, especially to the Right honourable, the Lord Provost, and other magistrates and officers of the Ancient and honourable Society." The whin-bush is the same as gorse or furze, and has a yellow flower resembling Scotch Broom. Alexander Hamilton to Dr. B. G. H——n, June 13, 1739, Hamilton Letter Book, 1739-43, Dulany Papers.

16. Record of the Tuesday Club, 1, 3, 4.

17. *Ibid.,* 1-65.

18. A small portion of the history is bound with the Record of the Tuesday Club, but the three volumes mentioned may be consulted at the Johns Hopkins University Library.

19. *Dict. of Amer. Biog.,* V, 498-99; VIII, 171.

20. Stephen Bordley to Witham Marshe, May 30, 1747, Stephen Bordley Letter Book, 1740-47, Maryland Historical Society.

21. He was replaced on March 30, 1752, probably on account of his poor health. Vestry Minutes of St. Ann's Parish, Maryland Hall of Records, Annapolis.

22. Hamilton also borrowed £100 in 1749 and £50 in 1750. *Maryland Archives,* 52, pp. 24-25.

23. Since the Annapolis Lodge did not receive its constitution from Grand Master Thomas Oxnard of Massachusetts until August 12, 1749, it seems certain that Alexander Hamilton was the first "Right Worshipfull Master" of the Masons in Maryland. Lawrence C. Wroth, *History of Printing in Colonial Maryland* (Baltimore, 1922), 197-98; Edward T. Schultz, *Freemasonry in Maryland* (Baltimore, 1884), I, 23.

24. He contributed generously to the Royal Infirmary at Edinburgh, to the Scots Charitable Society at Boston, and to other worthy causes. Alexander Hamilton to J. D——d, April 22, 1742, Hamilton Letter Book, 1739-43, Dulany Papers; *Virginia Gazette,* July 25, 1751; Oswald Tilghman, *History of Talbot County, Maryland* (Baltimore, 1915), II, 478-813.

25. In the *Maryland Gazette,* July 2, 9, 1752, he advertised: "To be Sold cheap, at the Subscriber's Shop, in Annapolis, a VARIETY of fresh Drugs and Medicines, Chemical and Galenical. Alexander Hamilton." He purchased his drugs from William Anderson of London. Anderson to Hamilton, April 10, 1751, Dulany Papers.

26. The full title is *A Defence of Dr. Thomson's Discourse on the Preparation of the Body for the Small Pox, and the Manner of Receiving the Infection,* 27 pp. The only known copy of this pamphlet is in the Huntington Library at San Marino, California, through whose courtesy the Institute of Early American History and Culture at Williamsburg has procured a photostat. The College of Physicians at Philadelphia kindly supplied a photostat of their rare copy of Dr. Thomson's *Discourse* for the Institute.

27. For the whole controversy, see Carl and Jessica Bridenbaugh, *Rebels and Gentlemen: Philadelphia in the Age of Franklin* (New York, 1942), 82, 265.

28. *Pennsylvania Gazette,* May 7, 1752.

29. Maryland Archives, 50, pp. 168-69.

30. *Ibid.,* 172, 176-77, 179, 180, 217.

31. *Ibid.,* 188-89, 219, 406, 416, 427-28.

32. Alexander Hamilton's will is in Liber 30, folio 106, and

the appointment of his wife as testatrix and her bond, dated July 16, 20, 1756, are in Liber 36, folios 309-10, Hall of Records.

33. *Maryland Gazette,* May 13, 1756.

34. Albert B. Hart, ed., *Hamilton's Itinerarium* (St. Louis, 1907), vii.

Notes: Itinerarium

1. In Maryland, on either side of the Bay, there were two main north and south roads which merged at Head of Elk. Dr. Hamilton had intended to cross on the ferry from Annapolis to Kent Island and thence ride northward; instead he traveled the main post road known as the King's Highway which followed the fall line. Clarence P. Gould, "Money and Transportation in Maryland, 1720-1765," Johns Hopkins University, *Studies*, 33 (1915), 125.

2. Mr. H——t was probably Samuel Hart who was a member of the Tuesday Club of Annapolis which Hamilton helped to organize in 1745. Joseph T. Wheeler, "Reading and Other Recreations of Marylanders, 1700-1766," *Maryland Historical Magazine*, 38 (1943), 44.

3. Mr. H————l was, possibly, Samuel Hasell who, born in Barbados in 1691, came to Philadelphia about 1715, and set up as a merchant. He held public office in that city, serving as mayor three times, and was a vestryman of Christ Church. In July, 1744, he was an alderman of Philadelphia. John R. Young, ed., *Memorial History of the City of Philadelphia from Its First Settlement to the Year 1895* (New York, 1895-98), I, 238.

4. In the summer of this same year, Witham Marshe kept a journal of a trip he made which followed, in part, the same route Hamilton traveled. Marshe reported that Mrs. Hughes kept the Patapsco Ferry at a point called Ferry Bar, and that he crossed to Whetstone Point. Witham Marshe, "Journal of the Treaty Held with the Six Nations by the Commissioners of Maryland and Other

Provinces," Massachusetts Historical Society, *Collections,* 1st ser., 7 (1800), 172. Hereafter cited as Marshe, "Journal."

5. The mariner may have been biased, but the fact remains that despite enjoying the most lucrative livings in all the colonies, the Anglican clergy of Maryland had the unsavory reputation of being indolent, high-living, and scandalous persons. William S. Perry, ed., *Historical Collections Relating to the American Colonial Church* (Hartford, 1870-78), IV, 324.

6. Dr. Hamilton did not overlook what was to become Maryland's first city, for in 1744 Baltimore was only "a scattered group of houses." In Moale's famous view of 1752 only twenty-five houses are shown. Clarence P. Gould, "Economic Causes of the Rise of Baltimore," in *Essays in Colonial History* (New Haven, 1931), 235, 249; Moale's aquatint in James T. Adams, *Provincial Society, 1690-1763* (New York, 1927), facing 202.

7. Edward Day kept the ferry on the south side of Gunpowder River. Marshe, "Journal," 172.

8. Now extinct, Joppa was in 1744 the county seat of Baltimore County. Located at the falls of Gunpowder River, it was the chief port of entry and major tobacco exporting town with tobacco warehouses and wharves fed by numerous "rolling roads" from the surrounding plantations. John T. Scharf, *History of Maryland* (Baltimore, 1879), I, 413-15.

9. Maryland was well supplied with taverns. A list of 1746 shows 845 licensed ordinaries. Every court house had at least one, and one could be expected near each ferry landing. Taverns were often not much more than grog shops, with a few rooms for travelers who were not fortunate enough to carry letters entitling them to stay at the great houses. Gould, "Money and Transportation in Maryland," 147n; Paul Wilstach, *Tidewater Maryland* (New York, 1931), 101.

10. When Witham Marshe visited Hugh Deane at Joppa a few weeks later, he also had to listen to these tedious accounts. "Here I waited on the Rev. Hugh Deane, who is parson of this parish. . . . He read to me some news mentioned in his European letters, concerning the Queen of Hungary, the King of Prussia, and the Lord knows how many other potentates; but as I was

neither politician nor author I gave but little attention to it."
Marshe, "Journal," 172.

11. Sangaree was a drink of wine and water, spiced and sweetened, which was popular in warm climates.

12. If ginseng was as remarkable as Colonel William Byrd reported, it is regrettable that Hamilton could not find any, for the Virginian wrote to a friend in London that "It is as hard to be found as Humility in our Sex and Constancy in the other and the Frugal hand wherewith Providence dispenses this Noble vegetable is a proof of its excellencies . . . tis as easy to propagate Chastity in that great city as it is ginseng in a garden." Nevertheless it was announced that the plant had been discovered growing near the Susquehanna River in 1738. William Byrd to Mr. Otway, *ca.* 1735-40, in *Virginia Magazine of History and Biography,* 9 (1902), 129; John F. Watson, *Annals of Philadelphia and Pennsylvania* (Philadelphia, 1844), II, 427.

13. Witham Marshe said he "baited at Mr. Treadway's ordinary" after crossing Susquehanna Ferry, and inasmuch as Treadway is an old Maryland name it can be assumed that his spelling is the correct one. Marshe, "Journal," 201.

14. The War of Jenkin's Ear which broke out between England and Spain in 1739 was, in 1744, about to merge with the Anglo-French struggle known as King George's War. The impression usually given in the history texts that this struggle affected the colonists very little finds no support from Dr. Hamilton, who found not only a lively interest everywhere on his tour but considerable apprehension of French attacks on the colonies.

15. A crowd is a Celtic musical instrument resembling the violin but with six strings.

16. The Lower Susquehanna Ferry was at Havre de Grace. The boat was drawn across by means of ropes wound on capstans by blindfolded horses driven in a circle about an upright drum. There were many ferries across this river but this one, a link in the road between Philadelphia and the South, was the most frequented. Wilstach, *Tidewater Maryland,* 187.

17. Monocacy was a town on a creek of the same name which is a tributary of the Potomac in Frederick County, in what was then western Maryland.

18. As Dr. Hamilton traveled northward, he found abundant evidence of the ardor of "New Light" followers of the English evangelist, George Whitefield, who had arrived in Philadelphia in November of 1739 on the first of his visits to this country. Whitefield was responsible for "the first great and spontaneous movement in the history of the American people"—the Great Awakening—which aroused the fears and repugnance of "Old Lights," especially the Anglicans, Quakers, and Congregationalists.

19. Mr. B——r was William Baxter, a Virginian. A good account of the Principio Company is given by William G. Whitely in *Pennsylvania Magazine of History and Biography,* 11 (1887), 63-68, 190-98, 285-95.

20. Elk Ferry crossed the river at Head of Elk, the present Elkton, Maryland.

21. William Lily's (1468-1522) Latin grammar, revised by Erasmus, was universally used in the eighteenth century. Emile Légouis and Louis Cazamian, *A History of English Literature* (New York, 1929), 208.

22. Bohemia Manor was an estate in Cecil County, Maryland, on the Elk River which was originally granted to Augustine Herman in the seventeenth century. Donnell MacClure Owings, "Private Manors: An Edited List," in *Maryland Hist. Mag.,* 33 (1938), 332.

23. The Reverend William Wye of St. Mary Anne Parish, Cecil County, Maryland, whom Hamilton identifies on his return trip. George Johnson, *History of Cecil County, Maryland* (Elkton, 1881), 18, 219.

24. Bohemia Ferry and Ferry House were at Bohemia Landing. Gould, "Money and Transportation in Maryland," 128.

25. Newtown's name was officially changed to Chestertown in 1780. Writer's Program, Maryland, *Maryland, A Guide to the Old Line State* (New York, 1940), 367.

26. In 1727 a settled post was opened to the Eastern Shore by way of Newcastle. It went once a fortnight in the summer and once a month in the winter and tied in with the already established royal post between Virginia and Maryland which went through all the northern colonies bringing and forwarding letters between Boston and Williamsburg, Virginia, in four weeks. Scharf, *History of Maryland,* I, 362.

27. Captain Paul Binney of Boston, a well-known ship-owner and trader at the head of Chesapeake Bay. *Maryland Hist. Mag.,* 26 (1931), 342.

28. William Alexander, a Scotsman, married the widow of Ephraim A. Herman, descendant of the founder of Bohemia Manor. In 1742, Mr. Alexander joined Col. Thomas Colville, Zebulon Hollingsworth, and five others to found Charles Town at Long Point on the west bank of North East River. Johnson, *History of Cecil County, Maryland,* 174; *Archives of Maryland,* 42, pp. 616-24.

29. Miss Coursey is identified by Hamilton when he visits Bohemia Manor on his return trip. See p. 195 and n. 388.

30. In February 1714/15, Ephraim Herman sold a tract, St. Augustine's Manor in present Kent County, Delaware, to Matthias Van Bibber of Cecil County, Maryland. Owings, "Private Manors: An Edited List," 334.

31. The Hollingsworths were a prominent family at Head of Elk, and one of them kept a famous tavern which stood on the main road, what would now be West Main Street, west of Bridge Street in Elkton. Writers' Program, Maryland, *Maryland, A Guide to the Old Line State,* 320.

32. A decade prior to 1744, tobacco culture had given way in Cecil County to the growing of wheat and corn for the Philadelphia market. Gould, "Economic Causes of the Rise of Baltimore," 227, 232*n.*

33. Delaware was not a part of Pennsylvania as Hamilton thought; it was a separate colony, although often referred to as "The Three Lower Counties." The Penns, as proprietors, chose one governor to rule both Pennsylvania and Delaware.

34. Newcastle was the oldest town in the Delaware Valley; it was the capital of the Lower Counties and, next to Philadelphia, the principal port of entry for the Scotch-Irish. Its population was possibly 1500 at the time of Hamilton's visit. Wayland F. Dunaway, *The Scotch-Irish of Colonial Pennsylvania* (Chapel Hill, 1944), 44.

35. The Indian King was a tavern on the up-river side of the town. Later the same structure was known as the Ship Tavern, and the site is now referred to as the old Stage Tavern. Federal Writers' Project, Delaware, *Newcastle on the Delaware* (Wilmington, 1937), 88.

36. Newcastle had an architectural style of its own, the houses facing each other across the green, which was laid out by Peter Stuyvesant, or along the Strand facing the river. Philadelphia imperialism had not yet affected the village. That it had is stated by Thomas J. Wertenbaker, *The Founding of America Civilization: The Middle Colonies* (New York, 1938), 253. Federal Writers' Project, Delaware, *Delaware, A Guide to the First State* (New York, 1938), 232, 235.

37. The Newcastle courthouse, one of the oldest in America, was built in 1676; one addition had been made in 1708 before Hamilton viewed it; another in 1767. George F. Bennett, *Early Architecture of Delaware* (New York, 1932), 45.

38. Newcastle had two churches, but probably the one Hamilton referred to was the Anglican church which was completed about 1710. The Presbyterian church, erected in 1657, was one of the oldest of the Calvinist denomination in America. Federal Writers' Project, Delaware, *Delaware, A Guide to the First State*, 240, 242-43.

39. Sir Robert Walpole, principal minister of George II, who fell from power in 1742.

40. Hamilton here refers to the fabric, a kind of linen, and not to the place of origin.

41. The ferry crossed a little above the place where the river flows into the Delaware, just below Wilmington.

42. Founded by Andrew Justison and Thomas Willing, 1730-32, as a real estate speculation, Willington possessed only about fifteen or twenty houses by 1735 when William Shipley, "the Father of Wilmington," settled there and produced a boom by building a market-house, wharf, and brewery. It became a borough, known as *Wilmington,* in 1739. In 1744 William Black found the houses "large and well Built, and tho' an Infant place, . . . there are now upwards of one hundred and fifty Famlies [*ca.* 1000 people] in the town, chiefly Merchants and Mechanicks. There was several Ships and other small Vessels on the Stocks a Building, and several other Branches of Workmanship and Commerce seemed to go on Briskly." William Black, "Journal," *Pa. Mag. of Hist. and Biog.,* 1 (1877), 239, hereafter cited as Black, "Journal"; Ernest S. Griffiths, *A History of American City Government* (New York, 1938), 435-36,

439; Federal Writers' Project, Delaware, *Delaware, A Guide to the First State,* 267-68.

43. William Black, reporting more fully, wrote, "The Court House and Prison is two tolerably large Buildings of Stone; there are in Town a Church dedicated to St. Paul, the Congregation are after the manner of the Church of England; a Quaker Meeting and a Sweed's Church [Lutheran]." On Sunday he and his companions sampled the Anglican and Quaker worship before returning to "our Inn, where we had a very good dinner." Chester had received its borough charter in 1701, and in 1744 it consisted of about one hundred houses. Black, "Journal," 240; Evarts B. Greene and Virginia D. Harrington, *American Population before the Federal Census of 1790* (New York, 1931), 118.

44. The King's Highway had formerly by-passed Chester, but in 1701 the town ordered a bridge built over the river in order to bring traffic through the town. George Smith, *History of Delaware County, Pennsylvania* (Philadelphia, 1862), 212-13.

45. Although only a hamlet, Darby (as it is spelled and pronounced) enjoyed the singular distinction of a subscription library founded in 1743—one of the earliest in the colonies. In 1761 it contained three hundred and sixty volumes. E. V. Lamberton, "Colonial Libraries of Pennsylvania," in *Pa. Mag. of Hist.,* 42 (1918), 216.

46. The Darby road to Philadelphia ran northeast to Gray's Ferry. John T. Scharf and Thompson Westcott, *History of Philadelphia, 1609-1884* (Philadelphia, 1884), I, 10.

47. As early as 1733 The Three Tons was termed "an Old accustomed House." *American Weekly Mercury,* May 31, 1733.

48. Philadelphia was on the eve of a period of great civic development which, however, did not become visible for a number of years after Hamilton's visit. Many fine brick houses were being built alongside dilapidated structures remaining from pioneer days. Urban congestion was evident. Carl Bridenbaugh, *Cities in the Wilderness: The First Century of Urban Life in America, 1625-1742* (New York, 1938), 305-6, 317-18.

49. In James Porteus and his associates of the Carpenter's Company (1724) and several gentlemen amateurs, the city had a notable coterie of master builders and architects. The "State House,"

as Hamilton labelled it meaning the *Stadt House,* was actually the Court House, a typical English town hall on pillars with a market below. In A. B. Hart's edition of the *Itinerarium* the "State House" and "Assembly House" are erroneously said to be one and the same building; the picture of the building that faces page 21 is in reality the Court House. The "Assembly House" is known to most Americans today as Independence Hall, to Philadelphians as the State House. It had been designed by Speaker Andrew Hamilton, and was opened for use in 1735 although it was not completed until 1747. Bridenbaugh, *Cities in the Wilderness,* 149, 306-7.

50. The "great church in Second Street" was the Anglican Christ Church which William Black described as a "very stately Building, but it is not yet finished." Black, "Journal," 411.

51. Whitefield's Church, begun in 1740 for the great evangelist and intended for a charity school, fronted on Fourth Street. In 1743, a group of Presbyterians led by Gilbert Tennent used it for their services. The Academy, later the College, of Philadelphia which became the University of Pennsylvania, opened in this building on January 7, 1751. Carl and Jessica Bridenbaugh, *Rebels and Gentlemen: Philadelphia in the Age of Franklin* (New York, 1942), 41 and illustration facing p. 58; Edward P. Cheyney, *History of the University of Pennsylvania, 1740-1940* (Philadelphia, 1940), 24-26, 60.

52. William Hogarth's caricatures of Englishmen were tremendously popular in the colonies as well as in England.

53. William Alexander was appointed Collector of Customs of the Port of Philadelphia; he died in January, 1745. *Pennsylvania Gazette,* Jan. 22, 1744/5.

54. Philadelphians patronized at least two coffee houses in this period, James' Coffee House and Robert's Coffee House. *Pa. Gaz.,* June 21, Aug. 23, 1744.

55. Dr. Thomas Bond, born in Calvert County, Maryland, in 1712 (the same year as Dr. Hamilton) did not study under the Scottish physician as is usually asserted (cf. *Dictionary of American Biography,* II, 434), but with Dr. John Kearsley at Philadelphia in 1734 and later in London and Paris; Hamilton did not take his degree at Edinburgh until 1737. Bond's work in clinical medicine and his role as founder of the Pennsylvania Hospital made him one

of the foremost colonial physicians. He was a member of Franklin's abortive Philosophical Society of 1743 and was prominent in the founding of the American Philosophical Society in 1769. Bridenbaugh, *Rebels and Gentlemen*, 263-64, 271-75, 336-39; and portrait facing p. 275.

56. It was customary in these years for gentlemen who planned to stay in a town for any length of time to take lodgings where quiet and privacy were assured; they dined at taverns.

57. Probably Thomas Venables who, at his death in January, 1751, was buried at Christ Church. Charles R. Hildeburn, "Records of Christ Church, Philadelphia, Burials, 1709-60," *Pa. Mag. of Hist.*, 7 (1883), 226.

58. In spite of Venable's opinion of freemasons, many prominent Philadelphians from the former Mayor William Allen, who was grand master, to Benjamin Franklin were members of St. John's Lodge. As we have seen in the Introduction, Dr. Hamilton was master of the Masonic Lodge at Annapolis in 1749, if not earlier.

59. Samuel Hasell was criticized for being a lax magistrate, because he not only refused to take notice of a complaint made to him against a person guilty of profane swearing, but (at another time) set an evil example by swearing himself. Scharf and Westcott, *History of Philadelphia*, I, 212.

60. Ebenezer Currie advertised as a merchant on Front Street, *Pa. Gaz.*, Feb. 2, 1743/4.

61. Captain John Mackey was commander of the *Tartar*, a new ship of 300 tons, eighteen carriage and twenty swivel guns, and 130 men. At the Crown and Thistle on Front Street "all gentlemen Sailors and Others" were invited to sign for "the Cruise of a Privateering Voyage against his Majesty's Enemies." *Pa. Gaz.*, May 24, June 28, 1744.

62. Dr. Phineas Bond, a younger brother of Dr. Thomas Bond, studied medicine at London, Paris, and Edinburgh. He had a special interest in botany and became an intimate of J. F. Gronovius at Leyden. With his brother he was a trustee of the Academy and College and a member of the American Philosophical Society. Bridenbaugh, *Rebels and Gentlemen*, 267, 309-10.

63. The Old Tun Tavern, later in the 1750's known as

Peggy Mullen's Beefsteak House, on Water Street was the meeting place of the Governor's Club. Joseph Jackson, *Cyclopedia of Philadelphia* (Harrisburg, 1931-33), IV, 973-74.

64. Philadelphia had the best water supply of any of the colonial cities. Bridenbaugh, *Cities in the Wilderness*, 373-74.

65. As early as 1686 Robert Turner wrote: "Building goeth on. Now many brave Brick houses are going up, with good Cellars. . . . We build most Houses with Balconies." *Ibid.*, 10.

66. William Black penned a charming description of activities on a market day during his visit to Philadelphia that summer. The market stalls extended from the rear of the Court House one whole block down the middle of High (or Market) Street. Black, "Journal," 405.

67. The "Great Meeting House" of the Quakers was located at Second and High Streets, across from the Court House, and an earlier structure was situated on the river bank at Front and Sassafras Streets. These were probably the ones Hamilton refers to, for a third was at Center Square, the present Penn Square, which was remote from the center of the city's activities at that time. Bridenbaugh, *Cities in the Wilderness*, 261; Scharf and Westcott, *History of Philadelphia*, II, 1242.

68. On Sunday, June 3, William Black wrote, "most of our young Company went . . . to Visit the Reverend Mr. Gilbert Tennent, a Disciple of the Great Whitefield, whose followers are Call'd the New Lights; we found him Delivering his Doctrine with a very Good Grace, Split his Text as Judiciously, turn'd up the Whites of his Eyes as Theologically, Cuff'd his Cushion as Orthodoxly, and twisted his Band as Primitively as his Master Whitefield could have done, had he been there himself." Black, "Journal," 412.

69. St. Joseph's Roman Catholic Church was founded in 1732 and was located in Willing's Alley. Cheyney, *History of the University of Pennsylvania*, 10.

70. The Baptist Church was erected in 1731 at Second and Mulberry Streets. Scharf and Westcott, *History of Philadelphia*, II, 1306.

71. For some time prior to 1704 the Presbyterians had joined with the Baptists in the use of a small store, but in that year they erected their first church, a small structure on Market Street which

was called "Old Butternut" from the trees that surrounded it. By 1744 the Presbyterians were on the way to becoming the most numerous religious denomination in the city, and Philadelphia was soon the colonial capital of Presbyterianism. A new Meeting House was going up at the northwest corner of Third and Arch Streets, and some Presbyterians, as has already been stated, were using the Whitefield church. Scharf and Westcott, *History of Philadelphia,* II, 856; Watson, *Annals of Philadelphia,* I, 448, 450.

72. George Thomas of Antigua was appointed governor in 1737. He immediately became involved in a losing contest with the pro-Quaker Assembly over the issue of paper money, and, when the war broke out, the matter of local defense. Conversely his conduct of Indian Affairs was highly successful. *Dict. of Amer. Biog.,* XVIII, 431.

73. In 1747 Benjamin Franklin succeeded in organizing an "Association" for defense. Carl Van Doren, *Benjamin Franklin* (New York, 1938), 184-86.

74. Dr. Hamilton went to Philadelphia, in fact took his entire journey, at the time that the Great Awakening was at its peak; hence his generalizations on the life of the times, like the comments of all travelers, fail to take such transient conditions into account.

75. Colonel Thomas Lee, President of the Council of Virginia, William Beverley, and six commissioners were appointed by Governor Gooch of Virginia to treat with the Six Nations at Lancaster. William Black, their secretary, kept a gossipy journal which has been quoted in these notes.

76. Henry Fielding's parody of Samuel Richardson's *Pamela* was published in England in 1742, just two years before Hamilton's tour.

77. Dr. William Salmon (1644-1713) wrote several well-received medical treatises, especially *The Compleat English Physician* (London, 1693).

78. The Lutheran Church, which had been built just one year previous to Hamilton's arrival in Philadelphia, was at the corner of Appletree Alley on Fifth Street. The Reverend Heinrich M. Muhlenberg was the minister. Watson, *Annals of Philadelphia,* I, 451.

79. Dr. Lloyd Zachary was an eminently successful physician.

Born in London, he came to this country at a very early age. After an academic course, he "was placed under Dr. Kearsley for professional training" and then spent three years abroad. He began practice about 1723. He was the health officer of the Port of Philadelphia and in charge of sick Palatines. Scharf and Westcott, *History of Philadelphia*, II, 1580.

80. France declared war against England on March 15, and England declared war against France on March 29, 1744. *Pa. Gaz.*, May 24, 1744.

81. Richard Peters, a former clergyman, was at this time a politician serving the Proprietary as secretary of Pennsylvania. With Benjamin Franklin he was one of the principal founders of the College of Philadelphia. Hubertis Cummings, *Richard Peters* (Philadelphia, 1944).

82. The Governor's speech is printed in the *Pa. Gaz.*, June 14, 1744.

83. This expedition of 1741, ambitiously planned by the English and enthusiastically entered into by the colonists, bogged down and was productive chiefly of bitterness by colonial scribes. Herbert L. Osgood, *The American Colonies in the Eighteenth Century* (New York, 1924), III, 497-501.

84. Charles Calvert, fifth Lord Baltimore, proprietor of Maryland.

85. If Hamilton had attended church he might have joined William Black in his comments: "I was not a little Surpris'd to see such a Number of Fine Women in Church. . . . I must say, since I have been in America, I have not seen so fine a Collection at one time and Place." Black, "Journal," 411.

86. Mr. Currie has already been mentioned. John Wallace was a merchant, and soon to join with three other "Directors" in founding the famous Philadelphia Dancing Assembly in the winter of 1748/9. *Pa. Gaz.*, Feb. 2, 1743/4; Thomas W. Balch, *The Philadelphia Assemblies* (Philadelphia, 1916), 18, 22, 24.

87. The famous "Log College," founded by the elder William Tennent to train "New Side" Presbyterian ministers, was located on this stream not far from where Hamilton crossed it. A. V. Alexander, *Biographical Sketches of the Founder and Principal Alumni of the Log College* (Princeton, 1845).

88. James Birket, traveling through Pennsylvania in 1750, wrote "Bristol has the name of a City but in England would make but a poor village." Ten years later, however, a mineral spring development made it one of the greatest watering places in America. James Birket, *Some Cursory Remarks* (New Haven, 1916), 69; Carl Bridenbaugh, "Baths and Watering Places of Colonial America," *William and Mary Quarterly*, 3d ser., 3 (1946), 167-71.

89. In 1744 three people are listed as licensed to keep a tavern in Bristol Borough, but the only one whose name resembles that of Hamilton's host at the Sign of the Crown was Malachi White. William W. H. Davis, *The History of Bucks County, Pennsylvania* (Doylestown, 1876), 836.

90. The Delaware Ferry at Trenton was run by John Williams. *Pa. Gaz.*, May 19, 1744.

91. This house near Trenton, belonging to Governor Thomas of Pennsylvania, was built about 1719 by Chief Justice William Trent of New Jersey, for whom the town was named. The mill was on the same property which was conveyed by his son, James, to William Morris who in turn transferred it to Governor Thomas in 1733. Trenton Historical Society, *A History of Trenton, 1674-1929* (Princeton, 1929), I, 40, 293.

92. Governor Lewis Morris (1671-1746), a talented but contentious individual, had been first Lord of the Manor in Morrisania, New York. He was the first governor of New Jersey after its separation from New York in 1738. *Dict. of Amer. Biog.*, XIII, 213-14.

93. James Birket also stayed at Bond's and, referring to the innkeeper as a fellow Englishman, declared that he probably came from Cockram near Lancaster, and that Mrs. Bond came from Warrington. An advertisement of 1745 calls Bond Elisha, but one of 1748 refers to Elijah. Birket, *Some Cursory Remarks*, 50; *Pa. Gaz.*, April 4, 1745, April 16, 1748.

94. Dr. Thomas Cadwalader, graduate of Rheims, was an outstanding Quaker physician and public figure. He served as burgess of Trenton, founded its library, became a manager of the Pennsylvania Hospital, and was a trustee of the College of Philadelphia. He owned a large estate near Trenton and lived on Queen Street. Bridenbaugh, *Rebels and Gentlemen*, 267-68; *Pa. Gaz.*, Feb. 2, 1742/3, Aug. 9, 1750.

95. Dr. Adam Thomson was a fellow-student of Hamilton in the Medical School at Edinburgh. See the Introduction for further details.

96. Princeton did not become an important community until the College of New Jersey was moved there during the following decade.

97. *How' s't ni tap* is commonly written *nehotep.*

98. James Leonard of Kingston advertised that he was handling subscriptions for John Dalley's road maps. *Pa. Gaz.,* Sept. 12, 1745.

99. Kingston, New Jersey, half way between New York and Philadelphia, was the place where the post riders exchanged mail with those coming from the other direction, rested, and returned whence they came. Federal Writers' Project, New Jersey, *Old Princeton's Neighbors* (Princeton, 1939), 91.

100. Virginia's commissioners and the Governor of Pennsylvania met with the Indians at Lancaster. *Pa. Gaz.,* June 21, 1744. See Paul A. W. Wallace's *Conrad Weiser* (Philadelphia, 1945) for a discussion of the meeting.

101. This type of wagon was used in what was perhaps the earliest long-distance stage-line in America. Trips from Trenton to New Brunswick were running in the summer of 1738. *Pa. Gaz.,* April 10, 1740.

102. When New Brunswick received its charter in 1730, it consisted of about 125 families. Federal Writers' Project, New Jersey, *New Jersey, A Guide to Its Present and Past* (New York, 1939), 299.

103. Paul Miller's tavern was on "Burnett's Street," the most public part of town. *New York Weekly Post-Boy,* Sept. 25, 1749.

104. Dr. William Farquhar, a "physician of great repute," practiced in New Jersey but spent much time in New York. E. Alfred Jones, "The Loyalists of New Jersey in the Revolution," New Jersey Historical Society, *Proceedings,* new ser., 3 (1918), 291; *Pa. Gaz.,* March 16, 1746/7.

105. The Raritan was always forded at New Brunswick until 1697 when John Inian established the ferry there. William A Whitehead, *Contributions to the Early History of Perth Amboy* (New York, 1856), 271.

106. Perth Amboy was not as old as Hamilton asserted, for it was not founded until 1684, about fifty years later than New

York. With Burlington, in West New Jersey, it shared prestige as the capital of the province in alternate years. Birket, *Some Cursory Remarks,* 48.

107. Birket reported a "Courthouse, a Goal, An Episcopal Church, A Presbyterian Meeting house And a pretty Market house but [I] believe but little use for it; I do imagine the Plan of this City has been laid out very regular by the Appearance of Some part of it being So thin Built and the houses and Gardens etc. So intersperst that its hard for a Stranger to form a Notion how the Streets ought to run, however the Houses that are Built are tollerable good and I imagine about 70 or 80 in Number." *Ibid.,* 48.

108. There was such a diversity or religious sects in Perth Amboy in its early days that no one clergyman was ever acceptable to all the settlers. It was not until the 1730's that permission was granted to erect a Presbyterian meeting on State, formerly Back, Street. Whitehead, *Contributions to the Early History of Perth Amboy,* 241.

109. See *ibid.,* 271-72, for a discussion of the ferries at Perth Amboy.

110. Cuckold's Town was the former name of Richmond on Staten Island. Ira K. Morris, *Morris's Memorial History of Staten Island, New York* (New York, 1898-1900), I, 298.

111. Woodbridge actually lies across Arthur Kill in New Jersey.

112. The Narrows Ferry was operated by Jacob Corsen. Isaac N. P. Stokes, *Iconography of Manhatten Island* (New York, 1915-28), IV, 622.

113. Better known as the Brooklyn Ferry, this was a monopoly of the Corporation of New York, and was under lease to Richard Baker. Arthur E. Peterson and George W. Edwards, *New York as an Eighteenth Century Municipality* (New York, 1917), 380.

114. The Cart and Horse was a popular tavern on what is now William Street between John and Fulton. Birket said it "prov'd to be very bad lodgings altho' 'tis a house much used." "Old Taverns of New York," *Journal of American History,* 18 (1924), 129; Birket, *Some Cursory Remarks,* 40.

115. William Jamison, High Sheriff. New York (City) Common Council, *Minutes* (New York, 1905), V, 99, 123.

116. Dr. Alexander Colchoun's chief claim to fame seems to

have been that he was stabbed and killed in a drunken brawl in June, 1749, by Oliver de Lancey. Stokes, *Iconography*, IV, 616.

117. Robert Todd's establishment (the present 101 Broad Street), next door to the coffee house, was frequented by the Governor and his friends and was the scene of many political conferences, concerts, and banquets. In 1730 it became the starting point for the Boston post. Stokes, *Iconography*, IV, 10, 531; George F. Marlowe, *Coaching Roads of Old New England, Their Inns and Their Stories* (New York, 1945), 118.

118. Archibald Home was also a member of the Council of New Jersey and a member of Franklin's American Philosophical Society of 1744. He seems to have died prior to August 10, 1744, when the *Pennsylvania Gazette* carried a poem in his memory. Cf. *New Jersey Archives*, 1st ser., 12, pp. 154-55n.

119. King George II of England and the governors of New York and Maryland.

120. The residence of Mrs. Robert Hogg was at the corner of Broad and William Streets. Martha J. Lamb, *History of the City of New York* (New York, 1877-96), II, 581.

121. New York houses were often four or five stories high, and most travelers, including Birket, commented that the gable ends faced the street. Birket, *Some Cursory Remarks*, 43-44.

122. Trinity Church (Anglican) was burned in 1776; a newer edifice today occupies the same site.

123. The old Dutch church was on Garden Street; the New Dutch Church, as it was then called, which had been erected in the years 1727-31 was on the northeast corner of Nassau and Crown (now Liberty) Streets. Stokes, *Iconography*, I, 251, 262.

124. This was the second city hall, or town house, erected in 1700 at the corner of Broad and Wall Streets where the old Sub-Treasury now stands.

125. The New York Exchange was at the lower end of Broad Street. Stokes, *Iconography*, IV, 602.

126. See below, p. 178 and n. 371.

127. Lambert Moore. Stokes, *Iconography*, IV, 582.

128. Thomas Jefferys. Common Council, *Minutes*, IV, 226.

129. Trinity church organ was built by John Klem of Philadelphia. A letter had been written to London in December, 1743,

for an organist, but none had arrived. Morgan Dix, ed., *A History of the Parish of Trinity Church in New York* (New York, 1898-1906), I, 98.

130. On Saturday, September 29, "His Excellency, our Governor, was pleas'd to appoint Stephen Byard, Esq; to be Mayor of this City in the room of the Honr. John Cruger, Esq; deceased." *New York Gazette,* Oct. 1, 1744.

131. There were at least two well-known coffee houses at this time. The Exchange Coffee House was on the northwest corner of Broad and Water Streets, and the Merchants Coffee House was at Wall and Water Streets. Stokes, *Iconography,* IV, 509, 607.

132. *The Journal of Proceedings in the Detection of the Conspiracy Formed by Some White People in Connection with Negro and Other Slaves* was written by Daniel Horsmanden, Recorder of the City of New York. This attempt to justify the hysterical measures taken against the so-called "Negro Plot" of 1741, and to arouse the citizens of Manhattan to the need for better regulation of blacks, was published in New York in 1744 just prior to Hamilton's arrival. As Robert Hogg's house had been robbed at the outset of the "conspiracy," it is quite possible that Hamilton found a copy there or was encouraged to buy one by the Hoggs' account of the incident.

133. The Reverend John Milne from 1728 to 1737 was the rector of St. Peter's church in Albany and subsequently at Shrewsbury in New Jersey. *Pa. Gaz.,* Oct. 27, 1743.

134. Mrs. Milne had been previously married to Killian Van Rensselaer and was the mother of Jeremiah Van Rensselaer. Thomas A. Glenn, ed., *Some Colonial Mansions and Those Who Lived in Them* (Philadelphia, 1898), I, 166.

135. Nutting Island was an old name for Governor's Island. John M. Hammond, *Quaint and Historic Forts of North America* (Philadelphia, 1915), 37.

136. William Cosby arrived in 1732. It was he who quarreled with John Peter Zenger and brought on the famous libel suit involving the freedom of the press. Cosby had a reputation for excessive profanity and violence. *Dict. of Amer. Biog.,* IV, 459.

137. Rip Van Dam, a prominent merchant and principal political opponent of Governor Cosby. *Ibid.,* XIX, 166.

138. Oliver de Lancey's house fronted on the Hudson near 34th Street. Lamb, *History of New York,* II, pt. 2, 88.

139. Anthony Van Leeuwenhoek (1632-1723), eminent Dutch student of natural history and inventor of the microscope.

140. The following item, taken from a London newspaper of September 20, 1738, was published in Philadelphia: Sept. 12, "died, Dr. Herman Boerhaave, the famous and learned Professor of Physick at Leyden, aged 69, much celebrated and consulted from all Parts of Europe." *Pa. Gaz.,* Jan. 18, 1738/9.

141. Philipse Manor was a conspicuous landmark, situated on a hill in Yonkers, commanding a view of the traffic passing up and down the Hudson. Edward H. Hall, *Philipse Manor Hall at Yonkers, New York* (New York, 1912), 76.

142. Dunderbarrack, or Dunderberg, or Thunder Hill: a mountain on the west bank of the Hudson opposite Peekskill. It forms the west side of the gateway to the Highlands, the name given to that district of the Hudson River from Peekskill to Cornwall. *The New York Tourist* (New York, 1842), 18.

143. St. Anthony's Nose: a mass of rocks on the eastern shore of the Hudson River where the present Bear Mountain Bridge crosses. Nelson Greene, *History of the Valley of the Hudson, River of Destiny, 1609-1930* (Chicago, 1931), I, 68.

144. There had been a legend about Doepper's, now Pollopel's Island, that when a ship came down the river and passed it, old skippers had a habit of christening new hands by sousing them in the current. By Hamilton's time the crew had learned to turn the tale to their own advantage. Clifton Johnson, *The Picturesque Hudson* (New York, 1909), 147.

145. Butter Mountain, now known as Storm King, is a few miles below Newburgh. *New York State Tourist,* 29.

146. Moodna Creek, formerly called Murderer's Creek, joins the Hudson between Canterbury and New Windsor. *Ibid.,* 29.

147. Dancing Hall is opposite Carthage. Wallace Bruce, *The Hudson River by Daylight* (New York, 1873), 49.

148. Navigators once divided the Hudson into fourteen "Reaches." *Ibid.,* 20.

149. Bruce relates that there were forty different ways of spelling Poughkeepsie, and that each year the Post Office had a new

one. The first house in the town was built in 1702 by one Van Kleek. *Ibid.,* 51.

150. Count Nikolaus Ludwig von Zinzendorf, founder of the Moravian Church in this country, traveled in America in the years 1741-43. Contrary to Hamilton's views, the Moravian Church required a high standard of Christian conduct and a strict discipline of its members. *Dict. of Amer. Biog.,* XX, 657-58.

151. Sopus Village: The name "Esopus" was once applied to the whole district of which Kingston is the center—the hills on the west and the island opposite. Esopus Creek empties into the Hudson River twenty miles north at Saugerties. Rondout Creek, which flows in at Kingston, used to be called Little Esopus. Ernest Ingersoll, *Rand McNally & Co.'s Illustrated Guide to the Hudson River and the Catskill Mountains* (Chicago, 1893), 141.

152. A conference of commissioners from Massachusetts, Connecticut, and New York to discuss a program for defense against the French. Osgood, *American Colonies in the Eighteenth Century,* III, 391.

153. Ancram, which was named in honor of the parish in Scotland where his grandfather had labored so long, was at this time occupied by Robert R. Livingston. It was built in 1730 near the water's edge in the southwest part of Livingston Manor. The family regarded the name as too ambitious for a second son and it was therefore changed to Claremont, and eventually Clermont. Edwin B. Livingston, *The Livingstons of Livingston Manor* (New York, 1910), 145, 475.

154. The name Rhinebeck was derived from the Rhine and Beekman, the original proprietor. It is opposite Kingston. *New York State Tourist,* 36.

155. This was the older Livingston Manor built by the first Lord of the Manor in 1699. Livingston, *Livingstons of Livingston Manor,* 483.

156. This was the locale of the Mahicans, a confederacy of the Algonquin stock, although the council fire had been moved from Schodac, near Albany, to Stockbridge, Massachusetts.

157. Charles de la Boische, Marquis de Beauharnois, Governor of New France, 1726-47.

158. Stephen Van Rensselaer became patroon in 1745 upon the death of Jeremiah. Glenn, *Some Colonial Mansions*, I, 156.

159. The Cohoes Falls are at the junction of the Mohawk and Hudson Rivers.

160. The Reverend Henry Barclay was a native of Albany. After graduating from Yale in 1734, and then receiving orders in England, he spent a number of years in the Mohawk country. In 1746 he went to Trinity in New York City as rector. Lamb, *Hist. of New York*, I, 585.

161. "Col. Skuyler" might have been either John Schuyler, who treated with the Indians and who died in 1747, or Peter, John's brother, who was reputed to have almost unbounded control over them. Glenn, *Some Colonial Mansions*, II, 77, 412, 414.

162. Probably Philip Livingston, who succeeded to the office of Secretary of Indian Affairs upon his father's death. *Ibid.*, I, 308.

163. John Collins who married Margaret Schuyler. *Ibid.*, II, 411.

164. Cornelius Cuyler, mayor of Albany, 1742-46. Joel Munsell, *The Annals of Albany* (Albany, 1850-59), V, 102.

165. The Albany Town House was on the northeast corner of Hudson Street and Broadway (then called Market Street). It burned in 1836. *Albany's Tercentenary* (Albany, 1924), 96-97.

166. A pass in Scotland where troops of William III were met by Scottish troops under Viscount Dundee in 1689. His death in the battle resulted shortly in the dissolution of the Scottish forces. John R. Green, *A Short History of the English People* (New York, 1894), IV, 1496.

167. Dirk Ten Broeck was the first of the family to be mentioned in the public records. He was mayor of Albany in 1747. His son married Elizabeth Van Rensselaer, sister of Stephen. Gorham A. Worth, *Random Recollections of Albany* (Albany, 1866), 44n; Munsell, *Annals of Albany*, V, 102.

168. Canso, an English outpost on the gut between Nova Scotia and Cape Breton, had been surprised and taken by the French on May 13, 1744, before news of the war with France had reached Boston. Thomas Hutchinson, *The History of the Colony and Province of Massachusetts-Bay* (Cambridge, Mass., 1936), II, 309.

169. The English Church was St. Peter's, erected in 1714 on State Street. Worth, *Random Recollections of Albany*, 39n.

170. Thomas Blood and several accomplices failed in an attempt to steal the crown jewels from the Tower of London in 1671. His pardon has always remained a mystery. An Edmund Blood was a resident of Albany in the first years of the eighteenth century and was, according to tradition, a grandson. Wilbur C. Abbott, *Conflicts with Oblivion* (Cambridge, Mass., 1935), 13, 147.

171. Namur was a citadel in the Netherlands which William III lost to the French in 1692. The French under the Duke of Berwick decisively defeated the English and their allies at Almanza, Spain, in 1707.

172. Probably Daniel Dulany, who was to be Hamilton's father-in-law.

173. Charles Rollin (1661-1741) was a French author of historical and other works, whose books enjoyed a great popularity in English translations. His *Ancient History* was perhaps best known. The volume Hamilton was reading was the *Method of Teaching and Studying the Belles Lettres, or an Introduction to Languages, Poetry, Rhetorick, History, Moral Philosophy, Physicks, &c., By Mr. Rollin,* the second edition of which was published at London in 1737.

174. A bar or obstruction to navigation near Castleton.

175. The fort at Albany was built in 1623.

176. The Reformed Dutch church was built in 1715, on the site of an earlier one, at the corner of State Street and Broadway. It was of heavy stone with high windows and a raised platform along each side originating from the days when the church was to be defended against Indian attacks. Worth, *Random Recollections of Albany*, 28n.

177. Dr. Hamilton often became confused over the various religious denominations. Here he probably means the Reformed Dutch or Calvinist faith and not the Lutheran.

178. Captain Edward Tyng, commander of the Province Snow, was thanked by the Town of Boston on June 26, 1744 "for the great Service he has done in taking and bringing in" a sixteen gun French privateer sloop from Cape Breton, commanded by "Capt.

Delabroitz and manned by ninety-four Men. . . ." Boston Record Commissioners, "Boston Town Records, 1742-1757," *Fourteenth Report* (Boston, 1885), 56.

179. Kinderhook was settled by the Dutch and Swedes. It was originally called Children's Point from the number of children that belonged to a Swedish family living there. *New York State Tourist,* 48.

180. The privateer, *Tartar,* commanded by Captain Mackey, sailed down Delaware Bay on July 1 and was overset in a sudden squall under Cape Henlopen. Mackey, the officers and most of the crew were saved. It was believed that the ship was badly ballasted and over-masted. Howard M. Chapin, *Privateering in King George's War, 1739-1748* (Providence, 1928), 189-90.

181. Daniel Horsmanden, author of the *Journal of Proceedings.* Common Council, *Minutes,* V, 99.

182. Oliver de Lancey was a famous soldier who became a Loyalist during the Revolution. *Dict. of Amer. Biog.,* V, 214.

183. Governor George Clinton, colonial governor of New York. He arrived in New York in September, 1743. *Ibid.,* IV, 225.

184. Possibly Henry Laughton who became Clerk of the Market in Boston in 1750-51. Boston Record Commissioners, "Boston Town Records, 1742-1757," 191.

185. John Hamilton, the son of former Governor Andrew Hamilton, was prominent in New Jersey political affairs and became governor in 1746. John O. Raum, *The History of New Jersey from its Earliest Settlement to the Present Time* (Philadelphia, 1877), I, 157, 225.

186. John Watts was one of New York's foremost merchants, a member of the Assembly, and a brother-in-law of Oliver de Lancey. *Dict. of Amer. Biog.,* V, 247.

187. Abraham de Peyster, Treasurer of the Colony. *Ibid.,* V, 247.

188. Dr. James McGraw, McGraa, or McGrath, began to practice in New York in 1740 and soon came to be regarded as one of its best physicians, notwithstanding, his austere manner and "original views." James G. Wilson, *Memorial History of New York* (New York, 1892-93), IV, 390-91.

189. That Commodore Peter Warren did make a large fortune

is evidenced by his building one of the handsomest houses in New York at No. 1 Broadway in 1745, and by his elaborate estate near Greenwich Village. He was reputed to have gained $2,000,000 in prize money. Arthur Pound, *Johnson of the Mohawks* (New York, 1930), 21.

190. Dr. Jean Astruc (1684-1766) taught medicine at the University of Paris. Among his best known medical studies was A Treatise on Venereal Diseases (1736), which circulated in manuscript. Preserved Smith, *History of Modern Culture* (New York, 1934), II, 118-19.

191. A visitor of some ten years later spoke of "Houses on one Story and a stoop to each, a roof longer than the Stud, Odd appearance." Samuel Curwen, "Journal of a Journey from Salem to Philadelphia in 1755," Essex Institute, *Historical Collections,* 52 (1916), 52, 78.

192. For fifty years after its founding, the Presbyterian was the only church in Jamaica. In 1702 a Reformed Dutch congregation was formed but the church was not built on the south side of Fulton Street until 1715. Grace Church (Anglican) was erected in 1734. Benjamin F. Thompson, *History of Long Island* (New York, 1839), 387, 391-92, 395.

193. Peters is the name of an old family in Hempstead, but the public house referred to must have been the Pettit Tavern at the Sign of the Guy of Warwick. Bernice Schultz, *Colonial Hempstead* (Lynbrook, N. Y., 1937), 24, 245.

194. Hempstead Plain was a prairie in the middle of a forest which served as an admirable grazing area for cattle. Ralph H. Gabriel, *The Evolution of Long Island* (New Haven, 1921), 30.

195. The first edifice of the Church of England on Long Island was that at Brookhaven, erected in 1730. Martha B. Flint, *Early Long Island* (New York, 1896), 258.

196. Curwen speaks of stopping on the eighteenth stage of his journey with Captain Hubbard, the Southold collector. Curwen, "Journal," 77.

197. Southold was settled by people from New Haven and was one of the oldest settlements on Long Island. Epher Whitaker, "The Early History of Southold, Long Island," New Haven Historical Society, *Papers,* 2 (1877), 2.

198. Oyster Pond was really a peninsula on the easternmost extremity of the North Fork of Long Island where the town of Orient now stands. Thompson, *History of Long Island*, 245.

199. "Quevedo's Visions" was one of the novels of the Spaniard Francesco Gomes de Quevedo y Villegas (1560-1645).

200. Gardiner's Island was purchased from the Indians in 1639 by Lion Gardiner, who named it Isle of Wight, but even before Hamilton's visit it had come to be known as Gardiner's Island.

201. In the *Vade Mecum for America: Or a Companion for Traders and Travellers*, 302, published at Boston in 1732, Deshon's was listed as the public house in New London.

202. "New London is the Capital of the County of that name And pleasantly Scituated upon the river about 5 miles from the Sea (or more properly the Sound that lyes between long Island And the Continent) And is Navigable for vessels that draw 20 foot water (or any vessels whatever) there is but few vessels belonging to this port which are Chiefly in the west india trade, But as it is one of the Chiefe ports in Connecticut Government Many vessels that are Owned in Other parts of the Government come here to Clear out and go under the Name of New Londonery, They have Some very good wharfs here which their vessels lay along Side of to load or discharge; The town Seems to Improve by the Appearance of their houses many of which Appear New and Neat all built of wood and Consists of one Street about A mile long by the riverside, Altho upon the Bank which is of a Moderate height and as Several lots on that Side the Street are not built it affords a fine prospect over the river and the Adjaient Country." Birket, *Some Cursory Remarks*, 33-34.

203. Captain Morpain, or "Morpang," was one of the most famous and feared of the French-Canadian privateersmen. He was said to have been in reality an Irishman named Murphy. Chapin, *Privateering in King George's War*, 45.

204. By 1750 Williams had been promoted to colonel. A dinner of salt pork, turnips, and thick cider led James Birket to record his disapproval of the "entertainment So Called." Birket, *Some Cursory Remarks*, 33.

205. The *Vade Mecum,* 202, lists Thompson's as one of the two public houses at Westerly.

206. The original spelling of Noyes. Margaret Allis, *Historic Connecticut* (New York, 1934), 136.

207. George Ninigret, or Charles, as Ezra Stiles recorded, was the sachem of the remnant of the once powerful tribe of Narragansetts. "The King or Sachem has an English House built on the Road," Stiles continues, adding that after 1752 there were no longer any wigwams in the Narragansett Country. Franklin B. Dexter, ed., *The Itineraries and other Miscellanies of Ezra Stiles* (New Haven, 1916), 108, 144.

208. Squire Hill's at Charlestown, R. I. Birket, *Some Cursory Remarks,* 32.

209. Block Island was named for Adrian Block, Dutch navigator—one of earliest explorers of Narragansett Bay. Edward Peterson, *History of Rhode Island and Providence Plantations* (New York, 1853), 65.

210. Conanicut, the island on which the present Jamestown is situated.

211. Robert Case's dwelling was on the southerly side of the road leading down the east slope of Tower Hill from the Post Road. Birket said it was "reckon'd one of the best houses of Entertainment in the Government." William D. Miller, "The Removal of the County Seat from Tower Hill to Little Rest, 1752," Rhode Island Historical Society, *Collections,* 13 (1920), 11*n;* Birket, *Some Cursory Remarks,* 31.

212. The *History of the Nine Worthies of the World* (London, 1687) was written by Robert, or Richard, Burton, a publisher who compiled numerous little books which sold for a shilling and had great popularity. *Dictionary of National Biography,* II, 15.

213. To cross over Narragansett Bay from South County to Newport it was necessary to take two ferries. The first was the Narragansett Ferry, which crossed from the mainland to Conanicut Island; the second connected Conanicut with Newport on the island of Rhode Island. There were in 1744 four ferries plying between Conanicut and Newport, two from each side. Caleb Carr and Benjamin Ellery operated the ferries from the Newport side.

Anna A. and Charles V. Chapin, *History of Rhode Island Ferries, 1640-1923* (Providence, 1925), 1-7.

214. Rose Island, so-called from the abundance of wild roses which once grew on the place. Peterson, *History of Rhode Island*, 37.

215. Newport market house which Hamilton saw was built in 1732 "at head of the Dock between the Carr and Tillinghast wharves," close to the Ferry. There was an older one at the foot of King Street, Bridenbaugh, *Cities in the Wilderness*, 351.

216. The Town House, or Colony House as it was actually called, was built facing the Parade, 1739-41, after plans drawn by Richard Munday, skilled master-builder of Newport. At the time of its completion it was one of the handsomest and finest public buildings in the English colonies. *Ibid.*, illustration p. 236, 311.

217. Being unacquainted with New England church polity, Hamilton always calls a Congregational church Presbyterian. Newport's Congregational church, the first in Rhode Island, was organized in 1720 by the Reverend Nathaniel Clapp, and in 1728 the second church was founded. *Boston News Letter*, Nov. 7, 1720; Bridenbaugh, *Cities in the Wilderness*, 419.

218. When the Meeting House was built on Marlborough Street in 1700, the Society of Friends included nearly half of the population of Newport. *Ibid.*, 104, 265.

219. There were, at this time, actually two Baptist churches: the regular Baptists, founded in 1639 and the oldest religious society in Newport; and the Seventh Day Baptists, formed in 1671, the interior of whose church is now preserved in the Newport Historical Society. This church was one of the loveliest in the colonies.

220. Trinity, one of the most impressive Anglican churches in America, was completed in 1726 by Richard Munday, leading colonial builder-architect, who appears to have adapted plans of Christ Church, Boston, and Wren's St. Andrew-by-the-Wardrobe, London, for his interior. The clock, which Hamilton mentions, was made by the famous clockmaker of Newport, William Claggett, and the organ was the gift of Dean George Berkeley. Norman M. Isham, *Trinity Church in Newport, Rhode Island; a History of the Fabric* (Boston, 1936), 38, 44, 58; George C. Mason, *Annals of Trinity Church, Newport, Rhode Island, 1698-1821* (Newport, 1890), 58n, 61n.

221. Captain John Griffiths of the privateer *Caesar* arrived on July 8 with a rich prize, the snow *Senora de la Rosara,* 200 tons, Captain Juan Gonsales de Valdez. Her cargo consisted of 150 tons of cocoa, 10,000 weight of Jesuit's bark, or quinine, seven Negro slaves, and 4,600 pieces of eight in specie. She was reported "much the best prize brought here this war," and paid 48 pieces of eight per prize share. On July 13 arrived the *Indian Queen Opess,* a schooner taken by Captain John Dennis in the *Prince,* with a prize cargo of 2,000 pieces of eight, 48 barrels of tar, and 50 boards. *Pa. Gaz.,* July 26, 1744.

222. The White Horse Tavern was operated by Jonathan Nichols; it stood on the corner of Marlborough and Farewell Streets. George C. Mason, *Reminiscences of Newport* (Newport, 1884), 179.

223. Dr. Thomas Moffatt, Edinburgh graduate, came to Newport in the 1730's in the wake of his uncle John Smibert, the painter. A bachelor, something of a philanderer, a collector of paintings and first librarian of the Redwood Library, he became more of a seeker for political office under the Crown than a medical practitioner. His obituary is in the *Gentleman's Magazine,* 57 (1787), 277-78.

224. Robert Feke's paintings are highly prized today. The first native American painter of talent, he worked in Boston, New York and Philadelphia as well as at Newport. Hamilton's is the most complete contemporary description of him that has been found. *Cf.* Henry Wilder Foote, *Robert Feke* (Cambridge, 1930) with James T. Flexner, *American Painting: First Flowers of Our Wilderness* (Boston, 1947), 130-47. In the latter volume, page 136, the *Judgment of Hercules* is reproduced.

225. Dr. James Keith lived in Newport for forty years, dying in 1781. *Newport Mercury,* Sept. 1, 1781.

226. Dr. John Brett was a native of Germany. He studied at Leyden, as did many of his associates, and was deemed a scholarly person. Included in his excellent medical library were 28 volumes of his Leyden lecture notes. *New York Mercury,* Oct. 28, 1754; Mason, *Annals of Trinity Church, Newport,* 68, 319.

227. Colonel Godfrey Malbone, Virginia-born merchant, made a fortune in the West India trade and privateering in King George's

War, becoming probably the richest man in Newport. Dr. Hamilton's description of the Malbone country house, with its marbleized quoins, architraves, and window trim belies any Holland influence, which in this country took the form either of urban or peasant architecture. Possibly it had stepped-gable ends and therefore appeared Dutch to the physician. This was one of the really great and impressive mansions of English America, and doubtless because of the connection of Malbone with the logwood trade to England, his house was one of the first in the colonies to have mahogany interiors. Many other gentlemen's seats were being developed in the environs of Newport at this time.

228. One of the values of Dr. Hamilton's journal is the fact that, like all of his contemporaries, he tended to spell phonetically. In 1698 Samuel Sewall also referred to Burden's Ferry, but the name of Borden is no longer pronounced in the old fashioned way. The Bordens kept the ferry and the tavern at the crossing from Newport to the mainland at Mount Hope Bay for many years. Chapin, *History of Rhode Island Ferries,* 164, 178-79.

229. Philip, sachem of the Wampanoags and son of Massasoit, was dubbed King Philip by the colonists. To describe King Philip's War of 1676 as "very troublesome" was to place a singularly mild interpretation on the most disastrous Indian war in New England annals. *Dict. of Amer. Biog.,* XIV, 534.

230. Bristol, Rhode Island, earned more attention from Birket, who commented upon its large meeting house and the regularity of the streets. Although its excellent harbor and flourishing shipbuilding industry impressed him, Newport appeared to draw off most of the trade, and he recorded the current saying that "Bristol is Only remarkable for its plenty of women and geese." Birket, *Some Cursory Remarks,* 26.

231. Daniel Hunt, inn-holder at Rehoboth. Edith M. Tilley, "More Items of Newport Interest in Old Boston Papers," Newport Historical Society, *Bulletin,* no. 74, (1930), 11.

232. This must have been the "Slack's" listed as the public house for the stop at Attleborough in the *Vade Mecum,* 201, and it was indubitably the place Birket had reference to when he said he stopped at "Mother Stacks, who I thought realy very Slack in her Attendance for twas with great Intreaty and fair words that we

obtained a Candle altho twas So dark when we lighted that we could Scarce See." Birket, *Some Cursory Remarks,* 25.

233. Pelatiah Man's in Wrentham, Massachusetts. *Records of the Colony of Rhode Island,* 5, p. 281.

234. E. Robbin's at Walpole was another of the well known stages for the travelers of those years. Birket, *Some Cursory Remarks,* 25; Curwen, "Journal," 76.

235. Possibly William Coffin, Boston merchant. Francis Goelet, "Journal," in *New England Historical and Genealogical Register,* 24 (1870), 55. Hereafter cited as Goelet, "Journal."

236. Robert Lightfoot, Oxford graduate and reader at the Inner Temple, became a prominent merchant and a vestryman of King's Chapel at Boston. In 1742 he purchased the iron works at Attleborough from Robert Saunderson, master of the forge, for £2,000. From 1752 to 1758 he served as Judge of the Court of Vice Admiralty for Rhode Island. Joshua E. Crane, "The Iron Works of Attleborough," Colonial Society of Massachusetts, *Transactions,* 7 (1901-1902), 91, 93; Dorothy S. Towle, *Records of the Vice-Admiralty Court of Rhode Island, 1716-1752* (Washington, 1936), 88.

237. Annapolis Royal in Nova Scotia had been captured and recaptured in the years of conflict but had finally been retained by the English under the Treaty of Utrecht, 1713.

238. A Joshua Barker presided over the Bunch of Grapes in 1749, but his previous location proves elusive. Annie H. Thwing, *The Crooked and Narrow Streets of Boston, 1630-1822* (Boston, 1920), 139.

239. The almshouse stood facing the Common on the corner of Beacon and Park Streets. *Ibid.,* 222.

240. Possibly Captain Samuel Hughes. Boston Record Commissioners, "Records of the Boston Selectmen, 1743-1753," *Seventeenth Report* (Boston, 1887), 274.

241. The first lighthouse in America was erected by the Colony of Massachusetts on Great Brewster (or Beacon) Island at the entrance to Boston Harbor and began operation on September 14, 1716. *Boston News-Letter,* Sept. 17, 1716.

242. William Hooper was another Scotsman, who had come to Boston in 1723. Although a Congregational minister when Hamil-

ton met him, he became an Anglican in 1746. Justin Winsor, ed., *The Memorial History of Boston, 1630-1880* (Boston, 1880-81), I, 229.

243. Thomas Lechmere, Surveyor-General of the Customs for the Northern Department (1721-27, 1742-60), was a prominent figure in Boston mercantile and social circles as well as vestryman of King's Chapel. Charles M. Andrews, *The Colonial Period of American History* (New Haven, 1934-38), IV, 202.

244. What Hamilton called the Townhouse was the State House which stood at the head of King (now State) Street. Erected three years after the loss of the frame townhouse in the great fire of 1711 as the meeting place of both town and colonial assembly, this "elegant" brick structure became the scene of some of the most exciting events of colonial history. Adjacent to it, wrote Joseph Bennett in 1740, "there are likewise walks for the merchants, where they meet every day at one o'clock, in imitation of the *Exchange* at London, which they call by the name of Royal Exchange too, around which are several booksellers' shops." Joseph Bennett, "History of New England," Massachusetts Historical Society, *Proceedings*, 5 (1861), 110.

245. Probably Thomas Hutchinson, at this time a member of the House of Representatives, where he was the stalwart champion of sound currency. *Dict. of Amer. Biog.*, IX, 439-40.

246. Goelet, who visited Boston a few years later, frequently spoke of his friend Captain John Wendal. Goelet, "Journal," 52.

247. Long Wharf was the most ambitious and important piece of construction at Boston. Opened for use in July, 1713, it extended 1600 feet into the water from the foot of King Street, and shortly thereafter Daniel Neal described it as "a noble Pier . . . with a Row of Warehouses on the North Side for the Use of the Merchants. The Pier runs so far into the Bay that Ships of the greatest Burthen may unlade without the Help of Boats or Lighters." Bridenbaugh, *Cities in the Wilderness*, 171-72.

248. Samuel Wethered was a noted tavern-keeper whose establishment was the resort of merchants and masters of vessels. It was centrally located across from the townhouse on the corner of Kilby and King Streets. *Boston Post Boy,* Oct. 17, 1743; Winsor, *Memorial History of Boston,* II, ix.

249. "We hear the Magazines belonging to his Majesty's Garrison at Placentia, [Newfoundland] were lately blown up, suppos'd by Treachery." Boston item of July 28 in *Pa. Gaz.,* Aug. 2, 1744.

250. Dr. William Douglass (1691-1752) was perhaps the leading colonial physician of these years. Although he opposed inoculation for the smallpox in 1721, he later relented in 1751, calling it a "most beneficial improvement." He founded the Medical Society at Boston in 1736. The same year he published a masterly account of scarlet fever in *The Practical History of a New Epidemic Eruptive Military Fever,* which is the first adequate description of this disease and antedates Dr. John Fothergill's so-called classic account by twelve years. Opinionated, dour, and irascible, Douglass was, nevertheless, an able man who, in addition to his medical contributions, wrote authoritatively on paper money in 1739 and published his widely-read, controversial work, *A Summary, Historical and Political, of the First Planting, Progressive Improvements and Present State of the British Settlements in North America* (Boston, 1749-51). *Dict. of Amer. Biog.,* V, 407-8.

251. John Arbuthnot, taverner of Essex Street, was chosen an auditor of the accounts of the Boston town treasurer in 1738. Boston Record Commissioners, "Records of the Boston Selectmen, 1736-1742," *Fifteenth Report* (Boston, 1886), 142, 195.

252. Thomas Perkins rented the town warehouse in 1736 for six months; he was also master of a vessel at this time. *Ibid.,* 15, 133.

253. The Reverend William Hooper's meeting-house was the West Congregational Church built in 1737 on Lynde Street. Winsor, *Memorial History of Boston,* II, 229.

254. The Reverend Stephen Roe, a young Irishman who had "no uncommon qualifications but the art of inveigling," became assistant to Commissary Price at King's Chapel in 1741. He was dismissed in 1744 for "bad behaviour" as is evident from Hamilton's remarks on page 129. Henry W. Foote, *Annals of King's Chapel* (Boston, 1881), I, 487, 494, 525.

255. They walked across the "Mill Dam" which separated the Mill Pond from the Charles River. Bonner's Map of Boston, 1722, in Bridenbaugh, *Cities in the Wilderness,* 146.

256. The Faneuil Hall visited by tourists today is not the origi-

nal market building designed by John Smibert and completed in 1742 which Hamilton saw. The latter structure burned in 1761, was rebuilt, and then later enlarged. "Funell" was the way the name was pronounced and also the way it was spelled on Peter Faneuil's tombstone. *Dict. of Amer. Biog.*, VI, 262; Samuel E. Morison, *The Maritime History of Massachusetts, 1783-1860* (London, 1923), 19*n.*

257. Hugh Vans was a prominent Boston merchant through whom many Rhode Islanders made their European purchases.

258. Captain Mangeau's sloop brought thirty-six persons who had been taken when Canso fell. So short were provisions that the French were forced to send their prisoners, "most of them Women and Children," to Boston. *Pa. Gaz.*, July 19, 1744, citing Boston papers of July 9.

259. Commencing on July 5, Alexander Carlile conducted an auction of "A curious and valuable collection of books on most subjects, just brought from Great Britain." His shop was in King Street, opposite to the Sign of the Blue Anchor. *Boston News-Letter*, July 5, 1744; George L. McKay, *American Book Auction Catalogues, 1713-1934* (New York, 1937), 43.

260. The Wendell family were Dutch, settling first in Albany; some of the family migrated to Boston. Jacob Wendell was colonel of the Boston regiment. He married the daughter of James Oliver and was an ancestor of Oliver Wendell Holmes. Winsor, *Memorial History of Boston*, I, 543-44.

261. Henrique, or more properly Hendrick, was a Mohawk chief. Converted to Christianity, he was in close contact throughout his life with those responsible for English policy on the New York frontier. His greatest oration, which was delivered at the Albany Congress of 1754, was printed in England. *Dict. Amer. Biog.*, VIII, 532. For the Iroquois deputies to the Conference to the Eastward in 1744, see *Pa. Gaz.*, July 19, Aug. 14, 1744.

262. John Smibert (1688-1751) came to Newport in 1729 with Dean Berkeley, but the next year he moved to Boston where he became court painter to the New England worthies. His nephew John Moffatt, brother of Dr. Thomas, soon joined him as a partner. Their studio was the first art center in the colonies and through them the great Renaissance tradition of painting was brought to

America. Here it was that talented young natives like Robert Feke, John Singleton Copley, and Charles Willson Peale received inspiration and perhaps advice. The *Continence of Scipio* admired by Dr. Hamilton was a copy of the painting by the French painter Nicolas Poussin and is reproduced on page 116 of Flexner's *American Painting: First Flowers of our Wilderness.* Henry Wilder Foote, "Mr. Smibert Shows His Pictures," *New England Quarterly,* 7 (1935), 14-28; Flexner, 112-29.

263. This "mad scheme" of taking the great French fortress of Louisbourg, on Cape Breton, was first proposed by William Vaughan, a merchant of Damariscotta, and was pushed to a victorious conclusion by Governor William Shirley of Massachusetts. Louisbourg fell on June 17, 1745. Francis Parkman, *A Half-Century of Conflict* (Boston, 1897), II, 56-133.

264. Dr. John Clark was a charter member of this earliest American medical organization. Dr. William Douglass wrote to Cadwallader Colden in February, 1735, "We have lately in Boston form'd a Medical Society of which this gentleman [Dr. Clark], bearer, a member thereof, can give you a particular account. We designed from time to time to publish some short pieces." *Letters and Papers of Cadwallader Colden,* II, 146-47 in New York Historical Society, *Collections* (New York, 1917-22).

265. The Sun Tavern faced Market Square and was just around the corner from Dock Square. Winsor, *Memorial History of Boston,* II, xxii.

266. John Tasker was a merchant and ship owner of Salem and Marblehead. Harriet S. Tapley, "Richard Skinner of Marblehead," Essex Institute, *Historical Collections,* 68 (1932), 9.

267. The Honorable Benjamin Tasker, President of the Council in Maryland. *Maryland Hist. Mag.,* 4 (1909), 192.

268. Possibly Captain William Fletcher, who was excused from serving as constable in 1738. Boston Record Commissioners, "Boston Town Records, 1729-1742," *Twelfth Report* (Boston, 1885), 216.

269. Samuel Clarke edited an edition of the first twelve books of Homer's *Iliad* (London, 1729) by royal command. The remaining twelve books were completed by his son in 1732. *Dict. of Nat. Biog.,* X, 443.

270. The Upper Ferry was generally known to Bostonians as

the Charlestown Ferry and was used by persons traveling to Cambridge or to the northward.

271. In 1750, according to Birket, "Charles Town is pretty Large and a Country town Scituate upon a Peninsula between Mistick river and Charles river and is Caled the Mother of Boston being Settled before it and parted from Boston only by Charles River over which there is a ferry very well Attended and the River here is as broad as the Thames at London. This town has two large Streets that Come down towards the ferry, and Handsome large Meeting House and Good Market place. It has but little trade as Boston is so near it. Most people in trade Choose to live there." Birket, *Some Cursory Remarks*, 17.

272. Nicholas Gilman, minister of Durham, New Hampshire, belonged to the "New Light" school. Two weeks after his ordination at Durham in 1742, the church was rent asunder over revival preaching. On occasion he would preach for eight hours; someone would then take him outside and walk him up and down until the screaming of the congregation drew him back to the meeting. After two years of this, his fame as the wildest of the New Lights had spread well beyond New England. Clifford K. Shipton, *Sibley's Harvard Graduates, 1722-1725* (Boston, 1945), VII, 341-42.

273. Mystic was a village of about 100 houses. Goelet, "Journal," 58.

274. Lynn was a small country town of about 200 houses. *Ibid.*, 56.

275. Marblehead was estimated to have had 450 houses in 1747; this would mean a population of about 3,600 rather than the figure Hamilton gives. Samuel Roads, Jr., *The History and Traditions of Marblehead* (Boston, 1880), 60.

276. Most travelers' accounts mention only the Fountain Inn, but Goelet indicates that Reid's establishment was still there in 1750. Goelet, "Journal," 58.

277. The Reverend Alexander Malcolm (b. 1687) was the rector of St. Michael's Church from 1740 to 1749 when he resigned and moved to Maryland. There he became a member of the Tuesday Club, probably through the offices of Dr. Hamilton. In 1721 Malcolm had published at Edinburgh *A Treatise of Music, Speculative, Practical, and Historical*. It was reprinted in London in 1730 and

1776. Essex Institute, *Historical Collections*, 74 (1938), 315*n;* *Wheeler,* "Reading and other Recreations of Marylanders," 49.

278. According to Birket, Salem was a "large Town, well built," with "many genteel large houses (which tho' of wood) are all plastered on the outside in Imitation of Hewn Stone," or "pland and Painted." Rustic work, as this was termed, enjoyed a considerable vogue among carpenter-architects in New England during this period. "Here is a good Harbour for Small vessels," continued the Quaker merchant, "and several good Wharfs and Warehouses." Goelet adds that the houses gave evidence of "Neat Building, but all of wood, and Covers a Great Deal of Ground, being at a Convenient Distance from Each other, and with fine Gardens back [of] their Houses." Birket, *Some Cursory Remarks*, 15-16; Goelet, "Journal," 58.

279. The Ship's Tavern, later known as Pratt's, was a large house at the head of Central Street. James D. Phillips, *Salem in the Eighteenth Century* (Boston, 1937), 22, 114, 168.

280. There were many Sewalls living at Salem. The one here mentioned was probably Stephen Sewall, a special justice of the Superior Court of Massachusetts, who in 1751 became Chief Justice. Shipton, *Sibley's Harvard Graduates*, VI, 561-67.

281. Richard Woodberry of Rowley was an itinerant exhorter. Thomas F. Waters, *Ipswich in the Massachusetts Bay Colony* (Ipswich, 1917), I, 122.

282. "Browne Hall," situated in Danvers near the Beverly line, was built in 1740 by William Browne for his young wife Mary, daughter of Governor William Burnet and granddaughter of Bishop Gilbert Burnet, who died in 1745 before it was finished. The great circular hall had a dome and a gallery running around it from which one could look down on the floor which was painted to resemble a mosaic. Ezra D. Hines, "Browne Hall," Essex Institute, *Historical Collections*, 31 (1896), 201, 209, 210-11.

283. Wachuset Mountain near Worcester.

284. John Vanderbanc, the "most successful English tapestry manufacturer" of the Queen Anne period, being particularly noted for his Chinoiserie. One of his tapestries can be seen in the Metropolitan Museum of Art. George L. Hunter, *The Practical Book of Tapestries* (Philadelphia, 1925), 224-25.

285. Less oppressed by New England theology, Francis Goelet, six years later, gained a very different impression of Mr. Browne, with whom he conversed on various subjects and whom he thought a gentleman of excellent parts well "adversed in Leaturate, a good Scholar a great Virtuoso and Lover of the Liberal Arts and Sciences having an extraordinary Library of Books of the Best Ancient and Modern Authors." Goelet, "Journal," 57.

286. Salem, according to Goelet, had about 450 houses. *Ibid.,* 58.

287. The five Presbyterian meetings were, of course, Congregational, for this was the birthplace of "the New England Way" in America. In 1716 a new Quaker Meeting House was built on Essex Street, and in 1736 the Anglicans opened St. Peter's on Prison Lane, over which two years later the Reverend Charles Brocknell, an Oxford graduate, came to preside. Phillips, *Salem in the Eighteenth Century,* 60-71, 102-12, 157, 161-62.

288. The watch house was ordered built on Leech Hill in 1704. Sometime prior to 1725 Leamon Beadle made the wooden representation of a watchman with his equipment which Hamilton mistook for a grenadier. Joseph B. Felt, *Annals of Salem* (Salem, 1849), II, 83, 496.

289. The Salem Ferry crossed the harbor to the town of Beverly.

290. Ipswich was a "pretty large Inland Town Scituated upon a fine river but not Navigable so high as the Town. There is a Large Presbyterian [Congregational] Meeting house in the Middle of the Town, the houses here seem to be mostly old And upon the decline. They have Some Coasting vessels that come to below the town at some distance." Birket, *Some Cursory Remarks,* 15.

291. Increase Howe operated a tavern in Ipswich for many years in the eighteenth century. Waters, *Ipswich,* II, 84, 128.

292. A stout defender of Whitefield, the Reverend John Rogers served as the Congregational minister at Ipswich for 45 years. Waters, *Ipswich,* II, 17.

293. Ebenezer Choate. Massachusetts, *Journal of the House of Representatives, 1742-1744* (Boston, 1945), 35.

294. Birket found that Newbury was "pretty well Built, and has 2 large presbyterian Meeting houses And one Episcopal Church

. . . . Here is carried on a Great trade in Ship building, I reckoned 26 upon the Stocks in the town besides what was Launched and then in the river and what was building in Other Parts Adjacent, I lodged at Ebenezer Choats." Birket, *Some Cursory Remarks*, 15.

295. The old square meeting house stood from 1700 to 1806. A new one was built in the years 1738-40. Joshua Coffin, *A Sketch of the History of Newbury, Newbury Port and West Newbury* (Boston, 1845), iii, 207, 212.

296. Carr's Island Ferry across the Merrimack was the chief crossing at Newbury. Coffin, *History of Newbury*, 207.

297. At Portsmouth, New Hampshire, "4 Principal streets meet in the nature of a + there, are pretty Streight and regular, through which you have a prospect of the country on every side; the other Streets are Irregular and Crooked with many vacant lots not yet built upon." Birket, *Some Cursory Remarks*, 8.

298. Here as elsewhere Dr. Hamilton means Congregational when he says Presbyterian churches. Queen's Chapel, named in honor of Queen Caroline, was the first Anglican church in New Hampshire. The Reverend Arthur Browne was its rector for many years. Everett S. Stackpole, *History of New Hampshire* (New York, 1916), I, 277-78.

299. "Spent the Evening at the Widdow Slatons . . . where I lodged and intend to do So during my Stay in this place being the best tavern for Strangers in town." Birket, *Some Cursory Remarks*, 3.

300. From 1691 to 1741 New Hampshire had the same royal governor as Massachusetts. Benning Wentworth (1696-1770), most flamboyant member of a famous family, became the first governor of New Hampshire after the separation. Shipton, *Sibley's Harvard Graduates*, VI, 113-33.

301. Fort William and Mary was built near Newcastle on Great Island at the mouth of the Piscataqua. In 1750 as Birket's ship approached the Piscataqua he noted that "this river makes a very Grand and Genteel appearance at the Entrance for On the Larboard hand going from the Sea you have the Ancient town of Newcastle with a fort upon the point." Birket, *Some Cursory Remarks*, 7; William G. Saltonstall, *Ports of Piscataqua* (Cambridge, 1941), 12, 21.

302. By Kitterick, Hamilton meant Kittery Point not far

from which William Pepperell, the hero of Louisburg, had his great mansion. Federal Writers' Project, Maine, *Maine: A Guide 'Down East'* (Boston, 1937), 249-51.

303. York, the shire town of the county of the same name, was the point farthest north and east that Dr. Hamilton reached. That Scots lived in York seemed to have escaped the physician's notice. Federal Writers' Project, *Maine*, 251; Charles G. Banks, *York, Maine* (Boston, 1935), II, 28.

304. The Lower, or Winnisimmet Ferry crossed the harbor from the town of Chelsea to the foot of North Street in Boston completing the shortest and most direct route from Salem and points to the eastward. Mellen Chamberlain, *Documentary History of Chelsea* (Boston, 1908), II, 111-14.

305. Archibald Pitcairne (1652-1713), physician and poet, was one of the most celebrated medical men of his time. In 1692-93 he was professor of physic at Leyden; later he practiced in Edinburgh where he was suspected of atheistical leanings because of his mockery of the puritanical strictness of the Presbyterian Church. *Dict. of Nat. Biog.*, XLV, 335.

306. The Scots Quarterly Society was actually called the Scots Charitable Society which, except for a brief time, has been in continuous existence since 1657. It became a model for similar organizations in other colonial cities. Bridenbaugh, *Cities in the Wilderness*, 81-82.

307. Friends of Samuel Waterhouse claimed that the owners of his ship had instructed him not to fight privateers, for he would only gain "rags, lice, and broken bones." His vessel, the brigantine *Hawk,* mounted 12 guns, 20 swivels, and carried a crew of 138 men. His defense was disputed by his owners. Chapin, *Privateering in King George's War*, 36, 39-40; *Pa. Gaz.*, Aug. 23, 1744.

308. Possibly Richard Philips (1661-1751), first Governor of Nova Scotia and Lieutenant Colonel of the New England regiment which became the 40th Foot. *Dict. of Nat. Biog.*, XLV, 181.

309. Lorenz Heister (1683-1758) was a celebrated German surgeon whose *Chirugie* (1718) became the standard textbook. Douglas Guthrie, *A History of Medicine* (Philadelphia, 1946), 244.

310. This might have been the well-known Hugenot merchant James Boutineau who lived near School Street, or his kinsman

Samuel Boutineau. Winsor, *Memorial History of Boston,* II, xxviii.

311. In 1750 Goelet wrote of stopping at the Sign of the Grey-hound where Jervis gave him "some choice Punch." This inn was a favorite stopping place for parties driving out from Boston and in 1744 was owned by John Grayton or Graton. Boston Record Commissioners, "Records of the Boston Selectmen, 1743-1753," 82, 174; Goelet, "Journal," 56.

312. The Mosquito Coast comprised the east coast of Nicaragua and a portion of the coast of Honduras where one of the New England ships engaged in the logwood trade could have procured the monkey.

313. Edward Holyoke (1688-1769), ninth President of Harvard, 1737-1769. Shipton, *Sibley's Harvard Graduates,* V, 265.

314. Matthew Cushing, class of 1737, Librarian. Colonial Society of Massachusetts, *Collections,* 15 (1925), clx, 131-37.

315. "Cambridge is well Scituated On Charles River which is Navigable to the Town and over which there is a very good wooden bridge but has no trade (being too near to Boston), the Inhabitants depend Chiefly on their Courts etc., being the Chiefe of a County And the Colledge etc. There are Some good homes here and the town is laid out very Regular, but for want of trade One 4th part of it is not built." Birket, *Some Cursory Remarks,* 18. Goelet reported the town to contain 100 houses. Goelet, "Journal," 62.

316. As Hamilton entered the quadrangle from the open west end he saw Stoughton College (1699) straight ahead; while on the left was Old Harvard (1677), which burned in 1764, and to the right was Massachusetts Hall (1720) with its "little clock," the only one of these now standing. Most of the books in this, the largest library in America, were lost in the fire. Curiously Hamilton neglected to notice Holden Chapel, a gem of colonial architecture, which was either completed or nearly so when he visited Harvard. Samuel E. Morison, *Three Centuries of Harvard* (Cambridge, 1936), 43, 59, 95.

317. Governor's Island had been granted to Governor John Winthrop for a garden. Samuel A. Drake, *Old Landmarks and Historic Personages of Boston* (Boston, 1900), 806.

318. The Fort was called the Castle and was situated on Castle Island in Boston Harbor.

319. John Phillips. Massachusetts, *Journal of the House of Representatives, 1742-1744,* 373.

320. Dr. Silvester Gardiner, a Rhode Islander, returned from the study of medicine abroad to practice at Boston in 1735. He had a wide and lucrative practice which enabled him to become an extensive land speculator. Gardiner, Maine, is named after him. *Dict. of Amer. Biog.,* VII, 139.

321. The three largest colonial towns compared favorably in size with most English cities, excepting only the metropolis of London. By actual census figures Boston's population in 1742 was 16,258; that of Philadelphia was estimated at 13,000, and of New York at 11,000. Bridenbaugh, *Cities in the Wilderness,* 303n.

322. William Shirley, one of the ablest of colonial governors and the guiding spirit in the capture of Louisburg in 1745. *Dict. of Amer. Biog.,* XVI, 120.

323. Hamilton was not the only one to call the Congregationalists of New England Presbyterians. The two denominations were almost exactly alike in creed, but they differed widely in church policy. Each Congregational church, especially in Massachusetts, acknowledged no superior authority like the Presbytery or the Synods of the Kirk of Scotland. The Connecticut churches came nearest to the Presbyterian in government.

324. Dr. Douglass's first pamphlet on currency was published anonymously in 1738; five years later his widely read *Discourse Concerning the Currencies of the British Plantations in America* appeared at Boston. Osgood, *American Colonies in the Eighteenth Century,* III, 350.

325. The abortive expedition of Sir William Phips against Quebec in 1690 had to be financed by the first American issue of paper currency, on the sudden return of the troops without any plunder. Hutchinson, *History of the Colony and Province of Massachusetts Bay,* I, 340.

326. The old hostelry in Dedham had been kept by Fishers as early as 1658. Later it belonged to the Ames family, famous almanac publishers. Mary C. Crawford, *Old New England Inns* (Boston, 1924), 210.

327. The first bridge was built over the Pawtucket (not Nantucket) Falls of the Blackstone River in 1713; it had been replaced

in 1735. The iron works, or forge, was below the falls on the west bank of the river. John W. Haley, *The Lower Blackstone River Valley* (Pawtucket, 1936), 34, 39, 43.

328. In 1749 and 1750 there were about thirty licensed tavern-keepers in Providence. The highest fees were paid by Joseph Angell, William Pearce and Jonathan Olney, eight pounds each. William R. Staples, *Annals of Providence* (Providence, 1843), 199.

329. These pictures were mezzotints sold by John Overton (1640-1708?) or his son Henry, who were the principal vendors of this form of art which enjoyed a great vogue in the colonies as well as in England. *Dict. of Nat. Biog.*, XLII, 384.

330. Providence Ferry was the ferry across the Seekonk River at Watchemoket; it was sometimes called the Lower Ferry to distinguish it from the Upper or Narrow Passage Ferry which also crossed to Rehoboth. Its proprietor was Josiah Fuller. Chapin, *History of Rhode Island Ferries*, 132-33.

331. This was Duncan Kelley's ferry across the Swansea, or Warren River, at Warren. In 1744 John Kelley operated the ferry. *Ibid.*, 148.

332. Sueton Grant came from Scotland to America in 1725, settling in Newport where he became a prominent sea captain, merchant, and public-spirited citizen. He had Smibert paint his portrait and collected prints and paintings. He died in September, 1744, of injuries received in an explosion of powder in Taylor's warehouse where he and other owners of the privateer *Prince Frederick* were inspecting stores. The explosion blew all present out of the building. *Boston Evening Post*, Sept. 24, 1744; *Pa. Gaz.*, Oct. 11, 1744.

333. Edward Scott, uncle of Sir Walter the novelist, was master of the Grammar School, an active member of the Philosophical Club, and one of the first directors of the Redwood Library. Mason, *Annals of Trinity Church, Newport*, 55*n*.

334. In 1730 Henry Collins, Peter Bours, Daniel Updyke, Edward Scott and several other gentlemen founded the "Society for the Promotion of Knowledge and Virtue by a Free Conversation." In 1735 the group numbered 24 and meetings were held at the homes of members every Monday night to "converse about and debate some useful question in Divinity, Morality, Philosophy etc."

Considering Rhode Island's fear of Captain Morpang and other French raiders, it is no wonder this "Philosophical Club" discussed current affairs at this time. *Newport Historical Magazine,* 4 (1883), 68.

335. General William Wade (1673-1748), Commander-in-chief of the army in England, who in 1745 failed to stop the advance of Bonnie Prince Charlie. Simon Fraser (1667?-1747) twelfth Baron Lovat, was a noted Jacobite intriguer. *Dict. of Nat. Biog.,* XX, 216; LVIII, 413.

336. John Van Meurs (1579-1639), was a Dutch classical scholar and antiquary. Many of his treatises and editions of the classics are printed in Gronovius's *Thesaurus Antiquitatum.*

337. In 1729 George Berkeley (1685-1753), Dean of Derry and later Bishop of Cloyne, landed at Newport where he lived two years on his farm at Whitehall. At that time the famous opponent of materialism wrote his *Alciphron, or The Minute Philosopher.* Benjamin Rand, *Berkeley's American Sojourn* (Cambridge, 1932).

338. When Dean Berkeley returned to England he gave his farm at Whitehall to Yale College, by which it has been leased ever since. Isaac Anthony kept it as a public house for several years, and one of his daughters, presumably the one admired by Captain Williams, was Susannah, who became a famous religious figure in Rhode Island. Gilbert Stuart's mother was also an Anthony. Manuscripts of the Colonial Dames at Whitehall, Middletown, R. I.

339. Jacob Hasey renewed his tavern license on June 11, 1744. Newport Town Council Records, IX, 35, Newport Historical Society.

340. Francis Bacon, Baron Verulam (1561-1626).

341. Samuel Pemberton of Boston, who married Mary Leach of Newport and maintained a home there. He probably derived his title of judge because he was justice of the peace for Suffolk County.

342. Captain Henry Bull, "a man of strong character," later chief justice of Newport County, was a grandson of one of the first settlers of Newport. Mason, *Annals of Trinity Church, Newport,* 62, 62n; "The Bull Family of Newport," Newport Historical Society, *Bulletin,* no. 81 (1931).

343. Joseph Wanton. Towle ed., *Records of Vice Admiralty Court of Rhode Island,* 224.

344. Fort George, on Goat Island, was in such a state of decay

that local and provincial authorities at the time of Hamilton's visit were trying to procure ordnance and military stores from England. Peter Harrison, soon to be the leading colonial architect, prepared admirable new plans for the works in 1745. French Wars: Fort George, 14-15, in Rhode Island Archives, Providence.

345. On the occasion of Newport's centennial celebration, 1738, the Reverend John Callender attributed civil disorders to "the unjust, unnatural, and absurd attempts to force all to be of one opinion, or to feign and dissemble that they are; or the cruel and impious punishing those, who cannot change their opinions without light or reason, and will not dissemble against all reason and conscience." John Callender, *Historical Discourse on the . . . Colony of Rhode Island and Providence Plantations* (Boston, 1739), 39, 163.

346. William Greene, Governor of Rhode Island from May, 1743 to May, 1745. *Dict. of Amer. Biog.*, VII, 575.

347. The ferry from Newport to Jamestown was operated by the Carr family. The Newport landing was at Carr's Lane, now the foot of Mill Street. The landing on the other side was the eastern end of Ferry Road, now Eldred Avenue. Rhode Island Historical Society, *Collections,* 24 (1933), 46.

348. Hamilton had now entered the country of the Narragansett Planters, whose farms were unequaled in size anywhere in the Middle or Northern Colonies. Using slave labor, they raised large numbers of livestock for market and produced dairy products and the well-known Rhode Island cheese. William D. Miller, "The Narragansett Planters," American Antiquarian Society, *Proceedings,* 43 (1933), 3-69.

349. Because of the prominence of the accused, the case against Silas Greenman, his brother, and father, who were charged with counterfeiting, was prosecuted and became one of the most celebrated in colonial New England. Richard L. Bowen, *Rhode Island Colonial Money and Its Counterfeiting, 1647-1726* (Providence, 1942), 39.

350. Paul Ruiz, as appears later. See below, 176.

351. Nicholas Lechmere was naval officer at New London and later collector at Newport. Frances M. Caulkins, *History of New London, Connecticut* (New London, 1852), 477.

352. Dr. Giles Goddard, postmaster at New London, whose

wife, Sarah Updike Goddard, and son William became famous printers. *Dict. of Amer. Biog.*, VII, 341.

353. Members of the Green family were engaged in the printing and publishing business "from Massachusetts to Maryland from the seventeenth century to the nineteenth." Deacon Timothy Green had been a printer at New London since 1714. His son Jonas published the *Maryland Gazette* at Annapolis and joined with his friend Hamilton to form the Tuesday Club. Jarvis M. Morse, *Connecticut Newspapers in the Eighteenth Century* (New Haven, 1935), 7; *Dict. of Amer. Biog.*, VII, 552.

354. James Davenport of Southold, Long Island, was a descendant of the founder of New Haven. He was an ardent and renowned enthusiast of this period, who later retracted his position. The burning of the books took place on March 6, 1743. Caulkins, *History of New London, Connecticut,* 450, 454.

355. "Guilford," wrote Birket, "is a large Country town with two Meeting houses of the Presbyterian [Congregational] Persuasion, one of the New and the Other of the Old light and a Church, And a large Spacious green in the Centre of the Town." Birket, *Some Cursory Remarks,* 35.

356. Israel Munson's tavern was one of four public houses shown on Wadsworth's *Map of New Haven,* 1748.

357. "New Haven is the Capital of the county, And covers a great deal of ground and has been laid out Regularly, but only built upon here and there it looks very indifferently, It is a Seaport and was Settled very early and was then the Capital of the Province, it is well Scituated for Trade being near the Center of the Government, Here the Councele and Assembly Sit in this Month, here is also the County Goal And two large Presbyterian meeting houses one of the Old the other of the new light, Likewise a Colledge for the Education of youth Called Yale Colledge, it is built of Wood And Consists of one Long Narrow fabrick with Brick Chimneys running up the back part of it at Convenient distances the whole seems to be very much decayed, (which has put them upon building A new one of Brick which Seems to be About 3 foot Above the Ground @ And will front towards a large Spacious green in the Middle of the Town, there is in this Colledge a Very pretty Library And well kept, their Books are many of 'em Much later date and

better Choose then those at Cambridge They are Obliged for a good part of them to the late Dean Berkley now Bishop of Cloyne in Ireland, they have also Some Curiossitys in this Library and Some Aparatus for Natural Experimental Philosophy." Birket, *Some Cursory Remarks,* 36-37.

358. John Benjamin of Stratford owned the ferry in 1733, was listed as a goldsmith in 1743, and for years Benjamin's Tavern stood at the corner of Broad and Beardsley Streets. William H. Wilcoxen, *History of Stratford, Connecticut, 1639-1939* (Stratford, 1939), 191, 493-94, 626.

359. The Anglican Church at Stratford was completed in the year of Hamilton's tour. *Ibid.,* 457.

360. The octagonal church edifice, with the pulpit placed in the center so that all might hear equally well, was passing out of fashion by this time, and the familiar New England meeting house was taking its place.

361. He crossed the Saugatuck River at the present town of Westport.

362. John Belding kept a public house at the Sign of the Ship. Curwen, "Journal," 80.

363. Rye Bridge, the boundary line of Connecticut and New York, at what is now Port Chester, New York.

364. Jonathan Law (1674-1750), Governor of Connecticut, 1741-50. *Dict. of Amer. Biog.,* XI, 41.

365. Actually, Connecticut was a separate colony with a charter of its own. Foreigners and persons from the South frequently assumed that Massachusetts ruled over the rest of the New England colonies; this certainly would have been strange doctrine in Connecticut, Rhode Island or New Hampshire. It is curious that Dr. Hamilton has not discovered his error by this time.

366. Kingsbridge was a toll bridge across Spuyten Duyvil controlled by the Philipse family. It connected with the Albany Post Road and also the Boston Post Road. Stephen Jenkins, *The Story of the Bronx* (New York, 1912), 186-89; Stokes, *Iconography,* IV, 609.

367. Turtle Bay was an inlet of the East River at about Forty-Sixth Street and was a favorite anchorage for British war vessels.

368. James De Lancey (1703-1760) was to receive from Governor Clinton on September 14 a commission as chief justice providing

for tenure during good behavior rather than pleasure which would give him confidence to act without scruple in building a political machine to control both Council and Assembly. *Dict. of Amer. Biog.,* V, 212.

369. Thomas Mathews (1676-1751), Vice-Admiral of the Red and Commander-in-Chief of the British Navy in the Mediterranean, whose conduct in the blockade before Toulon earlier in the year was soon to lead to his resignation and trial for neglect of duty. *Dict. of Nat. Biog.,* XXXVI, 43; *Pa. Gaz.,* April 19, 1744.

370. Mr. Bourdillion was apparently a Maryland merchant whom Hamilton knew well. He was doubtless a connection of the Reverend Benedict Bourdillon, rector of St. Paul's Church in Baltimore County. *Maryland Archives,* 42, pp. 418-20; Alexander Lawson to Daniel Dulany, Feb. 20, 1741, Dulany Papers, Maryland Historical Society.

371. This was the Mill Street Synagogue, home of the oldest Jewish congregation within the present United States. David De S. Pool, *The Mill Street Synagogue* (New York, 1930).

372. "Here are no Phtisies or Consumptions," wrote a visitor to New York about this time, "and so very few Physicians and Apothecaries that People live to a very great Age." New York was rich in quacks like Hamilton's companion. Stokes, *Iconography,* IV, 518.

373. This may have been the John Rhea who was listed as in business at Philadelphia in 1756. *Dict. of Amer. Biog.,* II, 67.

374. Commodore (later Baron) George Anson set out in 1740 to attack the Spanish colonies on the west coast of South America. After a hazardous trip in which his squadron was reduced to one lone ship, he crossed the Pacific and captured the "Manila Gallion" *Acapulco,* which sailed between Mexico and the Philippines. This great ship had on board a million and a half dollars in gold. On this voyage Anson circumnavigated the globe, anchoring at Spithead June 17, 1744. Alfred T. Mahan, *The Influence of Sea Power upon History, 1660-1783* (Boston, 1923), 261-62.

375. The French Protestant church on what is now the northeast corner of Pine and Nassau Streets. In 1731 there were two pastors: the Reverend Louis Rou, described as "brilliant but a little bad," and the Reverend Mr. Moulinar, "good but a trifle dull." The

elders tried without success to oust Mr. Rou. *Leslie's History of Greater New York* (New York, 1898), I, 138, 221.

376. Alexander Pope died May 30, 1744.

377. The Reverend Ebenezer Pemberton, pastor of the Wall Street Church, was the only minister in the city to open his pulpit to Whitefield. The result was a great increase in membership. Gabriel P. Disosway, *The Earliest Churches of New York and its Vicinity* (New York, 1865), 133-34.

378. In 1748 Peter Kalm recorded that "Woodbridge is a small village, the houses mostly of boards and shingled on the side walls. Elizabethtown is a small town about 20 miles from New Brunswick. It has some stone buildings. We lodged in Elizabethtown Point about two miles from the town." "New Jersey as it Appeared to Early Observers," New Jersey Historical Society, *Proceedings,* 5 (1920), 162.

379. John Heard is listed as a property owner in 1749. *New York Weekly Post Boy,* Sept. 11, 1749.

380. Possibly Thomas White, a lawyer and father of William White, first Episcopal Bishop of Pennsylvania. He advertised in June, 1745, for an indentured servant who ran away from his "Plantation" in Bristol Township, Pa. *Pa. Gaz.,* June 6, 1745.

381. The settlers of this community came chiefly from the Piscataqua in New Hampshire and gave the township the name of their native place. It was known as Piscataway for some years after its settlement. Whitehead, *Early History of Perth Amboy,* 401.

382. This iron works appears to have been earlier than any mentioned in Philadelphia County in Arthur C. Bining's list of eighteenth-century iron works in his *Pennsylvania Iron Manufacture in the Eighteenth Century,* in Pennsylvania Historical Commission, *Publications,* 4 (Harrisburg, 1938), 188.

383. Late in 1743 Dr. Adam Spencer came from Boston "justly recommended" as "an Experienced Physician and Man-midwife." He gave public lectures on the nature and diseases of the eye, and Franklin tells us his lectures on experimental philosophy in April 1744, first directed the printer's attention to the new field of electricity. Black, "Journal," 246; *Pa. Gaz.,* April 26, 1744; Bridenbaugh, *Rebels and Gentlemen,* 269-70, 323-24, 341.

384. John Mitchell (d. 1768), physician, botanist and map-

maker, lived at Urbanna, Middlesex County, Virginia, from *ca.* 1721 until 1746 when he went to London for his health. *Dict. of Amer. Biog.*, XIII, 50.

385. Aristotle's rules of drama were the three unities of time, place, and action which arose from the problems of production. Here Dr. Hamilton is being pedantic in taking the neo-classicists' attitude towards Shakespeare, which, of course, he was reading in a diluted version by Cibber, Dryden, Garrick, or Thomson.

386. From 1738 until Whitefield's opposition forced it to close, a Musical Club headed by Attorney-General Tench Francis gave exclusive little concerts. Bridenbaugh, *Rebels and Gentlemen*, 155.

387. John Mather was a prominent citizen of Chester. He lived on the northwest corner of Third Street and Edgemont Avenue. Henry G. Ashmead, *Historical Sketch of Chester, on Delaware* (Chester, 1883), 77.

388. Miss Coursey came of a distinguished Maryland family which lived in the neighborhood of Bohemia Manor. Dating from Henry, who settled in the province in 1654, the family soon achieved both wealth and fame. Possibly Miss Coursey was the daughter of William, who was a member of the Council when the government of the colony was restored to the Proprietor in 1715. Hester D. Richardson, *Sidelights on Maryland History* (Baltimore, 1913), I, 228; II, 81; *Maryland Hist. Mag.*, 30 (1930), 316.

389. Thomas Colville, and associate of the Hollingsworths and other leading families of the Elk region, was one of the commissioners sent by Governor Bladen of Maryland to the Indian Conference at Lancaster in June, 1744. Scharf, *History of Maryland*, I, 426.

390. Doubtless Dr. Hamilton regarded Dr. Peter Boucelle as a quack, because he treated the "yaws," a term covering most skin diseases including syphilis, but upon discovering that he had married Catherine, daughter of Colonel Augustine Herman of Bohemia Manor, and was the stepson of Peter Sluyter the Labadist, the physician changed his opinion. Delaware Historical Society, *Publications*, II, 22, 43.

391. Dr. Christopher Witt, or de Witt, came to America from England in 1704. He was a thorough naturalist, a skilled physician known as "the Hermit of the Wissahickon." He lived in German-

town, Pennsylvania, where he kept the first botanical garden in the English colonies and dabbled in astrology. John W. Harshberger, *The Botanists of Philadelphia and Their Work* (Philadelphia, 1899), 42.

392. William Black reported Northeast to be "Compos'd of two Ordinaries, a Ghrist Mill, Baker-house and two or three Dwelling Houses." He also stopped at Smith's ordinary, where he "Drunk the best Cask Cyder for the Season that ever I did in America." Black, "Journal," 236-37, 247.

393. William Rogers was host of the tavern on what is now St. Paul and Baltimore Streets in Baltimore. Annie L. Sioussat, *Old Baltimore* (New York, 1931), 44-45.

394. "Arrived at James Moore's ordinary at the head of Severn river about one o'clock," wrote Witham Marshe on June 18, 1744, "but such a dinner was prepared for us, as never was seen or cooked in the Highlands of Scotland or the Isles of Orkney. It consisted of six eggs fried with six pieces of bacon, with some clammy pone or Indian bread." Marshe, "Journal," 171.

INDEX

O

Oversleigh, 70

Overton, John, mezzotint engraver, 149, n. 329

Oyster Pond, L. I., 95, 96, n. 198

P

Painting. *See* Art

Palatines in Pennsylvania, 22

Paper money. *See* Currency

Parker, Mr.: 80, 89, 92, 103, 108; flirts with girls, 90, 91, 96

Peale, Charles Willson, quoted, xiii

Peddlers: in Southold, L. I., 95; in Stonington, Conn., 160; in Walpole, Mass., 104

Pemberton, Samuel, Judge, 155, n. 341

Pennsylvania: 14; staples of, 29

Perkins, Thomas, 109, n. 252

Perth Amboy, N. J.: 37; buildings, n. 107; charter of, n. 106; churches, 38; description of, 38

Peters, Richard, Secretary, 25, 26, n. 81

Philadelphia: 13; architecture, 18, 21; awnings in, 21; buildings of, n. 49; churches: 18; Anglican, 22; Baptists, n. 70; Christ, n. 50; Lutheran, 24, n. 78; Presbyterian, 22, 190, n. 51, n. 71; Quaker Meetings, 22, n. 67; Roman Catholic, 22, 190, n. 69; Whitefield's, 22; compared with New York and Boston, 193; cost of living in, 29; culture of, 29; environs described, 18; expansion of, n. 48; few fortunes in, 193; Hamilton's opinion of, 192; inhabitants described, 28, 193; lack of public diversions in, 22; market, 21, n. 66; opinion of Maryland in, 28; plan of, 18; promising future of, 193; public buildings, 18; streets, 18; water supply, 21, n. 64; women described, 29

Philip, King of the Wampanoags, 104, n. 229

Philips, John, 143, n. 319

Philips, Richard, 137, n. 308

Philipse, Adolph, Speaker of New York Assembly, 175

Phips, Sir William, expedition to Quebec, n. 325

Physical News, The, 137

Physicians: at Attleborough, Mass., 148; at Boston tavern club, 108; at Boston, club of, 137; at Long Island, quacks, 91; at Treadway's, Md., 7; drunken, at New York, 179; empirics at Albany, 65; letters to Boston, 103; mentioned: Anderson, Dr., 11; Astruc, Dr. Jean, 87, n. 190; Boerhaave, Dr. Hermann, 52, 87, 137, n. 140; Bond, Dr. Phineas, 21, 189, n. 62; Bond, Dr. Thomas, 19, 189, n. 55; Boucelle, Peter, yaws-doctor, 167, 195, n. 390; Brett, Dr. John, 156, n. 226; Cadwalader, Dr. Thomas, 31, n. 94; Clark of Boston, 131; Clark, Dr. John, 138, n. 264; Colchoun, Dr. Alexander, 42, 43, 47, 48, 174, n. 116; Douglass, Dr. William. *See* under name; Farquhar, Dr. William, 37, n. 104; Gardiner, Dr. Silvester, 143, n. 320; Goddard, Dr. Giles, 160, n. 352; Harrison, Maryland midwife, 199; Heister, Dr. Lorenz, 137, n. 309; Dr. Hull of Southold, 95; Kearsley, Dr. John, on smallpox, xx; Keith, Dr. James, 102, 153, n. 225; Knox, David, of Edinburgh, 49; McGraw, Dr. James. *See* under name; Milner, Dr., of Bohemia Manor, 196; Mitchell, Dr. John, n. 384; Moffatt, Dr. Thomas. *See* under name; Pitcairne, Dr. Archibald, mentioned, 132, n. 305; Rosaboom, Dr., medical training of, 67; Salmon, Dr. William, n. 77; Shakesburrough, Mr., surgeon, 65; Spencer, Dr. Adam, man-midwife and electrical experimenter, n. 384; Thomson, Dr. Adam. *See* under name; Witt, Dr. Christopher, n. 391; Zachary, Dr. Lloyd, 25, n. 79; of a man o' war at New York, 84; Physical Club of Boston, 115, 116; popular antipathy to, 53; unnamed, travels to Long Island with Hamilton, 80

Piscataway, N. J., 186, n. 381

Placentia, Newfoundland, magazine explodes, 107, n. 249

VERMONT

MOHAWK R.

Mohawk

Cohoes Falls

Schenectady

Cohoes

Albany

NEW

MASSACH

Lower Schodack
Island

Motaling Island

Kinderhook

HUDSON R.

Ancram

The Comp

Wanton Island

Rinebeck

CONNECTICU

Esopus

Esopus Island

Poughkeepsie

CONNECTICUT R.

Butter Mt.

Polopel Island

HOUSATONIC R.

Nllingworth

YORK

Canada Hill

New Haven

Nian

Anthony's Nose

SAUGATUCK R.

Branford

Guilford

Sayb

Dunderberg

Stratford

Milford

LONG ISLAND SOUND

King

Fairfield

HUDSON R.

Horse
Neck

Norwalk

Browns

Rye

Stamford

Southold

NEW

Setauket

Hubba

Fanning's

New
Rochelle

Brewster's

JERSEY

Kings Bridge

Huntington

LONG

ISLAND

New York

Jamaica

Hempstead

EXPLANATION OF ROUTE

Annapolis to
York, Maine

York, Maine
to Annapolis